PRISON LIFE
IN VICTORIAN ENGLAND

PRISON LIFE
IN VICTORIAN ENGLAND

MICHELLE HIGGS

TEMPUS

First published 2007

Tempus Publishing
Cirencester Road, Chalford,
Stroud, Gloucestershire, GL6 8PE
www.tempus-publishing.com

Tempus Publishing is an imprint of NPI Media Group

British Library Cataloguing in Publication Data.
A catalogue record for this book is available from the British Library.

ISBN 978 0 7524 4255 6

Typesetting and origination by NPI Media Group
Printed in Great Britain

CONTENTS

ACKNOWLEDGEMENTS

While writing this book, I received help and advice in locating information and illustrations from a number of different sources. I would like to express my gratitude to the following:

The staff of Gloucestershire Archives, Lancashire Record Office, Worcestershire Record Office, the County Record Office Cambridge, Birmingham City Archives, Birmingham Central Library and The National Archives; Karl Vaughan, Mary Wall and Alan Longbottom.

Special thanks are due to Garry Morton of the Wandsworth Prison Museum for his identification of uniforms and places in specific photographs and for his advice about all aspects of prison life.

I would also like to thank the following people who were so generous with their time and their research:

Carolyn Alty, Anthony Baker, John Brake, Noelene Cummins, Sharon Floate, David Fry, Jim Halsey, Roger Harpin, Caroline Haycock, Christopher J. Hogger, Lyn Howsam, Wendy Corbett Kelley, Heather Leonard, Lyn and Jim Owers, Dominic Pinto, Brian Randle, Rita Richardson, Kenneth Scott, Peter Smith, Patrick Thomas, Graham Wells and Brian Wollaston.

Finally, I would like to thank my husband Carl for his patience and forbearance, and my family and friends for their encouragement during the writing of this book.

ILLUSTRATIONS

INTRODUCTION

In December 1857 at the Warwick Winter Assizes, George Beasley, a thirty-four-year-old brick maker from Birmingham, was convicted of stealing lead fixed to a building. He had a previous conviction so he was sentenced to four years' penal servitude (imprisonment with hard labour) in a convict prison. George was released in March 1861 after serving three years and three months of his sentence. He had earned nine months' remission from his sentence for good behaviour.[1]

Those sentenced to imprisonment in Victorian local prisons had a much harder time as they had no prospect of reducing their sentences with good behaviour. In April 1897, William Anderson, a sixty-year-old labourer, was convicted at the Wigan Sessions of two offences of stealing a jacket. He was given two separate sentences of eighteen months' hard labour to run concurrently in a local prison. This meant he had to endure three years' hard labour. Like George Beasley, William had experienced sentences of penal servitude and he would undoubtedly have preferred it to imprisonment in local prisons.[2]

In the nineteenth century, as George Beasley and William Anderson discovered, the experience of a man or woman convicted of a crime and sent to an English prison differed significantly, depending on which prison he or she was sent to. Before 1877, those, like George Beasley, who had committed a serious crime or who were convicted of several offences and were serving out long sentences of three years or more in a convict prison, were more likely to experience cleaner accommodation, better living conditions and more humane treatment. By contrast, at local prisons, in which shorter-term sentences were served, standards of accommodation and sanitation were far lower and treatment, particularly in terms of the hard labour prisoners were expected to undertake, was often more severe.

The reason for this was partly historical. Convict prisons had been built, funded and run by the government from their inception. Local prisons did not come under government control until 1877 and, until then, were run by justices for each county. They often accommodated their prisoners in eighteenth-century buildings which were no longer fit for purpose. In local prisons, sentences could be as little as a few days up to a maximum of two years, although this maximum was rare. With so little time, local prison staff had no chance to get to know their charges as they could in convict prisons. No local prison was the same as the justices in each county might have different ideas about the purpose of prison. If they saw it as a deterrent, treatment was necessarily harsh. If it was seen as an attempt to reform prisoners, more emphasis might be placed on religion and education.

There were also stark differences between conditions and treatment at convict prisons such as Pentonville and Millbank, as reported by Charles Dickens in 1850. Dickens commented that 'In no other country but this does Justice – blind as she is – administer cocoa and condign misery to the same degree of crime with the same hand.'[3]

If the Victorian English prison was so harsh and severe, why were there so many reports of petty criminals repeatedly re-offending to ensure they were convicted and sent to prison again? The sad truth must be that they were willing to exchange their liberty for better food, accommodation and care than they had at home. A similar motive inspired countless workhouse inmates and vagrants to deliberately destroy property or refuse to work in order to get sent to prison. The prison diet was arguably more generous than that of the workhouse.[4]

The differences between convict and local prisons extended to the pay and working conditions of the staff. Local prison officers were paid significantly less and endured less favourable working conditions than their convict prison counterparts. This disparity continued right up to the end of the nineteenth century.

This book has been written to describe what life was really like in prison for the Victorian convict or prisoner, and also for the prison officers who looked after them. Using original prison records, contemporary sources and testimony from convicts, prisoners and prison officers, the book examines every aspect of the Victorian English prison to bring this fascinating period of social history to life.

1

THE COURT SYSTEM AND SENTENCING

In the nineteenth century, anyone charged with a petty criminal offence could be tried locally by a Justice of the Peace at the monthly Petty Sessions or at the Quarter Sessions held four times a year at Epiphany, Easter, Midsummer and Michaelmas. This is the equivalent of today's magistrate court.

More serious criminal offences such as murder, rape and burglary were referred to the Assizes. England and Wales was split into regional circuits and two or three times a year, royal justices visited each circuit to hear the most serious criminal cases.

While awaiting trial, men and women charged with a criminal offence were usually remanded in custody and kept in prison. The exception was if he or she could afford to pay for bail costs. Those awaiting trial for a serious criminal offence might have to wait several months before the case was heard.

Victorian criminal terminology can be a little confusing. Not everyone convicted of a criminal offence was known as a 'convict'. This term was reserved for those convicted of a felony (i.e. a serious criminal offence, usually involving violence) and sentenced to penal servitude. Penal servitude, often abbreviated to P.S. in criminal records, is defined as imprisonment with compulsory hard labour. In the Victorian period specifically, penal servitude was introduced in 1853 as a substitute for 'all crimes punishable by transportation for less than fourteen years'.[1] The convict was admitted to a government-run prison where he or she undertook a period of separate confinement before completing the sentence with a period of hard labour. The minimum sentence for penal servitude was three years, increased to five years in 1864 for a first offence, and seven years for subsequent offences.

Anyone convicted of a more minor criminal offence was known as a 'prisoner'. He or she could receive a sentence of anything from a few days up to a maximum of two years, with or without hard labour. The sentence would be served in a local prison, run by county justices until 1877 when all prisons came under government control.

One might think that a prisoner convicted of a minor offence and sent to a local prison might receive better treatment than the convict who had committed a serious offence. However, it has been argued that someone sent to prison 'as the result of a minor offence…would be treated more severely than had [they] committed one of the great crimes. Commit a grave offence (short of murder), and [they] would be punished ostensibly more with an eye to reformation than had [they] been modest in [their] crime'.[2]

Prior to 1877, there were distinct differences between local and convict prisons in accommodation, discipline, work tasks and general treatment of prisoners or convicts. After 1877 it was intended that there be more uniformity between convict and local prisons.

However, even after this time, 'so distinct were local from convict prisons, and so separate their administrations, that there was great ignorance, even by the staff, of how the other's system was run'.[3] One Who Has Endured It, a gentleman convict, was sentenced to five years' penal servitude and held locally at Newgate during his trial. After his sentence, he was removed to the convict prison of Millbank. He wrote that 'everyone, warders and officials, were perfectly ignorant of the system and discipline pursued at the convict establishments. Not one knew anything of convict life'.[4]

The Central Criminal Court in London, also known as the Old Bailey.

The cells at the Old Town Hall, Boston, Lincolnshire.

Opposite: Expenses incurred in removing a prisoner from the New Bailey Prison, Salford to Wakefield Gaol, 1866. These expenses included cab and rail fares (3rd class) and a personal allowance for the prison officer. (QSP 3747/81 – courtesy of Lancashire Record Office)

New Bailey Prison. Salford
17th March 1866

Expences incurred in removing Prisoner
Thomas Scarborough to Wakefield Gaol

Cab fare to Railway Station.	„	1	„
2 Fares per Railway Manchester to Wakefield Officer and Prisoner 3d class @ 3/3	„	6	6
Cab fare at Wakefield to Gaol	„	1	6
Officer returning per Railway from Wakefield to Manchester	„	5	4
Officers 1 days Allowance (Personal)	„	6	„
	1	„	4

Examined, approved & ordered to be paid
John Magadder

John Kay, Visiting Justice

A convict was entitled to earn remission from his or her sentence for good behaviour. From 1857, the amount of remission available was 'on a sliding scale of from one-sixth for the shortest sentence of penal servitude to one-third remission for those serving fifteen years or more'.[5] However, a prisoner sentenced to a local prison for a maximum of two years did not have the option of remission, no matter how well behaved he or she was. He or she would have to serve every single day of the sentence. It has been argued that many prisoners 'preferred three or four years of penal servitude to two years of hard labour'.[6]

This lack of remission applied to the vast majority of convictions as in 1877, three-quarters of prison sentences meted out by English magistrate courts were for one month or less. In the higher courts, over one-quarter of all prison sentences were for three months or less.[7] Local prisoners were finally able to earn remission from their sentences from 1898 onwards.[8]

2

TYPES OF PRISON

At the beginning of the nineteenth century, there were several different types of prison in England. Small towns had a bridewell, which was originally a 'house of correction where paupers were put to work'.[1] In addition to a bridewell, county towns were often the location for the county gaol.

These bridewells and gaols were run on a profit basis by the gaoler, who did not receive a salary. He charged fees from the inmates for the 'provision of food and bedding, light and fuel, or transfer to better accommodation'. Disease was rife in these overcrowded prisons and it was said that in the late eighteenth century, 'a committal to prison was in fact equivalent, in many cases, to a sentence of death by some frightful disease; and in all, to the utmost extremes of hunger and cold'.[2] Indeed, some eighteenth-century prisons 'were so dilapidated that heavy leg-irons were a cheap substitute for building repairs'.[3]

Since 1776, convicts sentenced to transportation had been housed on the 'hulks' for two years prior to departure for Australia. These were decommissioned naval vessels moored in the Thames estuary and on the South Coast. As the hulks were managed by a private contractor, to whom the government paid a fee, they were 'prone to corruption and abuse of all kinds'[4] and the convicts awaiting transportation endured terrible insanitary conditions on board.

Eighteenth-century prison reformers such as John Howard and Elizabeth Fry campaigned rigorously for better conditions on both the hulks and in the prisons. Some improvements were made but it was not until the early nineteenth century that significant changes to the prison system began to take place.

CONVICT PRISONS

A step towards replacing the hulks with a land-based prison was taken when the building of the Millbank Penitentiary in London was begun in 1816 and completed some five years later. Millbank was on the site of today's Tate Gallery and was built as a holding prison for all convicts awaiting transportation. In 1842, Pentonville, also in London, was built as a 'model' prison for the separate system. However, it was not until 1857 that the hulks were finally closed.[5]

The convict service was established in 1850 when Millbank, Pentonville and the hulks came under the control of the government. By 1853 when the Prisons Act introduced penal servitude as a substitute for transportation, there were twelve government-run convict prisons in England.

Wakefield, Leicester and Millbank acted as holding prisons for male convicts at the start of their sentences. They were then transferred to Pentonville for a period of separate confinement. Before the end of transportation, convicts at Pentonville were supposed to be 'the pick of the criminal crop'.[6] They were young, fit and healthy and deemed suitable for reformation. In Pentonville, they were taught a trade which theoretically would equip them with the skills needed to earn a living overseas.

After twelve months, or nine months from 1853, male convicts were transferred to a public works prison at Chatham, Portsmouth or Portland. Before 1853, convicts sentenced to fourteen years or more transportation would be transported at the end of their time at the public works prison.

The convict prison at Aylesbury. Built in 1847 as a county gaol, it became a women's prison in 1890.

There were also two prisons for male invalid convicts who were not capable of the labour required at the public works prisons. These were at Woking and Dartmoor. One Who Has Endured It was sent to Dartmoor to complete his sentence of penal servitude. He commented: 'Dartmoor is called a Convict *Invalid* Station and…it really is a healthy place though so disagreeable. Being of a rheumatic constitution I gave myself up for lost when I saw the first two or three wet fogs, but during the three years I spent there I never felt one twinge.'[7] Parkhurst on the Isle of Wight was used for male juvenile offenders until 1864 and for adults after this date.

Female convicts went first to Millbank for a period of separate confinement, and on moving through two further 'stages' or classes, they were transferred to Brixton.[8] The 'very best behaved women' who progressed through two further stages were sent to Fulham Refuge, which was 'the most distinctively feminine of the early convict prisons'.[9] Here, women were taught skills in household cleaning, cooking and laundering which might equip them for a job in service after their release.

By 1867, the number of convict prisons had been reduced to nine plus an asylum for criminal lunatics at Broadmoor and the refuge for female convicts at Fulham.[10]

LOCAL PRISONS

While the convict prisons were being developed with a staff of paid officers, local prisons remained under the control of local justices. They continued to resist reform because the increased expenditure would lead to an extra burden on the rates. The salaried gaoler remained a 'rarity'.[11]

Successive Acts of Parliament failed to rectify the problem. The passing of the 1823 Gaol Act:

provided for quarterly reports by the justices to the Home Secretary, systematic inspection by the justices, payment of a salary to gaolers, abolition of private trading by gaolers, improved accommodation, supervision of females by females, and the keeping of work journals by the gaoler, the chaplain, and the surgeon, which were to be presented to the Quarter Sessions. There was also insistence upon productive labour, education and religious observance.[12]

The old prison at Southampton.

Although the details of the Act looked good on paper, there was no mechanism to force local prisons to undertake reforms and no inspectorate to supervise them. More importantly, the Act only applied to a small minority of prisons: 'those of the county justices, of the Cities of London and Westminster, and seventeen provincial towns'.[13] The London debtors' prisons and 150 gaols in so-called minor municipalities were not affected by the Act.

In 1835, the government rectified the lack of an inspectorate by appointing five inspectors to produce detailed reports on the state of local prisons. They still had no powers of enforcement but publishing the reports meant that deficiencies were immediately in the public domain. From 1844, any proposed building plans of new prisons or alterations to existing plans had to be referred to the newly appointed Surveyor General of Prisons. It was no accident that in the six years after the building of Pentonville, 'no fewer than fifty-four new prisons were built...affording 11,000 separate cells'.[14]

By 1862, one-third of local prisons in England and Wales 'admitted fewer than twenty-five prisoners in the whole year, and one-seventh received fewer than six prisoners. Some local prisons were completely unoccupied'.[15] To compensate for this, some of the overcrowded prisons in the towns and cities contracted with county prisons to house their overflow of prisoners. Such prisoners were usually serving months rather than a few days or weeks because removal costs to a county prison had to be taken into account.

This happened in March 1868 at Worcester. The Visiting Justices reported that 'To meet the pressure on the female side, [they]...felt compelled to enter into an arrangement with the County of Hereford for the Reception in the Prison of that County of five female prisoners, at a weekly cost of ten shillings each.'[16]

Finally, in 1865, the Prison Act 'formerly amalgamated the jail and the house of correction' into an institution called a prison.[17] It was arguably this piece of legislation which forced the local prisons to begin the process of falling into line with the convict prisons. Based on the recommendations of the 1863 Committee '...the Act decreed a staff complement which had to include a gaoler, a chaplain, a surgeon and a matron for women...and forbade the employment of prisoners as staff'.[18] Crucially '...the grant from the central government to the local authority could be withdrawn if the latter failed to comply with the Act'.[19] From this time onwards, 'the convict service was the model for the new local service'.[20]

Her Majesty's Prison at Bodmin, Cornwall.

PRISONS AFTER 1877

After the Prisons Act of 1877 came into force on 1 April 1878, 113 local prisons were taken over by the government. A period of review followed and by 1881-2, there were just sixty-five local prisons remaining. In 1886, both Coldbath Fields and Clerkenwell were closed with the prisons at Holloway and Pentonville adapted to accommodate extra numbers. Later, Pentonville, the much lauded model for the separate system, was downgraded from convict to local prison.[21] Despite this legislation, convict and local prisons 'continued to operate independently of each other....'[22]

In 1898-9, it was reported that a hard labour term in a local prison still began with a period of 'strict separation' for the first month, while the convict serving a term of penal servitude still underwent a period of six months' separate confinement. This was a reduction from the traditional nine months. Also in the 1898-9 Report it was pointed out that in the local prison, a prisoner was 'eligible' for associated labour after a month, but this was a privilege, not a right.[23]

Towards the end of the nineteenth century, the Prison Act of 1898 'drew the convict and local services together, although...pay scales [of staff] remained different...Other provisions allowed local prisoners to earn remission, limited the use of corporal punishment in prison [and] allowed a part of payment of a fine to be accepted in lieu of imprisonment.'[24]

3

THE SILENT AND SEPARATE SYSTEMS

At the beginning of the Victorian period, two different penal systems were in use in English prisons. Under the separate system, prisoners were kept in strict confinement in separate cells, day and night, for all or part of their sentence, with breaks for chapel and exercise. Under the silent system, prisoners were confined to their separate cells at night, but during the day the prisoners were allowed to work together in 'association' while strict silence was enforced. Both systems had been trialled in America in the 1820s and 1830s and both had their advocates and critics.

THE SILENT SYSTEM

Versions of the silent system were introduced at Wakefield and Coldbath Fields in 1834. In March 1834, the governor of Wakefield reported that 'Four extra Assistants as Superintendents were appointed to carry out American system of silence, they acted as overlookers of the wardsmen who were appointed in every workshop'.[1] Two months later he reported, 'Silence was very irksome to the men. 533 deprived of their food'. In December 1834, Governor Chesterton of Coldbath Fields reported no resistance in establishing the silent system as 'the established rule of the prison'.[2]

At Preston, where the introduction of the separate system was limited by the lack of cell accommodation, it was necessary to use the silent system as well. The Revd Clay, the chaplain of the prison, reported that in the workroom:

> the 'silent system' is applied to a number of prisoners varying from forty to eighty, all of whom are under summary conviction. They are seated upon forms, are about nine feet apart from each other, all facing the direction of the officers' raised desk, and all employed in picking cotton, except a few who are undergoing the punishment of compulsory idleness. At meals the same order is observed; and in taking exercise, still under vigilant superintendence, they walk about 30 feet apart. Throughout the discipline it is not merely that the silence of the tongue is observed - but the eye and the hand are mute. No sign, no look – whether of recognition to a fellow prisoner or of curiosity towards a visitor – is permitted, nor is it often attempted. To some persons all this may seem unnecessarily severe. I am fully satisfied that it is otherwise.[3]

BENEFITS OF THE SILENT SYSTEM

The main benefit of the silent system was that it allowed 'association' for prisoners to undertake their work tasks in workrooms although they were forbidden to speak. This meant there was no risk of any of the feared side-effects of separate confinement, such as mental illness or debility of muscles or joints.

'A Convict at Work in His Cell – He pauses in his task as he hears sounds of the outer world' – Convict Life at Wormwood Scrubs Prison drawn by Paul Renouard. (*The Graphic*, 19 October 1889)

PROBLEMS WITH THE SILENT SYSTEM

Inevitably, the rule of silence proved to be very difficult, if not impossible, to enforce and therefore the system was ineffective. Excessive punishments were necessary and in 1836 at Coldbath Fields, 'there were no less than 5,138 punishments for talking and swearing'.[4] As a result, more staff were required to monitor and observe prisoners, and to enforce the rules and regulations.

It was commented that 'The silent system of discipline has its advocates, but the arguments in support of the advantages of association, however strictly regulated it may be, leave so much obvious evil untouched, that there can be no question as to its being wrong in theory, and if so, it will be difficult to prove it right in practice.'[5]

THE SEPARATE SYSTEM

The separate system was designed to prevent association of prisoners with each other which was considered to be contaminating. Separate confinement in a cell by himself allowed the prisoner time to reflect on his crime and his future. It was believed that 'he would come to welcome the visits of the chaplain, whose encouragement would assist the awakening of conscience'.[6]

Although prisoners were prevented from talking to each other by being confined to their cells, they could converse with the governor and other members of prison staff who visited them there. This 'distinguished the separate system from solitary confinement, where isolation was complete'.[7]

The Prisons Act of 1835 advocated the separate system as the best form of discipline for English prisons. As a result, Pentonville was built as a model prison for separate confinement between 1840 and 1842. By 1856, 'two-thirds of English prisons had wholly or partially adopted the [separate] system'.[8]

At first, the period of separate confinement at Pentonville was to be eighteen months. This was reduced to twelve months in 1848. At the beginning of 1852, 'there occurred an *unusually large* number of cases of mental affection among the prisoners, and it was therefore deemed necessary to increase the amount of exercise in the open air, and to introduce the plan of brisk walking, as pursued at Wakefield'.[9] As a result, the period of separate confinement was again reduced in 1853, this time to nine months.

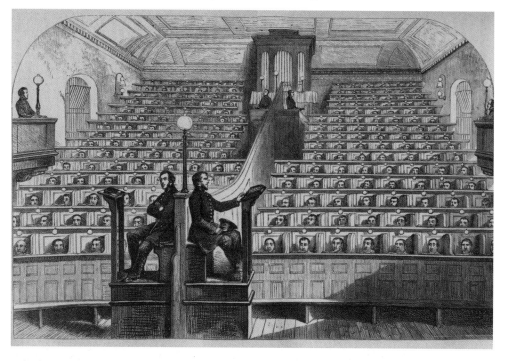

The chapel at Pentonville arranged under the separate system. (From Mayhew & Binny)

Until 1853 at Pentonville, convicts were required to wear masks while exercising so that they could not see one another. This practice was abandoned when Colonel Jebb, in his Report on the Discipline and Management of Convict Prisons for that year, declared

> …the mask or peak does not prevent prisoners from recognising each other in the prison; moreover, that as prisoners see each other before they are brought to the prison, come in considerable bodies, and are assembled together when they leave the prison, it would be desirable to discontinue it, since the use of it appears calculated to depress the spirits of the men, without obtaining any corresponding advantage.[10]

On a visit to Pentonville, Henry Mayhew discovered that separate confinement was widely disliked by the prisoners. He found that a:

> curious privilege granted to well-conducted prisoners in Pentonville, is the liberty of labouring; for so terrible is separate confinement found to be, without occupation, that one of the forms of punishment peculiar to this prison is the stoppage of a man's work, and forcing him to remain in his own cell in a state of idleness throughout the day.[11]

BENEFITS OF THE SEPARATE SYSTEM

For those in favour of the separate system, the main benefit was that it prevented contamination and corruption of vulnerable new prisoners by hardened criminals. The Revd John Clay, the chaplain at the Preston House of Correction between 1821 and 1857, was an outspoken advocate of the separate system. He believed that the prison operated as 'a seminary of sin' and 'wherever the association of prisoners is permitted, there the work of corruption is still going on!'[12]

Female convicts undertaking exercise with conversation at Aylesbury Prison. This privilege was granted after serving the first nine months of a sentence. (Supplement to *The Sphere*, 12 December 1908, courtesy of Karl Vaughan)

The Revd Clay argued that in the ordinary imprisonment of the jail 'the newly sentenced convict is placed in a ward, or upon the tread-wheel, where there is either no supervision at all, or merely a formal one, and where the prisoner is left to all the evils of an unbridled intercourse with spirits more wicked than himself'. In solitary confinement 'he is removed from the court of justice, while the solemnities and anxieties of his trial are still sobering and saddening his mind, into a solitary cell, where, left alone with his own thoughts, he may reflect upon his crime and its consequences, and weigh the pleasures of sin against the pains which followed undisturbed by the jeers and scoffs of the hardened and irreclaimable...'[13]

When new blocks of separate cells were introduced at the Kirkdale House of Correction in 1848, the chaplain, the Revd Richard Appleton, noted their beneficial effects: 'With few exceptions, these [separate] cells are much preferred by the prisoners to the old workrooms... They for the most part make a good use of the opportunity afforded them of learning to read, write and cypher, and study, with tolerable diligence, the various books with which they are plentifully furnished.' He added that he did not see 'any tendency in it to overthrow, or even enfeeble the mind.'[14]

By confining the prisoners or convicts to individual cells, the separate system was 'a corner-stone of control' for the prison staff.[15] It was far easier to enforce discipline on individuals than groups of prisoners. In addition, contamination was stopped because communication was restricted. This, in turn, 'prevented collaboration'.[16]

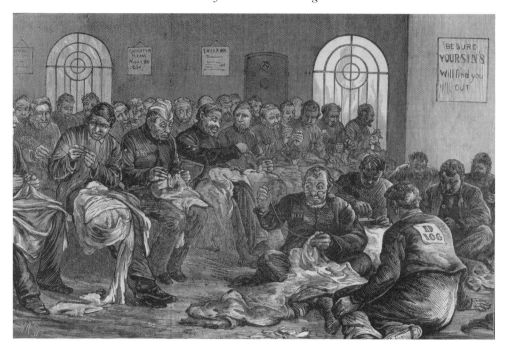

The needle-room at the Clerkenwell House of Correction. (*Illustrated London News*, 17 January 1874)

PROBLEMS WITH THE SEPARATE SYSTEM

It was considered vital to monitor the effects of separate confinement on a prisoner's mental and physical health, hence the medical officer's duty to make regular examinations of such prisoners. Michael Davitt, a Fenian convict sentenced to fifteen years' penal servitude in 1870, found his nine months of separate confinement in Millbank to be 'the most onerous part of his sentence'. His health suffered considerably and, after eight months, on the orders of the medical officer, he was granted an extra half-hour's exercise a day. He wrote: 'That human reason should give way under such adverse influences is not, I think, to be wondered at: and many a still living wreck of manhood can refer to the silent system of Millbank and its pernicious surrounding as the cause of his debilitated mind'.[17]

At Preston, the separate system was adapted for the boys. Their daily routine included two hours' brisk exercise which 'preserves their bodily health; and, being taken in company, though without communication, keeps also their minds in vigour'. The Revd Clay noted that at Wakefield, the boys were put in close confinement at first but 'on their suffering from debility and contraction of the joints' the system was relaxed, and the boys were permitted 'to play at leapfrog and other similar recreations'.[18]

The requirement for separate cells meant that prisons had to be modified to provide the new accommodation. However, many of the local prisons were still operating from eighteenth-century buildings which were unsuitable to adapt into separate cell accommodation. Consequently, new prisons had to be built at considerable cost. As this re-building took a long period of time, in practice many prisons adopted a hybrid version of the silent and separate systems to suit their individual requirements.

4

ARRIVAL IN PRISON

For the first-time prisoner or convict, life behind bars was truly a world away from the norm. Many prisoners, especially those with long-term sentences, would have experienced a taste of prison life if they had been on remand awaiting trial.

REMANDED PRISONERS

Before trial, all remanded prisoners were to be kept separate from the convicted prisoners. Remanded prisoners were entitled to procure for themselves or receive 'at proper hours, food and malt liquor, clothing, bedding, or other necessaries' if they so wanted.[1]

One Who Has Endured It was a remanded prisoner in Newgate in 1867. He recalled:

> I could either have the prison allowance of food or order in what I wished for, under certain restrictions, from an eating-house on the opposite side of the Old Bailey... At first I had in my meals from outside; but in a few days I found every shilling I possessed would be needed by my family and for my defence, and I determined to accept the full brunt of my position and put up at once with the prison fare.[2]

Remanded prisoners could also wear the prison dress which was to be of a different colour from that of the convicted prisoners. If their own clothes were insufficient or unfit for use, they would be required to wear prison dress. Prisoners on remand had the option of employment but were not 'compelled to perform any hard labour'[3] and were allowed books and writing materials.[4] They were entitled to be visited by a solicitor or other such legal representative, 'care being taken that, so far as is consistent with the interests of justice, such prisoners shall see their legal advisers alone...'[5]

RECEPTION

Prisoners brought from the courts to the larger prisons were usually transported in a hearse-like omnibus, well known as the 'Black Maria'. One convict described the experience:

On mounting the steps I was ushered into a passage running up the centre from end to end of the 'bus', with a number of doors on each side, through one of which I was gently pushed, and found myself shut up in a close box, with a seat, not too well ventilated nor too clean, and out of the gratings of which I vainly endeavoured to catch a glimpse of the world I was leaving. On the seat, much to my surprise, were two large slices of bread, which I afterwards found by my own experience had been the allowance given out to some prisoner who had left the gaol in the morning, and had either been discharged or had forgotten to eat what in prison slang is called his 'toke' or 'chuck'. No sooner was the outer door shut and locked, and the vehicle commenced its journey, than I was made aware of the presence of fellow travellers calling to

The 'Black Maria' prison van at the House of Detention. (From Mayhew & Binny)

each other with inquiries as to how they got on before the magistrate, what sentence they had received…[6]

Once convicted and brought back to prison, each prisoner or convict was given a number by which he or she would be known. This number might change if the prisoner was transferred between prisons. This was the first phase of dehumanising the prisoner: until release, he or she would no longer be known by his or her name.

On admission to prison, all prisoners were searched and 'all dangerous weapons, articles calculated to facilitate escape, and prohibited articles' were confiscated. Female prisoners could only be searched by female officers. If a prisoner had money or other valuable effects, they were placed in the custody of the gaoler or governor until the prisoner's release. Tobacco and spirituous liquor was forbidden in prison unless by a written order of the surgeon. No gaming was allowed in any prison and the gaoler or governor had the power to seize and destroy all dice, cards or other instruments of gaming.[7]

HYGIENE

When admitted to prison, all prisoners were to have a tepid bath, unless exempted by the medical officer. In addition, for the purposes of health and cleanliness, the hair of male criminal prisoners was cropped but not cut 'closer than may be necessary'. The hair of female prisoners could not be cut without their consent 'except on account of vermin or dirt, or when the Surgeon deems it requisite on the grounds of health…'[8]

One Who Has Endured It recalled that 'About four or five days after my sentence…a warder entered my cell with another prisoner to crop and shave me. …I was clean scraped and my hair clipped to about half to three-quarters of an inch long.'[9]

MEDICAL EXAMINATION

Once bathed, the prison medical officer undertook a rudimentary medical examination of each new prisoner or convict. The height, weight and detailed physical description of each new arrival was noted for the records. This included the colour of hair, eyes and complexion, and other distinguishing features such as scars and birthmarks. The medical examination was designed to allow the medical officer to determine whether prisoners were 'fit for hard labour, or light labour, or the hospital, or the observation cell, according to his rapid judgement'.[10]

UNIFORM

Convicted prisoners were required to wear full prison dress. In local prisons where short sentences were served, the prisoner's clothes were returned to him or her upon release, unless it was necessary to destroy them because of hygiene issues. In such cases, clothing was to be provided.[11] In convict prisons, the clothes worn when convicted were often forfeited and a new set of clothes was provided upon release from prison.

One Who Has Endured It described what happened when he returned to Newgate after his conviction and sentence:

> I immediately came under another class, and my real imprisonment commenced. On arrival I was marched downstairs to the same floor as the baths. There I stripped off the clothes of a free Englishman to don those of a convict. I had been previously told that whatever clothes I wore or had when convicted would be forfeited; I took care therefore not to wear too good a suit, and all the extra clothes I had in the prison for change I had sent away previously; so what I stood upright in was all I 'forfeited to the Crown'.[12]

Convicts wore similar uniforms across England:

> Each man was dressed in a short loose jacket and vest, and baggy knickerbockers of drab tweed with black stripes, one and a half inches broad. The lower part of their legs were encased in blue worsted stockings with bright red rings round them; low shoes and a bright grey and red worsted cap, which each man wore in accordance to his own taste, completed the costume. ...All over the whole clothing were hideous black impressions of the Broad Arrow, the 'crow's foot', denoting the articles belonged to Her Majesty.[13]

At the local prisons, both the colour and style of uniforms varied from prison to prison. Kirkdale prisoners were issued with 'articles as would have been an appropriate costume for the "artful dodger" – a coat of dirty brown shoddy, full of patches, a pair of trousers, and vest of same material'.[14]

At Bodmin Gaol, the prison shirts were made of 'cotton or flannel, of a smock-style without buttons'.[15] The colour of the uniform varied according to the offence committed. Male minor offenders wore grey and females wore blue. Men convicted of felony had a red and grey striped uniform and women wore blue and white stripes. Men who were not sentenced to hard labour wore a black and yellow checked uniform. In cold weather 'thick warm capes were issued for wearing while exercising outdoors'.[16]

Susan Willis Fletcher, a prisoner at Tothill Fields, was provided with an outfit consisting of:

> brown serge prison-dress...with a not unbecoming white hat. The stockings are blue with a red stripe, and very coarse. There is one white flannel skirt and a flannel under vest if the prisoner is wearing one at the time of admission; but there are no drawers...a brown serge petticoat, skirt and jacket, and blue check handkerchief to wear under the jacket, and another for the pocket (very coarse and rough) and a white cotton cap.[17]

Above: Entrance to the convict prison at Grove Road, Portland. (Courtesy of Wendy Corbett Kelley)

Left: A view of the same entrance to the convict prison at Portland with officers at the prison gate.

One Who Has Endured It discovered that:

> Every article was quite new and had never been worn; consequently their stiffness was not at
> all conducive to their comfort. Among them were a new flannel, under-waistcoat, and pair of
> drawers. It was August. ...I tried to shirk them, but the principal, seeing what I was at, stopped
> me saying, 'Put them on now; when you get to your cell you can wear them or not as you like,
> but if you don't take them now you will have none all the winter'.[18]

RULES AND REGULATIONS

When new prisoners and convicts had been examined, bathed and dressed in their new
uniform, a principal warder read out the long list of rules and regulations which they had to
follow. One prisoner recalled: 'As it took him about three quarters of an hour to read them, by
the time he had got to the last rule I had forgotten all the others...'[19] Punishable prison offences
included disobedience of prison regulations, common assaults by one prisoner on another,
profane cursing and swearing, indecent behaviour, irreverent behaviour at chapel, using insulting
or threatening language to an officer or prisoner, absence from chapel without leave, idleness or
negligence at work and wilful mismanagement of work by any convicted criminal prisoner.[20]

STARTING A PRISON SENTENCE

Once a prisoner or convict received his or her sentence, a new life in prison started immediately.
For the family of the prisoner, a different ordeal began. If the prisoner was the breadwinner
of the family, and they had no other means of support, it was often necessary for them to ask
for help from the parish. In cases where outdoor relief was not offered, the family would be
expected to enter the workhouse.

Even if the family could support themselves, there was still a strong stigma attached to being
a relative of a prisoner. At the time of the 1851 census, Samuel Benbow, a twenty-two-year-old
pearl button worker, was in the District Borough Gaol of Birmingham. It is not known what
offence he had committed or the length of his sentence.

Samuel had married Elizabeth Smallwood two years earlier and on the 1851 census she and
their one-year-old daughter Sarah Ann were living with her parents. Elizabeth was named as
Smallwood, not Benbow. It is not clear if this was an error on the part of the census enumerator
or whether Elizabeth herself preferred to be known as Smallwood to avoid the stigma associated
with Samuel's imprisonment.[21]

CONDEMNED PRISONERS

Special rules applied to all condemned prisoners sentenced to execution at their trial. The gaoler
or governor had to search him and remove any articles which were deemed to be 'dangerous
or inexpedient to leave in his possession'. If the condemned prisoner was female, she would be
searched by the matron or other female officer. A condemned prisoner was confined to a cell
apart from the other prisoners and was 'placed day and night under the constant charge of an
officer'. This was primarily to prevent any attempt to commit suicide. The prison chaplain was
to have free access to the condemned prisoner, visiting the cell regularly throughout the day.
If he or she was of a different religious persuasion to that of the Established Church, he or she
could be visited by a minister from his or her own religion. With the exception of religious
ministers, Visiting Justices or prison officers, condemned prisoners could not receive visits from
anyone else unless the Visiting Justices ordered otherwise.[22]

5

DAILY ROUTINE

Like that other Victorian institution, the workhouse, the prison was run like a well-oiled machine to a strict timetable where every minute of the day was accounted for. For the convict or prisoner, this fixed routine would have punctuated the day and may even have helped them to get through a sentence. On the other hand, such an intensive routine was relentless with little respite.

For the convicts at the public works prisons, the daily routine was necessarily different as they went out of the prison six days a week to work. However, all the other convict prisons had similar timetables on which many of the local prisons based their own.

MORNING

Prisoners and convicts alike were woken at dawn by the sound of the prison bell. This could be any time between 5 and 6 a.m.[1] but it varied from prison to prison and from season to season. Unlocking the cells in the morning was the time when prisoners had a quick wash with the water from their buckets and cleaned their cells and tinware. They were then let out a few at a time to empty and refill their buckets with clean water. Later in the nineteenth century, when the insanitary water-closets were removed from the cells, this was also the time for the emptying of slop-buckets. Bedding had to be rolled up correctly and everything had to be spick and span in the cell.

One Who Has Endured It described the morning routine at Millbank. After the prison bell had rung at 6 a.m.:

> the warders arrived and threw open the cell doors. Scrubbing brushes and cloths were served out to each cell, and with the water he has washed in, the prisoner cleans the floor of his apartment. Then each in turn, as he is called by the warder, every man brings out his bucket and pewter to the sink to empty and replenish with clean water. Beds must be rolled up and stowed, everything in its place, and the man dressed by seven o'clock, when the bell goes for chapel.[2]

If a prisoner or convict wanted to see the governor, doctor or chaplain he had 'to "sport his broom" and lay his little hair-broom on the floor at the door directly the cell is opened in the morning'.[3] This was the signal for the warder to come to him and take down his requirements on a slate, on which he made up his morning's report. Breakfast was served to prisoners in their cells by those whose turn it was to be orderlies for the week. They assisted the warders in 'carrying up the bread baskets, cocoa, tea and gruel cans, the dinners and all the other things required'.[4] After breakfast, the morning was taken up with work tasks, chapel and exercise.

EXERCISE

Depending on the routine of each prison, all prisoners and convicts were to take half an hour or an hour's exercise outside 'except those already engaged in heavy work'.[5] Supervised exercise was staggered so that some prisoners might exercise after breakfast before chapel, some after chapel and so on.

Special yards were created for the purpose, in which prisoners were to exercise in silence. 'Exercise' usually consisted of marching around the yard with a specified distance between each prisoner. Convicted prisoners sentenced to fourteen days or less were not allowed to go out to exercise, unless the medical officer specifically ordered it.[6]

HYGIENE

Once a week during exercise, groups of prisoners were sent to the bath-house. At Millbank, the arrangement was that prisoners would alternate between having a complete wash in one week and washing just their feet the following week. This was also the time for shaving the male prisoners who were never allowed to shave themselves.[7]

In a study of convict life at Wormwood Scrubs in 1889, *The Graphic* reported that generally the prisoner did not regard his fortnightly bath:

> …as a luxury, and would in most cases be very much obliged if the warders would not bother him with these little attentions. He has not become accustomed to baths in most days of his liberty…The baths are side by side – between fifty and sixty of them…The water is kept at a temperature of fifty-five degrees, and the general verdict is that it is cold – stone cold – horribly cold. Sometimes it is at sixty degrees, but it is still objected to, and secretly anathematised.[8]

To ensure that prisoners kept the minimum standards of hygiene required, they were provided with a regular supply of soap, towels and combs. In terms of clean clothing, every prisoner was to be supplied with clean linen including shirt (whether of linen, cotton or flannel), stockings and handkerchief, at least once in every week.

When one convict arrived at Millbank, he was given 'clean sheets, a clean towel, with a piece of soap, a small horn-comb, and a little brush, like a nail-brush, which…was for my hair. The soap…was my allowance for a fortnight…' and every alternate Saturday he was given a similar piece. He was also provided with '…a small bag, containing some rags and bath brick, with which to keep my tin and pewter things bright and clean'.[9] However, one item was missing and when he begged for a toothbrush, he was told by the chief warder: 'If you are particular about your teeth, my man, use a corner of your towel.'[10]

AFTERNOON

An hour was allowed for dinner which was usually around midday. At this time, prisoners were locked in their cells. As an educated prisoner, One Who Has Endured It highly valued this time: 'During that hour a man's time was his own, and I used to hurry over my dinner that I might have as long as possible to enjoy my reading'.[11]

After dinner, the prisoners undertook more work until supper. For those entitled to it, although not daily, the afternoon might be the time for school instruction, for others it might take place in the evening after supper. The arrangements for such instruction were different from prison to prison.

EVENING

After supper, which was generally between five o'clock and half past five, prisoners were locked into their cells. In the prisons where convicts were undergoing separate confinement, they were expected to work in their cells for a further hour. For some prisoners, this might be the time for

The exercise yard at a Victorian prison, possibly Wakefield.

Convicts exercising at Pentonville wearing masks to prevent them seeing one another. This practice was abandoned in 1853. (From Mayhew & Binny)

Visiting Day in Newgate where prisoners on remand were held before trial. (*Illustrated London News*, 1 March 1873)

their school instruction. For others, this was a period of 'relative liberty'.[12] Before lights out at about nine o'clock, prisoners were allowed to read books they had borrowed from the library.

When all the lights were extinguished, the prison officers who had come on duty earlier put on felt overshoes which were supposed to deaden the sound of their footsteps and minimise any disturbance of the prisoners. One Who Has Endured It recalled that:

> At regular intervals throughout the night, the night watch comes round, looking into every cell. By placing the bull's-eye of his lantern against the glass of the window, and peeping through the spy-hole in the door, he can see very well if a man is in bed or not, asleep or awake. Many a time have I been woken up with the sudden flash of the bull's-eye in my face.[13]

SUNDAY

On Sundays, no work was required of the prisoners or convicts. It was a comparatively lazy day because the prison bell for getting up did not ring until around seven o'clock. There were two church services which prisoners had to attend and the men and women still had their regular exercise.

Although Sunday was a day of rest from the daily grind, prisoners often found it to be long and slow with less routine to punctuate the day. One convict commented that after the men's second exercise 'it is a long time to bed time…'[14]

ASSOCIATION ROOMS

First- and second-class convicts were entitled to be accommodated in the association rooms, rather than in individual cells. Here, there was much more liberty and the convicts could talk

'Husband, Wife and
Father' – Convict Life
in Wormwood Scrubs
Prison IV, drawn by Paul
Renouard. (*The Graphic*,
26 October 1889)

quietly. These larger rooms were usually far healthier than the cells. Similar 'dormitories' were
in place in many of the local prisons.

One Who Has Endured It described the association rooms at Dartmoor. Each of the four
large rooms could accommodate sixty-eight prisoners and the floor of the building

> was divided down the centre, by a wooden partition, into two long rooms about 100 feet in
> length by 30 in width. These rooms were divided into three equal portions lengthways by two
> rows of strong wood posts, with rails, 2 feet 6 inches from the ground. The centre portion was
> the gangway, and the two sides were where the men slung their hammocks at night and sat
> in the day. Along the walls were shelves – one at the top, 3 feet wide, and one below, 1 foot
> wide.[15]

Although being in the association room was considered a great privilege, One Who Has
Endured It lamented the fact that 'a man had no privacy, was never by himself. I used to miss
my wash nearly all over every morning very much. A great deal…depended on the men one
was associated with in the bay as to whether there was peace and comfort or otherwise'.[16]

VISITS FROM FAMILY AND FRIENDS

Remanded prisoners were allowed to see their family and friends at reasonable hours twice a week without any order. They might receive additional visits with an order issued by the Visiting Justices. They could also send letters twice a week and receive letters whenever they were addressed to them.[17]

At Newgate, certain days of the week were visiting days for remanded prisoners:

> The friends of prisoners not convicted are allowed to come and see them and converse through wire gratings – two gratings, with a space of some three or four feet between them, in which stands or sits a warder. Any parcels of clothes or other not prohibited articles are passed first to the warder to see there are no 'contraband' things among them, and then, after examination, they are handed by him to the prisoner. Either half-an-hour or an hour…this visiting goes on; the prisoners…stand in a row against these railings, and their friends opposite. Everyone is talking at once with his own friend, and the consequence is a perfect Babel…[18]

Once convicted, different visiting rules applied. A convict undergoing a sentence of penal servitude was entitled to receive rare visits from family and friends, provided he or she had 'earned his proper quota of marks'. In the first year, convicts could receive a visit every six months, in the second year every four months and every three months after that.[19]

In local prisons, arrangements were slightly different. Once a prisoner was convicted, he or she was not allowed to see relatives and friends until the first three months of imprisonment had passed. After this period, they could receive visits once every three months.[20]

When visits did take place, the circumstances were hardly conducive to a happy reunion. In most prisons:

> the prisoner is either locked up in a large iron cage or in a large wooden box, with a small aperture covered with wire netting, through which he is allowed to peer. His friends are placed in a similar cage, some three or four feet distant, and two warders stand between, to listen to, and, if they wish, stop or interrupt the conversation such as it may be.[21]

WRITING AND RECEIVING LETTERS

In the Victorian convict prison, even the writing and receiving of letters from family and friends was rationed to the same extent as visits. This was because such communication from the outside world was considered a privilege to be earned. This privilege could be forfeited if a convict had cause to lose any 'marks'.

On being transferred from one prison to another, convicts were allowed to write home within fourteen days of their arrival. One convict commented: 'This I knew would be a great comfort to those at home. I could tell them I was well, and also inform them where I was, for of course no intimation is otherwise given to the friends of prisoners as to where they may be sent to…'[22]

After this first letter, convicts could receive and write a letter every six months in the first year. By the second year, this had increased to every four months and then every three months after that.[23] In the local prisons where the maximum (and rare) sentence was two years, the number of letters a convicted prisoner could receive or send was also restricted to once every three months.[24]

All letters were censored and read by the governor or chaplain before despatch. One Who Has Endured It was told 'to confine my writing to the ruled lines – not to write between them or to cross my letter'. He 'was not to give any information respecting any other prisoner, or any prison news; was not to write to any improper person, or to use any improper language'.[25]

6

LIVING CONDITIONS

The overall physical state of a prison in terms of its accommodation, atmosphere, ventilation and sanitation had an enormous influence on the life of a prisoner or convict.

THE CELL

As the 'physical hub of the new prisoner's unfamiliar future'[1], the cell was where he or she spent his waking and sleeping hours. The cells were more rudimentary in the public works prisons where convicts spent most of the day working outside. They were described as 'nothing but a small corrugated iron kennel with a stone or slate floor'.[2]

In other prisons, the cell was 'a whitewashed cube 7 feet by 13, with a barred window of ground glass at one end, and a black painted door at the other…'[3] Once the prisoner was locked in, the cell became a dark place with very little daylight to penetrate the gloom. Oscar Wilde recalled: 'It is always twilight in one's cell, as it is always midnight in one's heart.'[4]

Inside the cells at Millbank there were:

> …three blankets, a rug and two coarse linen sheets…a wooden platter and spoon, a wooden salt-box, two tin pint-mugs, a bright pewter chamber utensil, an ordinary school slate, a large wooden bucket or pail, with wooden flat hoops, and fitted with a close-fitting lid, a short-handled hair-broom or brush, a stiff mill-board with a copy of the prison rules and regulations, and a small gas-jet, without tap, protruding from the wall about 4 feet from the ground…[5]

One Who Has Endured It found the bucket with its lid to be an extremely useful multi-functional item: 'It contained the water I washed in, and which I could change twice a day. It formed my seat when at work, and my table when I sat on the bed-place, or platform and had my meals. It always stood near the centre of the cell floor, immediately opposite the inspection aperture'.[6]

In the cell:

> the hours of repose were curtailed, and any attempt to doze, relax, or fall into a reverie after six hours of labouring on the treadwheel or grinding the crank was foiled by requiring the prisoner, under threat of even more drastic punishment, to sit on a backless stool or his upturned slop pail and by setting as a cell task a stiff quota of oakum picking.[7]

No personal possessions were allowed in prison – 'not a picture or even a photograph of the prisoner's wife or child – to break the monotony of the cell wall, or to keep alive any feeling of family affection'.[8]

One Who Has Endured It also commented on this cruel regulation:

> Nothing was allowed to be sent to any prisoner, not even the photograph of a wife or child. This I cannot but think a mistake; anything that tends to soften and humanise a man's heart can

do him no harm – far otherwise. The sight now and then of the face of a loved one…would have kept more than one man I came in contact with from breaking prison rules.[9]

Built into the cell door was a spy-hole, through which prison staff could look at any time of day and night to observe the prisoner. This meant that 'No matter how you would place yourself in your cell, standing, sitting or lying down, that cursed eye seemed to follow you'.[10]

THE BED

On arrival in his cell, a convicted criminal prisoner under the age of fifty would have found a plank bed without a mattress to sleep on. He was to sleep on this for the first month of his sentence or for the whole of his sentence if it was for less than a month. He would have the same amount of bed clothes as the other prisoners. This rule was rigorously enforced unless the surgeon deemed the prisoner unfit, from his state of health, to be deprived of a mattress.[11]

One Who Has Endured It described the bed at Millbank: '…a raised wooden platform, extending right across the cell…At one end of this platform was a step…This platform was my bed-place, on which the straw mattress was laid, and the step acted as bolster, on which I made a pillow of my clothes, no pillow being provided'.[12]

Oscar Wilde wrote that the plank bed 'caused him to shiver all night long and that, as a consequence of its rigors, he had become an insomniac'.[13] Michael Davitt made the same complaint.[14]

Under prison regulations, sheets were to be washed not less than once a month and blankets as frequently as required. The sheets of prisoners receiving medical treatment were to be washed

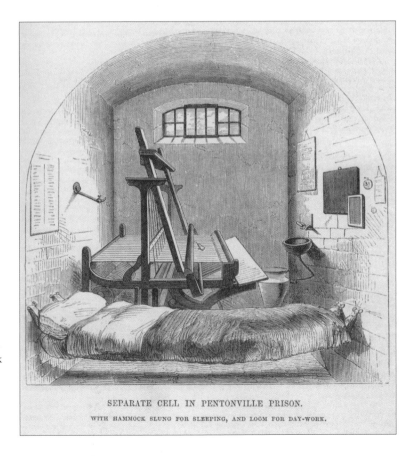

A separate cell at Pentonville, shown with the hammock for sleeping and a loom for working at during the day. (From Mayhew & Binny)

SEPARATE CELL IN PENTONVILLE PRISON.
WITH HAMMOCK SLUNG FOR SLEEPING, AND LOOM FOR DAY-WORK.

Above left: A Victorian prison cell door, possibly at Wakefield.

Above right: The interior of a Victorian prison, possibly Wakefield, showing the different landings.

A dormitory or 'association room' at Coldbath Fields Prison. (From Mayhew & Binny)

as often as the surgeon deemed necessary.[15] However, the standard of washing seems to have varied greatly from prison to prison. One Who Has Suffered It reported that his prison blankets and rugs were never washed.[16] In 1879, Michael Davitt told the Royal Commission on the Penal Servitude Acts that the bedclothes were 'sometimes soiled with faeces'.[17]

The hammock continued to be used in both local and convict prisons throughout the nineteenth century. One prisoner commented on the hammocks at Dartmoor: 'There is one luxury a convict certainly has, and that is a good comfortable warm bed... There is no bed in a hammock, but a man has two good blankets (three in winter), a capital rug, and two stout coarse linen sheets, with a wool or hair pillow. A great many of the prisoners never slept in such good beds when free men. Men have told me repeatedly, especially men from agricultural districts, that they were better fed and had better beds in prison than ever they had in their lives before'.[18]

COLD

Prisoners and convicts who wrote about their experiences in prison all commented on the extreme cold of the cell. The anonymous author of *Pentonville Prison From Within* complained of:

> the horrible sensation of cold in the morning in those cheerless...cells. It was not so much the intensity of the cold...as the abominable feeling of always waking cold, and the hopeless and helpless feeling that there was no prospect of going to sleep again, and no possible way of getting warm till the bell rang and you were allowed to get up and put on your clothes.[19]

Jabez Balfour, a convict at Portland, recalled that 'it was so cold in winter that the very warders of the night patrol used to make their rounds of the peep-holes with blankets wrapped about their heads and shoulders. But if they suffered from the cold, what was it to us prisoners?'[20]

NOISE

A prison could be a noisy place. One convict described the noise caused by the simultaneous shutting of the cell doors at Dartmoor:

> The entire block of 400 cells being all framed in iron there was hardly a door slammed to in the whole building that did not more or less vibrate throughout every cell. The effect when every cell door in the whole hall was slammed to at once, as they were on certain occasions, such as school nights, was like a volley of musketry.[21]

The man next to One Who Has Endured It's cell at Dartmoor had either struck or threatened an officer and had been 'bashed' or flogged. He was condemned to a punishment of wearing fetters:

> a heavy chain, one end of which was fastened with riveted rings round each ankle, and the middle of it was held up to his waist by a strap. Night and day, in bed and out of bed, did he wear these chains, and every time he moved in bed they clanked and rattled; and sometimes in turning round they would strike against the corrugated iron partition of the cell; not a very cheering sound to hear in the dead hours of the night.[22]

Another prisoner recalled:

> When the door banging is done, night is not silent. They choose this time when all the prisoners have gone to bed, for administering the cat-o'-nine-tails to men who have been

sentenced to that punishment. You are awakened by the voice of the doctor calling to a warder, as he stumbles along the dark walls towards the room where the dread chastisement is administered. Then there are the frantic and furious cries of the unhappy victim, and his hellish, dismal howls continue to resound through the otherwise silent patches of the night, long after the operation is finished.[23]

VENTILATION

The majority of prisons would have had the same problem with ventilation as the New Bailey Prison in Salford. Here, the prisoners tried to 'stop uncomfortable draughts by stuffing their unglazed windows with rags' while the administrators wanted to maintain a degree of ventilation to promote good health.[24] The 'small, cold, dark, and rather clammy cells'[25] were the perfect breeding grounds for all forms of lung disease, including tuberculosis.

SANITATION AND DRAINAGE

After 1880, repairs and alterations were undertaken at sixty-two prisons with most of the work completed by 1884. Improvements were made to heating, lighting and sanitation. It was reported that 'Sanitary work of the ordinary kind has continued to receive a large amount of attention, indeed there are few prisons where some improvement has not been made to bring it into keeping with modern sanitary ideas'.[26]

A major problem discovered when the local prisons were taken over was that almost every cell had its own water-closet. Unfortunately, the design of the basins and the connection to the sewers 'were such as to release vile and unhealthy gases through the cells and into the whole of the prison, and also, through the untrapped water pipes, into the cisterns and general water supply'.[27]

All these water-closets were removed by 1890 except in Newgate and in the female prisons of Manchester, Strangeways and Plymouth. Although better designed water-closets were available from 1889, cost constraints meant prisons took the 'cheaper option of communal landing and yard laboratories, and slop-buckets for overnight sanitation'.[28]

In Pentonville, when prisoners had to use chamber-pots during the night 'owing to the nature of the food...the fact is made known by a nasal telegram, almost over the whole ward...there was no adequate means of escape for the foul air that collected in the central hall of the prison, and the smell there of a morning was enough to knock you down'.[29]

MEDICAL FACILITIES

Every prison was supposed to have a separate wing or area reserved for hospital use. However, the hospital wing was not necessarily a healthier place than the standard cells. At the end of the nineteenth century in the hospital wing at Pentonville, the author of *Pentonville Prison From Within*:

> ...slept no better at nights...vermin abounded in the hospital cell. I woke...to the dismal sound of cockroaches dropping in great haste and hurry from the ceiling, walls, and wooden sideboard, and it was not long before I felt and found one running nimbly across my face, as I lay, only raised a few inches from the boarded floor on my plank bed.[30]

INFECTIOUS DISEASES

While many prisoners were already suffering from infectious diseases before their convictions, prison itself was an ideal breeding ground for potential epidemics. After the local prisons came under government control in 1877, each prison was individually inspected with regard to the state of the buildings. By July 1880, Dr Robert Gover, the Medical Inspector of Prisons, had issued detailed instructions to bring the prisons 'up to and maintaining them in the highest attainable sanitary condition, and of protecting their inmates, as far as possible, from the operation of all cause of preventable disease'.[31]

In 1882, priority was given to the rebuilding of Shrewsbury Prison as it had been home to numerous epidemics. Dr Gover described the general condition of the prison:

> The cells were not only badly arranged as regards closet provision, but were in many instances ill-paved and germ-sodden, so that efficient and precise disinfection was impossible....the whole area of the prison buildings was furnished with badly arranged and imperfectly constructed drains, which in many cases were simply brick culverts. Typhoid fever was endemic... [and] affected the staff as well as the prisoners to such a degree that there were sometimes more than half a dozen cases at one time. Diarrhoea was also constantly present...

Dr Gover reported a 'remarkable improvement in health' after the rebuilding was complete.[32]

Throughout the 1880s, an ongoing programme of improvements to reception buildings was under way. Many local prisons lacked this important facility altogether which had to accommodate examination rooms, clothing stores, the disinfecting apparatus, baths and holding cells.[33]

The prison authorities justified the expense of providing such reception buildings:

> A large proportion of the prisoners who form the population of our prisons are of diseased and impaired constitutions, victims of dirt, intemperance, and irregularity, and the sins of the fathers in these respects are visited on the children 'to the third and fourth generation'. The accurate medical examination of these on reception, the cleansing of them and their clothing from vermin and dirt, the due apportionment of labour, and, in many cases, their immediate medical treatment, have necessitated the provision of proper reception buildings, apart from the rest of the prison, where these processes can be carried on, and risk of carrying infection into the prison obviated.[34]

When there were instances of infectious disease in prison, special sick cells were used to isolate the afflicted. Some large prisons, such as Birmingham, Holloway and Maidstone, had superior facilities for dealing with infectious cases. These included isolation wards with separate entrances and accommodation for nurses.[35]

PREVENTION OF SUICIDES

As well as improving accommodation and sanitation, steps were taken to modify prisons to reduce opportunities for prisoners to attempt suicide. By 1890, padded cells were available at most prisons for those who had attempted suicide, as well as for insane and epileptic prisoners. Modifications were made to window catches, bars and ventilators and handrails were installed on stairs. The alarm bell handles, which were 'shaped so prisoners could suspend themselves from them', were removed from all cells and replaced by drop handles or electrical bells.[36]

Towards the end of the 1880s, wire netting was fitted across galleries between the first-floor landings at Clerkenwell, Holloway, Pentonville and other prisons with a high turnover. This was extended to all prisons by the 1890s.[37]

DIETARY AND HEALTH

Throughout the Victorian period, the quantity of food provided to prisoners and convicts was a contentious issue. While the diet was meant to be a deterrent, it also had to provide sufficient sustenance to enable prisoners to complete their work tasks.

The quantity of food provided was not equal in convict and local prisons. In 1863, the diet in convict prisons was reduced on the recommendation of a Board of Medical Officers because of 'the allegedly excessive amounts of food given to convicts, compared with what was given to local prisoners and soldiers'.[1] The quality of the food also varied greatly from prison to prison.

DIETARY

Prison diets varied according to the labour the prisoner was undertaking, and to which class he or she belonged. They were based on the dietaries recommended by Sir James Graham in 1843 for use in local prisons. These dietaries, which were adapted for use in convict prisons, consisted of six main ingredients: bread, gruel, potatoes, meat, soup and cocoa. However, not every prisoner received all the ingredients in their meals because there was a graduated scale of diets for various terms of imprisonment. Generally, prisoners had bread and gruel for both breakfast and supper. The only variation occurred at dinner when there were alternate days for meat with potatoes and for soup.

The infamous no. 1 diet which consisted simply of bread and gruel was 'as close to starvation as an institution could come'.[2] This was given to prisoners without hard labour during their first seven days of imprisonment.[3] On admission to prison, it was the medical officer's responsibility to identify all those unfit for the no. 1 diet or hard labour, or both. As many of the prisoners were in poor health on arrival at prison, the consequences of being subjected to this diet while working on the treadwheel or crank were dire. Misdiagnoses could prove fatal. The no. 1 diet was eventually discontinued.[4]

The gruel, also known as stirabout or skilly, was 'composed of equal parts of oatmeal and Indian meal'.[5] The stirabout was extremely disliked by both male and female prisoners. Members of the Gladstone Committee who visited prisons between 1894 and 1895 noticed large quantities of stirabout were discarded. Upon investigation, Dr Walker of Holloway reported that 'three-quarters of the stirabout was refused' because the Indian meal was so unpalatable.[6]

Miss Gee, the matron at Liverpool, reported that 'nineteen out of twenty women would not eat the no. 1 scale'. This mainly affected the drunks who could not eat the stirabout. Miss Gee explained:

> They come in tipsy the night before; then the next morning they do not feel very grand, and they are given cold water to drink. I think it would have a good effect if they had a pint of gruel. In the old days they had a pint of gruel night and mornings, and bread in the day-time. I think that it is better than the stirabout.[7]

By contrast, One Who Has Endured It enjoyed the 'very good thick gruel, sweetened with treacle' which was provided at Millbank, a convict prison.[8]

The bread was also variable in quality. Varying amounts of potatoes, soup, meat and cocoa were used in the other classes of diet. The cocoa was made with 'three quarters of an ounce of the solid flake, and flavoured with two ounces of pure milk and six drachms of molasses'.[9] Cocoa was recommended because it 'contains a good deal of that oily element which, if we could manage it, should always exist in food…'[10]

After 1864, suet pudding could be used as a substitute for meat.[11] However, this was not liked at all by the prisoners. One prisoner reported to the Gladstone Committee that, 'no matter how hungry a man might be, his stomach would naturally turn from it'.[12]

Overall, One Who Has Endured It thought the food at Millbank was 'plain but good and well cooked, and, considering the little exercise the men have, not insufficient. The soup was really most excellent, evidently made from heads and shins of beef, well stewed, and thickened with pearl barley and vegetables'.[13]

Under the 'progressive' dietary of the local prisons, the food allowance in the early stages was decidedly meagre. Few prisoners stayed long enough in local prisons to progress beyond the first or second stage of the dietary to benefit from 'a marginally improved allowance'.[14]

The lifestyle of habitual offenders meant they would be imprisoned for a week or two on 'minimum diet, debilitating labour, and depressing conditions', and after a short time on the streets, would return to prison for more of the same. Such people included drunks, beggars, tramps, prostitutes, nuisances and petty thieves, and 'the cumulative effects of the prison dietary on such people serving life by instalments…were devastating and destructive'.[15]

After 1892, a special dietary for all prisoners on the day of their reception was introduced. This was similar to the no. IV scale, and 'was intended to be a life-jacket for the destitute and famished, pending their medical examination, and the possible award of a restorative dietary'.[16] The reception day scale was 'breakfast: 8 oz bread, 1 pint cocoa; dinner: 12 oz bread, 4 oz preserved meat and supper: 8 oz bread, 1 pint porridge'.[17]

At the end of the nineteenth century, the anonymous author of *Pentonville Prison From Within* was sentenced to six months in the prison. By this time, Pentonville had been downgraded to a local prison. The author wrote of the prison diet:

> For breakfast (about 7.45 a.m.) I was given a pint of tea and a six-ounce bread roll; no butter. I then worked and took an hour's exercise, and at 12 midday a tin containing two potatoes and some beans and fat bacon (a gruesome and nauseating mixture, slimy and apt to cause sickness) and a five-ounce brown roll was thrust into my cell. I then worked at sewing sandbags until five in the evening, when a pint of cocoa and an eight-ounce brown roll (dry bread as before) was thrust into my cell. That was tea and supper combined. I had no more food till 7.45 the next morning. I soon turned into a pale and trembling mortal as a prisoner in His Majesty's Prison. These trembling fits, accompanied by faintness, regularly overtook me about an hour before the next 'meal' was due.[18]

On Tuesdays and Fridays dinner consisted of a 'peculiar, thick, stringy and doubtful soup' while on Wednesdays and Saturdays it was a pudding made of 'a hideous chunk of putty-like suet'. Thursday's dinner 'was the best of the week, and consisted of a piece of steak floating in a couple of inches of gravy at the bottom of its tin'.[19]

The author added 'a careful examination of the potatoes was always necessary as on tearing them in half, the interior was often found to be a mass of foul, black, spongy disease – a great disappointment to a starving man'.[20]

Oscar Wilde 'reported to friends, and in articles published after his release, that the food was revolting and insufficient, that diarrhoea was so common that astringent medicines were issued as a matter of routine, and that on three occasions he had seen prison staff vomit when they unlocked cells in the morning'.[21]

HUNGER

Visitors to Victorian prisons frequently commented that the prisoners and convicts complained of feeling hungry. Michael Davitt, a Fenian convict, served eight years of a fifteen-year sentence

Left: Page from Jabez Steane's journal showing dietary at Abingdon, 1857. (Courtesy of Anthony Baker)

Opposite: Female convicts at work in the bakery of Aylesbury Prison. (Supplement to *The Sphere*, 12 December 1908, courtesy of Karl Vaughan)

of penal servitude. He described the dietary as a 'scale of scientific starvation'. He added: 'There is no bodily punishment more cruel than hunger – that remorseless, gnawing, human feeling which tortures the mind in thinking of the sufferings of the body, and tending to make life an unbearable infliction under a denial of the elementary cravings of nature'.[22]

The hunger was so extreme that Davitt recalled how, 'he had seen men devour candle ends, the grease provided for their boots, the marrow of the putrid bones they had been set to break and grind, and even a used poultice retrieved from the prison garbage heap by the cesspool'.[23]

Prisoners in the local prisons of the 1870s were 'more likely to be emaciated than overweight' and they performed their labour at the treadwheel for six hours a day on a diet of 'oatmeal, bread, and water, after nights and days of extreme discomfort'.[24]

Ticket-of-leave-man recalled how desperate some men were for food:

Owing to my weak state of health I was unable to eat the allowance of bread, and the prisoner who came round to empty the slops, noticing I did not consume it, asked me to give it to him. Knowing that I should be punished if detected for so doing, he even suggested that I should place it in the receptacle among the unpleasant accumulations of the day, and that he would take it from there. To such extremity of hunger was the poor fellow driven that he would even have done this to obtain extra food.[25]

ILLNESS

Changes to the dietary could bring about a deterioration in the health of prisoners and convicts. Serious scurvy was rare in Lancashire until after the adoption of the government dietary of 1843, which reduced the allowance of potatoes. In 1847-8 the Kirkdale medical officer reported between twenty and thirty cases of scurvy, 'a disease we never knew before'.[26] Nutritional deficiency also contributed to other diseases, either by lowering resistance or by creating specific symptoms such as cirrhosis of the liver, 'debility' or 'exhaustion', anaemia and possibly 'fits'.[27]

The poor physical condition of many prisoners caused problems for the authorities. In 1837, Inspector William John Williams argued that:

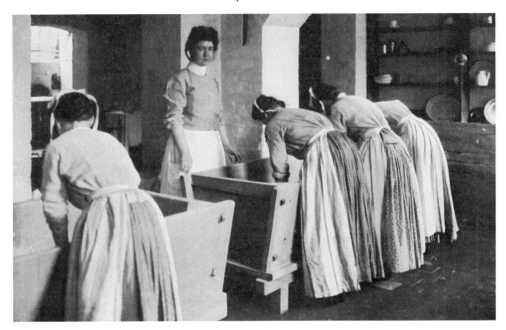

One of the most serious and increasing obstacles to good discipline is the common practice of tramps and prostitutes, when infected with foul diseases, (not admitted into public infirmaries), committing some slight offence for the purpose of obtaining medical treatment in prisons. Their committals are generally for one or two months to hard labour, which they seldom or never undergo, oftentimes passing the entire of the term in hospital; and many of the females are scarcely discharged a month, ere they return again for surgical care.[28]

This reliance on the prison as a source of medical treatment was observed by the Revd John Clay at Preston. He attended a dying woman who 'sinking under disease, and recollecting the attention she had received, some years before, in the hospital of the prison…committed a trifling theft in order to obtain admission to it again'.[29]

COMPARISON BETWEEN WORKHOUSE, FREE LABOURERS AND PRISON DIETARIES

A study from 1862 carried out by Dr Edward Smith investigated the dietaries of the poor labouring classes. The results revealed that:

farm workers, still the poorest group of regularly employed labourers, and a group whose toil fairly closely resembled that of the prisoner on the treadwheel, or at the crank, consumed more than twelve and a quarter pounds of bread, one pound of meat, six pounds of potatoes and half a pound of sugar per week, together with small quantities of dairy produce and fats.

This was still greater than the prison dietary.[30]

However, the prison dietary compared favourably with the dietary offered in the workhouse. This was the explanation given for the behaviour of countless workhouse inmates, particularly vagrants, who destroyed property in order to be admitted to prison for a short term. In 1878, a reporter for the *Sheffield & Rotherham Independent* went undercover in the casual ward at the Sheffield Union Workhouse where he met a vagrant known as 'Prison Jack'. Jack regularly tramped around the country until the cold weather set in.

...his habit was to seek shelters, for the winter months, and this he did by insulting the 'Screw' as they called the workhouse governor while staying in the 'Spike' – the workhouse; or, if opportunity did not serve for this, a favourite plan was to tear up his clothing, or burn the oakum he was set to pick; any of which vagaries would result in his being taken before the 'beak' and 'quadded'...[31]

According to the *Justice of the Peace* publication of March 1866, 'at Pentonville Prison a convict gets 140oz of bread a week, and at Millbank Prison 150oz, so that, as regards 'the staff of life', the convict has the advantage over the pauper'.[32] In the workhouse, able-bodied paupers received 96oz of bread per week.[33] In addition, the maximum amount of meat given in any London workhouse to 'able-bodied paupers' was 'below the minimum given in any London convict prison, that minimum being 30oz'.[34] Given that vagrants were fed an even more inferior diet than the workhouse inmates, prison was clearly an attractive proposition to them.

The overfeeding of convicts was regularly highlighted as a dilution of prison deterrence. Writing to *The Times*, William Tallack, of the prison-reforming Howard Association, argued that 'Humane prison officers state that certain classes of prisoners are so well fed and well treated that the necessary conditions of due deterrence for the protection of society from crime and violence are thereby weakened'. He also contrasted the convict dietary with that of able-bodied paupers in the workhouse. The convict was given 280 ounces of solid food a week, the pauper 166.[35]

ROLE OF THE MEDICAL OFFICER

It was one of the medical officer's many duties to make recommendations regarding the prison dietary. At Easter 1845, the medical officer of the Gloucester County Gaol and Penitentiary recommended that 'as the Potatoes become of bad quality during the ensuing Quarter the adoption of such proportion of boiled Rice with Treacle as shall on consideration be deemed to afford an equal quantity of Nutrient to the Potatoes abstracted...'[36]

He also recommended that the 'quantity of Bread in the Dietary of Class 5 in the new Prison Regulations be increased both at Breakfast and Supper to 8 ounces and that Breakfast throughout the year be served before hard labour commences...'[37]

A year later, the poor quality of potatoes was still raising concern. After a special investigation by Thomas Evans MD, John W. Wilton and Thomas Hickes, the prison medical officer, it was commented that potatoes:

> form part of the prison Diet in its solid plainly boiled state and as a constituent of the Soup. For each pound of plainly boiled Potatoes we would substitute four ounces of Rice flavoured with onions, salt and pepper, and supply the absence from the Soup by adding to it double the present amount of Rice and Onions. In the event of a total failure or marked deterioration of the quality of the potatoes, we recommend a moderate supply of Green or fresh Vegetables such as Cabbages, Greens and Turnips with a full allowance of condiments for Prisoners subject to prolonged confinement.[38]

Prison medical officers had the power to override recommendations about the dietary by the central prison authorities if they believed it was in the best interests of the prisoners. In June 1868, George Edwin Hyde, the medical officer of Worcester Prison, recommended:

> that fresh beef be given as the meat ration on Mondays and Fridays, instead of the South American beef which was recommended by the Commission on Prison Dietaries 'as an economical substitute for the more expensive English beef'. The use of South American beef will...be confined to the making of soup, in conjunction with an equal portion of English beef.[39]

8

DISCIPLINE

In 1865, there were 'only about one thousand wardens to cope with an average prison population of eighteen thousand'.[1] With such a high ratio of prisoners to prison officers, strict discipline was paramount to maintain control. The answer, which was linked to the rules and regulations, was the 'stage' or 'mark' system. This system was attractive to the prison administrators and staff because 'it provided maximum control, allowed minimal indulgences, and yet needed the fewest possible additional punishments'.[2]

DISCIPLINE IN CONVICT PRISONS

In convict prisons from 1853, the 'stage' system was used to enforce discipline and to reward good behaviour. Penal servitude was divided into three stages. In the first stage lasting nine months, the convict spent his or her time in solitary confinement. In the second stage, the convict worked in close association with other prisoners 'under a close and strict supervision'.[3] The third stage was the period after release when he or she was kept under the supervision of the police.

Within the 'stage' system, the convicts were divided into classes. Convicts could be promoted into the next class by earning 'marks'. There were a maximum of eight marks available to earn per day which could be gained by hard work.

For the first twelve months, the convict was in the probationary class and wore a registered number printed on a drab badge on the left arm, and no facings on the jacket. For the second year in the third class, the convict wore a black badge and facings with the number printed in red on the badge. The probationary and third classes carried 'no privileges with them'.[4]

After two years, if convicts had earned a full complement of marks, or so soon as they were earned, they were promoted to the second class. They wore a yellow badge and facings with their number printed in black. Members of this and of the first class were known as 'tea men' because they had the privilege of having 'one pint of tea every evening instead of gruel'.[5]

After three years and with the required number of marks, the convict could be promoted into the highest, or first class and wore a blue badge and facings with the number printed in black. If a convict was reported for any infringement of rules or misconduct and was punished, he or she might lose marks and privileges 'for such time as the governor or deputy may determine', besides having bread and water for so many days. It was technically possible for 'some unruly characters [to] pass their whole time in the probationary class'.[6]

If a convict was moved from the first or second class, he or she had to spend some time in the third class and lose the privilege of having tea. This, 'among prisoners, is termed "smashing the teapot" and when a man is restored to his class, and has his tea, it is said he has "had his teapot mended" or "got it down the spout"'.[7]

The highest incentive offered to the convict by the 'stage' system was the opportunity to earn remission from his or her sentence. One Who Has Endured It, sentenced to five years' penal servitude, noted that: 'It is very seldom a man goes through a whole term of service without losing some marks. I reckoned very quickly that it was just possible I could get twelve months and three weeks remission off my five years. I actually got off twelve months and ten days'.[8]

The flogging ward and chain room at Newgate Prison. (*Illustrated London News*, 29 December 1888)

DISCIPLINE IN LOCAL PRISONS

A version of the stage system was extended to local prisons in 1877. The system was made up of four stages and prisoners could be promoted to the next stage if they had earned 224 marks, at a maximum rate of eight per day. As twenty-eight days had be spent in each stage before promotion could be achieved, this meant that, despite good behaviour and hard work, prisoners with short sentences were confined to the early stages.[9]

Prisoners had to earn a minimum six marks per day by completing their prescribed work task. To earn seven or eight marks, the prisoner had to put in an extra effort to achieve more than his or her quota. If a prisoner failed to earn the six marks by falling short of it, he would automatically be charged with idleness. Allowances were made for new, inexperienced prisoners until they became used to the new work tasks.[10]

In the first stage, the prisoner was kept in close confinement and put to hard labour for between six and ten hours a day. For the first fourteen days, he would lie down to sleep on a hard plank bed without the comfort of a mattress. These were the conditions experienced by all short-term prisoners sentenced to four weeks' imprisonment or less.[11]

On promotion to the second stage, labour was less arduous and could be performed in association, instead of in close confinement. These prisoners could earn a maximum release gratuity of up to one shilling and could borrow one book from the library each week, in addition to the educational books they already had access to. If eligible, they could also receive school instruction.[12]

Third stage prisoners were entitled to an increased maximum release gratuity of 1s 6d and to two library books each week. Perhaps a more coveted privilege was the permission to send and receive a letter and to have a twenty-minute visit from family or friends.[13]

At the fourth stage, prisoners were entitled to an increased rate of gratuity up to a maximum of 10 shillings over the whole of the sentence. They could be considered for special employment, for instance in a maintenance party, they could write and receive a letter and have a half-hour visit after reaching 112 marks and this could be repeated every time they reached 224 marks.[14]

Unlike convict prisoners, prisoners in local prisons could not earn remission from their sentences, despite good behaviour and hard work. In addition, if local prisoners were ill and unable to work, they were not allowed to earn their marks while convicts might be allowed them, at the discretion of the governor.[15]

PUNISHMENT OF REFRACTORY PRISONERS

In cases of mild refractory behaviour such as idleness, insubordination or fighting, the prison governor had the power to order a penalty of confinement in the punishment cell on a diet of bread and water. The maximum penalty the governor could impose without permission from the Visiting Justices was three days in the punishment cell on a diet of bread and water. However, this could be repeated if there were breaks in between.[16]

For more serious offences, the governor would report to the Visiting Justices who would investigate the charges. If found guilty, the prisoner might be subjected to a maximum of fourteen days in a punishment cell. If the prisoner had already been convicted of a felony or sentenced to hard labour, he might also receive a sentence of corporal punishment. However, this only applied to serious offences such as 'assaults, threats to staff, false accusations against staff, damage to property and as the punishment for the persistent repeat offender'.[17] The use of 'dark cells' was banned after 1878 and was replaced with cells 'containing nothing in the way of furniture except a raised platform of hard wood on one side large enough for the occupant to lie down on, with a piece of wood fastened at one end for a pillow'.[18]

The governor had to record all punishments for prison offences in a punishment book. In order to prevent abuse of power or maltreatment of prisoners, certain safeguards were attached to the meting out of corporal punishment. Under the terms of the 1865 Prison Act, no prisoner was allowed to be put in irons or under any form of mechanical restraint, except in case of urgent necessity, and for no longer than twenty-four hours without an order from a Visiting Justice. If corporal punishment was deemed necessary, it had to be carried out with the governor and medical officer in attendance. It was the medical officer's duty to 'give such orders for preventing injury to health as he may deem necessary…' The governor had to enter in the punishment book the time and date of the punishment, the number of lashes and any orders given by the medical officer.[19] From 1878, the surgeon had to certify whether a prisoner was fit enough to be subjected to 'dietary punishment or confinement in the punishment cell'.[20]

With regard to corporal punishment, prisoners under the age of eighteen could only be birched. Prisoners over the age of eighteen could be subjected to the 'cat' or the birch for a maximum of thirty-six strokes. Both the 'cat' and the birch rod had to be manufactured to a design approved by the prison authorities.[21]

Refractory prisoners caused real problems for the staff of prisons across England. In February 1871 at Worcester, the governor reported that a prisoner named Robert Ray had fastened:

the door of his cell on the inside so that the officers could not enter. At 7pm I ordered the doors forced open and found that prisoner had pulled down the piping & otherwise damaged

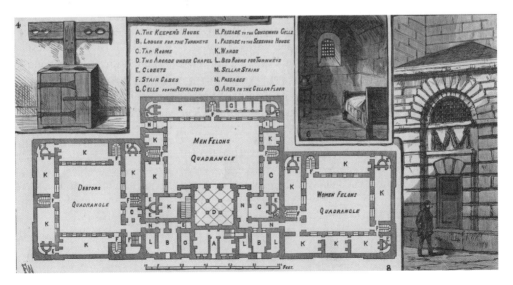

A plan of Newgate Prison together with a view of the flogging block and a cell for prisoners condemned to death. (*Illustrated London News*, 29 December 1888)

Convicts
returning from
work at Portland.
The convicts are
being counted
back in to prison.

the cell fittings & torn his bedding. I removed him to the light punishment cell, so that he could be attended to & seen by the warders through the open prison gate.[22]

The following day, the Visiting Justices sanctioned Robert Ray's removal to the light refractory cell. However, at 3pm he was reported to be 'very violent and refractory'. The governor visited him and:

found that he had removed a number of bricks from the wall in his cell, broken the thick glass in the window & destroyed the water closet. On the officers attempting to enter the cell he threw pieces of brick at them through the open iron door. It being necessary for the safety of the warder that mechanical restraint should be used...ordered prisoner placed in irons for 48 hours.[23]

Robert Ray continued to be disruptive and is mentioned again in the governor's journal of March 1871:

I have carefully watched this man since his committal, and I am of opinion, that he is not insane. He is at all times perfectly coherent, has no delictions that I can discover, and all his acts of violence and insubordination show premeditation... I think he is accountable for his conduct, he is wickedly disposed and has a violent temper, and I believe that he is deliberately taking advantage of his supposed insanity to escape his sentence...[24]

A riot at the Great Yarmouth Union Workhouse led to the ringleader, Charles Girdlestone, being arrested after seriously injuring a policeman's hand. This man, a twenty-two-year-old labourer, was the 'terror of the workhouse' and his behaviour was so violent he had to be transported to the court handcuffed and 'strapped down on a barrow' accompanied by seven policemen. It was reported that 'he used the most violent and disgusting language and resembled a maniac rather than a human being'. Charles was sentenced to forty-two days' hard labour while three other guilty paupers had to work the treadmill for twenty-one days. Whilst in prison, Charles Girdlestone's violent behaviour led to him being flogged and a soldier from Norwich was sent for 'whose vigorous application of the cat reduced Girdlestone to obedience'.[25]

Vagrants were often disruptive prisoners and were considered to be a blight on English prisons. In September 1871, Thomas Pursey, a vagrant imprisoned at Worcester Prison, repeatedly refused to work on the treadwheel. His punishment was twenty-four lashes with a cat o'nine tails. This appears to have had the desired effect because three days later the governor reported that 'The refractory prisoner Thomas Pursey went to work at the wheel this morning'.[26]

9

WORK

Under prison regulations, if a male prisoner over the age of sixteen was sentenced to hard labour, this was to be of the first class 'during the whole of his sentence, where it does not exceed three months, and during the first three months of his sentence where it exceeds three months'. He was to work for not more than ten or less than six hours (exclusive of meals), subject to the medical officer's approval. After three months, the justices could prescribe second class labour, which was less severe than labour of the first class. By 1877, the maximum period in which a prisoner was to undertake first class hard labour was reduced from three months to one.[1]

If the medical officer deemed any prisoner to be unfit for hard labour of the first class, he could order he be kept at hard labour of the second class. The surgeon could also certify that a prisoner was unfit to be kept at either class of labour. Prisoners sentenced to hard labour for periods not exceeding fourteen days could be kept in separate confinement at hard labour of the second class.

Those who were not fit enough for hard labour of either class were to be employed in a trade. There was no hard labour on Sundays, Christmas Day, Good Friday or on days appointed for public fasts or thanksgivings.[2]

HARD LABOUR

Hard labour of the first class was usually work at the treadwheel, shot drill, crank, capstan or stone-breaking. In practice, this varied from prison to prison and other work tasks were in use as hard labour.

In 1863, the Carnarvon Committee, made up of members of the House of Lords, was appointed to look at discipline in English prisons. Upon investigation, they discovered that there was a distinct lack of a definition for 'hard labour'. The committee members believed that only the treadwheel and the crank could be classed as hard labour but 'in some prisons mat-making was considered light labour…in others it was defined hard labour'.[3]

When the Prison Act of 1865 was passed, it was decreed that 'the treadwheel, crank, capstan, shot-drill and stone-breaking were listed as acceptable types of first class hard labour, and such others as the justices wished to provide had to be approved by the Secretary of State'.[4]

However, as late as 1879, it was discovered that 'mat-making, coir-plaiting, oakum-picking, weaving, rope beating, net-making, twine-spinning, sugar chopping and blacksmithing were all variously used and represented as first class labour'.[5]

In 1866 at the Kirkdale House of Correction, hard labour of the first class for male prisoners under the age of fifty consisted of work on the treadwheel or crank, shot drill or stone-breaking. For those over fifty, male prisoners might also undertake weaving of 'cocoa matting, ticking for beds, linsey, woolsey and such like heavy weaving, making cocoa yarn mats by hand on a frame with a beater about 5lbs in weight, weaving of mats and carpets, rope and oakum beating or work at platting and chipping machines'.[6]

Hard labour of the second class at Kirkdale, usually for those in weaker health, could include: 'Weaving of calico, shoemaking and clogging, tailoring, tin-plate working, coopers' and turners' work, painting and whitewashing, splicing cocoa yarn for weaving, winding bobbins, picking cotton and wool by task-work, opening and teasing hair and cocoa fibre by task work and picking oakum by task work.'[7]

Prisoners might also be asked to undertake joinery, stonemasonry, bricklaying, plumbing or smiths' work for repairing the prison and making and repairing its furniture.

Those prisoners not sentenced to hard labour were expected to pick cotton, wool or oakum by moderate task work, to undertake light hand-loom weaving and to clean and sweep rooms, passages and yards.[8]

Employment in the necessary services of the prison could, in the case of a limited number of prisoners, be deemed hard labour of the second class. This was considered a reward for industry and good behaviour.

At the Leeds Borough District Gaol and House of Correction, trades carried out included tailoring, shoemaking, joinery, weaving, mat-making and bookbinding. Prisoners were also employed in picking oakum and wool, picking and preparing silk and winding fancy wools. The females were employed in knitting and needlework.

The chaplain of the Leeds Borough District Gaol and House of Correction argued that:

employment is without doubt a very necessary element in the means of reformation, and there is no reason why it should not be made productive; but it is mistaken economy to sacrifice the system of separate confinement, merely to swell the profits of the manufactory. Many trades may be pursued with equal and some with greater advantage by prisoners in their separate cells, and if all persons committed for short periods...were, as a general rule, placed in separate confinement, the labour and employment where association is indispensable might be followed by prisoners who had passed satisfactorily through a period of probation in separate confinement. Associated labour might thus not only be held out as a privilege to the well conducted, but would also assist the officers very materially in testing the character of the prisoners.[9]

In 1851 at the Northallerton House of Correction for the North Riding, prisoners worked the treadwheel and the cranks. Some of the prisoners were also employed in tailoring, shoemaking and knitting stockings for the use of the prison but there was 'much difficulty in procuring any sort of work in the neighbourhood, they are not therefore kept fully employed'. When associated, the prisoners were under strict supervision and silence was strictly enforced.[10]

At the Exeter County Gaol and House of Correction in 1853, the prisoners were employed in stone-breaking which they undertook 'in 25 partitioned cells in the yard opening to the south, and having a passage down the front and a box for the inspecting officers'. Although the prison had twelve hard-labour cranks, they were only used for the 'vagrants, workhouse offenders, and other prisoners considered incorrigible, and also those who have been frequently imprisoned'.[11]

In 1852, at the Gloucester County Gaol and Penitentiary, the criminal prisoners were employed in weaving cloth and making cocoa-fibre mats. Various kinds of cloth were manufactured at Gloucester including sacking, tarpaulin, woollen cloth for prisoner's clothing, neck-handkerchiefs, pocket handkerchiefs, calico for shirts for prisons, linen for shirts for the lunatic asylum, linen sheeting, bed-casing and toweling.

At the time of the inspector's visit, six men were employed in tailoring and twelve in shoemaking, half of whom could make a complete shoe. Twenty-three were picking oakum, five were cleaning the prison and two were whitewashing it. The treadwheel was also used, with fifty prisoners working on it. Eight prisoners were employed in washing. Work for the female prisoners included washing, needlework, knitting and cleaning.[12]

The treadwheel at Coldbath Fields Prison. (From Mayhew & Binny)

A prisoner at crank labour in the Surrey House of Correction. (From Mayhew & Binny)

THE TREADWHEEL

Invented by William Cubitt in 1818, there was no ambiguity about whether or not the treadwheel was appropriate for hard labour of the first class. Contemporary illustrations of prisoners working on the wheel fail to 'convey the motion, the noise, the palpable strain and smell of intense physical effort'.[13] One prison medical officer commented that novice prisoners on the treadwheel or those incapacitated through drink found the wheel 'very trying, if not dangerous'.[14] When working the treadwheel, the prisoner had to lift 'his body up three feet at each step'.[15] Until 1880, the task was not standardised and the height the prisoners were required to climb varied from prison to prison. The Prison Discipline Society advised that each male individual should complete '12,000 feet of ascent per diem' which was akin to climbing the Matterhorn.[16] However, at York prisoners climbed 6,000 feet, at Stafford it was 16,630 feet while at Salford's New Bailey it was 19,400 in summer and 14,450 in winter.[17]

The intense physical effort required by prisoners working the treadwheel raised concerns about their state of health and whether the quantity of diet allowed to them was sufficient. In 1844, at Gloucester Gaol and Penitentiary, John W. Wilton, a Member of the College of Surgeons, reported that, 'The two working prisoners who do not complain [about the diet] have only been in the penitentiary one Month, but they are both losing flesh – as indeed is almost universally the case when men first come over to the Penitentiary & the labour of the wheel – of 25 who came over exactly one month ago – 2 are in Hospital, the remainder 23 have all lost weight from 2 to 9 pounds – the average loss being 4 pounds 2 ounces, these men…are asking for more Bread so that if more causes operate to reduce and depress the system, it does not appear to be to any great extent, or the stomach would not covet an increase of food – I therefore infer that the supply is not adequate to sustain them in their full strength under the increased bodily exertion, to which they are now subjected'.[18]

In June 1868 at Worcester Prison, it was recommended by the medical officer George Edwin Hyde that 'no prisoner be worked on the treadwheel before breakfast, and that a corresponding period of hard labour in the cell be substituted…'[19] By June 1872, he recommended that the class 1 prisoners working on the treadwheel 'be allowed one pint of gruel for breakfast and supper daily, in addition to the ordinary diet of that class'.[20]

Prisoners would do almost anything to avoid working on the treadwheel. In 1850, the surgeon at the House of Correction at Kirton-in-Lindsay reported that:

> They frequently swallow soap, which has the effect of purging them and bringing on a low fever, during the continuance of which it is impossible to put a man on the wheel. They formerly ate large quantities of salt, in order to bring on fever, and to prevent this they were deprived of their salt bags… I think it very desirable as a matter of health, as well as in a moral point of view, that some other employment should be substituted for the treadwheel labour; and as an immediate measure, I would recommend that, during the last quarter of an hour before breakfast, and the last half-hour before dinner and supper, the prisoners should leave the wheel and walk about to cool themselves gradually, instead of going straight into the cold passages to get their meals.[21]

Working the treadwheel could be extremely dangerous for those new to the task, or those who were simply exhausted. At Stafford, 'one man fell off the wheel from sheer exhaustion. The cry "a man down" was soon raised, and the mill at once stopped, but not until he had been terribly crushed by it…one of his legs was broken'.[22] The medical officer of Worcester Prison reported that in the second quarter of 1872, there had been three serious accidents at the treadwheel – 'one lacerated wound of hand, one dislocation of shoulder and one very severe injury to foot'.[23]

In September 1873, Dr Briscoe, one of Her Majesty's Inspectors of Prisons, visited Worcester Prison. He suggested the desirability of 'employing prisoners at remunerative labour instead of on the treadwheel, and expressed his readiness to certify the looms at present in use as fit for the purposes of first class hard labour'. These looms were used to make mats.[24]

By 1880, a standardised six-hour treadwheel task was introduced which prisoners worked in two equal shifts. Prisoners were allowed five minutes' rest between each fifteen-minute session on the wheel and the speed of the wheel was regulated to allow an ascent of 32ft a minute.[25] However, high costs meant that many prisons used the crank, capstan and stone-breaking instead of replacing their treadwheel with a standardised version. By 1890, there were still in use 'cranks connected to pumps, mills operated by prisoners in separate compartments, water-pumping capstans and unproductive fixed-resistance cranks in cells'.[26]

THE CRANK

Another form of hard labour which 'as often as not ground nothing but the air' was the crank.[27] It comprised 'a wheel set against cogs that exercised a resisting pressure, and turned by a handle weighted at will to fix the amount of effort required to make a revolution'.[28]

The cranks could be set up for productive labour. At Leicester, they were 'linked to the production of firewood'[29] while at the Leeds Borough District Gaol and House of Correction, the prisoners were employed, sixteen at a time, to pump water by crank machinery, for the use of the prison. In 1851, the governor reported that the 'two hard-labour cranks have had a deterring effect with the class for which they are principally used (the vagrants)'.[30]

In 1850, the Kirkdale House of Correction dispensed with their old treadwheel in favour of crank labour. The building which contained the treadwheel was fitted up as workshops for blacksmiths, turners and other such journeymen.[31]

Under an unscrupulous governor, the crank could be used as a vicious form of punishment. When investigations were carried out at Birmingham Prison in 1854 into alleged cruelties, it was found that there was a 'system of wanton and unmitigated tyranny, inflicted by way of punishment for failure to perform impossibly heavy tasks upon the crank'. At Birmingham, the daily task was to perform 10,000 revolutions by 6 o'clock although the crank was found to call for much greater efforts than the weights attached to them appeared to imply. If the prisoner failed to complete the task in the time allowed, he 'was kept in the crank cell until late at night, and if the work was not done, he was deprived of his supper, receiving no food till eight o'clock next morning, when he was given only bread and water'. A special punishment jacket was introduced to deal with those who failed to comply.[32]

SHOT DRILL

The third recommended form of first class hard labour was shot drill. This was not adopted by many prisons. There were a number of different versions but at Lewes it consisted 'of stooping down (without bending the knees) and picking up a thirty-two pounder round shot, bringing it slowly up until it is on a level with the chest, then taking two steps to the right and replacing it on the ground again'.[33]

MAT-MAKING

Another form of labour which could be undertaken in cells was mat-making. Manchester Merchant was 'taught in a few days how to trim fancy mats. The work was clean and not hard, and I was not under any task, as some mats required much more trimming than others'.[34] One Who Has Tried Them spent two months mat-making 'yet I could never manage to make a mat in less than two days. ...men who were certified fit for first class labour were required to make ten of these same mats in the week'.[35]

Until 1878, mat-making at Wakefield Prison was a highly profitable enterprise, producing a gross revenue of £40,000 a year. Before nationalisation, other local prisons also made profits from their prisoners' labours, including making up clothes for contractors, manufacturing all sorts of brushes for home and foreign markets, the extensive manufacture of boots and shoes and large sales of various other articles.[36]

OAKUM PICKING

Oakum picking had many advantages for the prison authorities. No instruction was needed and prisoners of any physical strength or mental capacity could perform the task. In addition, it 'could be performed in silence in absolute cellular isolation, and…was rendered all the more "penal" in character because of its very unprofitableness'.[37]

One Who Has Endured It described his introduction to oakum picking at Millbank:

> After breakfast the taskmaster warder came in, bringing with him the 'fiddle' on which I was to play a tune called 'Four pounds of oakum a day'. It consisted of nothing but a piece of rope and a long crooked nail. He first showed me how to break up the block of junk and to divide the strands of the rope. The 4 lbs. in three small blocks did not look so very much after all, but when pulled to pieces and divided into strands it seemed to grow wonderfully in size, and my heart began to sink. …Then when the strands were all divided, he showed me how to pull them to pieces, and how to use the fiddle to help me…I set to work…I made but slow progress, and found it hurt my finger and thumb ends, for they were quite unused to any such work…[38] …When a prisoner had picked his 4 lbs. his time was his own, and he might do what he liked, but I never did complete my quantum. I had to work away till the time for collecting the oakum arrived, about 9 p.m. The first day I did not do six ounces…[39]

It was the kindly chaplain who showed him that by 'beating and rubbing [the strands] …together, they are softened very materially, which rendered the after-work of picking them to pieces much easier'.[40]

Oakum picking was also a favourite task set for workhouse inmates. The chaplain at the Gloucester Gaol and Penitentiary included in his report for Michaelmas 1855 the comment of one prisoner who said 'he would come again after his sentence expired as he found that he was more comfortable in prison having better fare and clothing, and less work, as in the Workhouse he was obliged to pick 3 lbs of Oakum per day, whereas in prison even when sentenced to hard labour, he was only required to pick 2lbs'. As a result, at the next sessions in January 1856, the amount of oakum to be picked was increased to 2½lbs.[41]

At the 1896 Departmental Committee on Prisoners' Education, the Revd M.T. Friend, who had been a chaplain at Reading Prison for twenty-four years, commented that 'even though it was against the rule, men worked even on Sundays' to meet their oakum quota. According to the Revd Friend, prisoners had no time for reading: 'They go picking at their oakum as soon as they have swallowed their dinner. I believe the oakum is weighed, but as soon as one lot is taken out another lot is put in'.[42]

TAILORING AND SEWING

In the convict prisons, all prisoners who were not sufficiently fit to undertake hard labour at public works prisons were employed mainly in the domestic services and rough tailoring required for the prisons themselves.[43] This might include making up clothing, knitting stockings or sewing sacks.

One Who Has Endured It completed his sentence at Dartmoor, which was an invalid convict prison. He 'became a very fair "botcher", as those who knew nothing of tailoring before they came to prison were called'.[44] In his tailoring gang at Dartmoor, the men were not supposed to talk to one another but plenty of conversation in a low tone took place. The officers appear

The oakum shed under the silent system at the Clerkenwell House of Correction. (*Illustrated London News*, 17 January 1874)

to have turned a blind eye to this 'so long as a man does not neglect his work, and it is done in moderation…unless they are in a bad humour'.[45]

GARDENING

Most prisons had a garden in which vegetables were grown by the prisoners. To be in a gardening gang was considered a real privilege. At Dartmoor, the gang generally consisted of 'well-conducted men who are doing the last twelve or six months of their time. A large amount of very fine vegetables are grown here, the best of which are sent to market'.[46]

CONVICT WORKS PRISONS

Convicts were sent to one of the public works prisons at Chatham, Portland, Portsmouth or Dartmoor to serve out the remainder of their sentences. At Chatham, the convicts were tasked with excavating the basins on the Medway. This was heavy, manual work which also involved concreting foundations, brick-laying and stone-dressing as well as loading and unloading of materials.[47] At Portland and Dartmoor, the difficult and dangerous task of stone-quarrying was carried out.

Other outdoor work at Dartmoor consisted of turf-cutting, trenching and agricultural cultivation.[48] The so-called red-collar men worked on the farm and were 'generally old men who have a knowledge of horses, cows and farm life'. Considered a highly privileged gang, they 'dressed in blue with red cuffs and collars and went out to feed the horses and cows before breakfast…'[49]

10

RELIGION

IMPORTANCE OF RELIGION

Religion was an integral part of prison life with compulsory daily attendance at chapel, a service twice on Sundays and regular visits from the chaplain. It has been argued that 'not many prisoners attended service with a sense of devotion, its main attraction was probably a little light relief from the grinding monotony of prison existence and the chance to mix with others...'[1]

The quality of the service and therefore the prisoners' interest in it depended entirely on the calibre and personality of the chaplain. The Revd John Clay, who was known to be devoted to his work, boasted that at Preston 'the prisoners assemble for daily and Sabbath worship under circumstances which make them regard the Holy service as the greatest solace and advantage of their condition'.[2]

The logistics of getting all the prisoners in and out of chapel was akin to a military manoeuvre. This was especially true of prisons which housed both males and females. At Millbank, One Who Has Endured It reported that: 'Each ward is marched off to chapel in its turn, and on receiving a signal that the way is clear of other prisoners, along the corridors we marched in silence. Such is the rule, though there were many whisperings together among some of the men, which was always checked by the warders'.[3] Another prisoner commented that 'It took nearly half an hour to get the prisoners out of the chapel, and the same time to get them in. They were taken in and out very slowly, with the view of avoiding any disorder'.[4]

ARCHITECTURE OF CHAPELS

The prison authorities were anxious to ensure that silence and separation were maintained on the way to chapel, during chapel and on the way back to the cells. When first constructed, prison chapels had been designed with stalls to separate prisoners and reinforce the principles of separate confinement. This meant the prisoners were a 'segregated congregation'[5] and the objective of collective worship could never be achieved.

The arrangement of separate stalls was described by one prisoner:

> The chapel was arranged in rows of upright coffins (no other word will so well convey an idea of their appearance to the reader), each tier raised some two feet higher than the one in front, like the pit of a theatre, thus allowing the prisoner to see the chaplain, governor and chief warder, who were placed in a sort of gallery facing them, but quite preventing their seeing each other, or indeed looking anywhere but straight to their front.[6]

Prison authorities held the mistaken belief that the stalls 'would impede prisoners' clandestine communications...'[7] This was never the case as the time in chapel was specifically used by the prisoners to communicate with one another. Loud singing was 'the perfect cover...for illicit conversation'.[8]

According to Henry Mayhew:

The prison chapel under the separate system at Lincoln Castle.

> The chapel is the great place of communication among prisoners under separate confinement. Such communication is carried on either side by the convict who occupies (say) stall No. 10 leaving a letter in stall No. 9 as he passes towards his own seat, or else by pushing a letter during divine service under the partition-door of the stall; or, if the prisoner be very daring, by passing it over his stall. Sometimes those who are short men put their mouth to the stall-door, and say what they wish to communicate, whilst pretending to pray; or, if they be of the usual height, they speak to their next door neighbour while the singing is going on.[9]

Although the Revd John Clay, the chaplain of the House of Correction at Preston, strongly advocated the separate system, this did not extend to seating arrangements for chapel services at the prison. In 1854, he explained that:

> For some years, a screen was placed in the Chapel which prevented the female prisoners, who sat in a gallery, and the male prisoners, who sat below, from seeing each other. As the good effects of our better discipline continued to develop themselves, it appeared to me that the screen might be dispensed with. It betokened mistrust and suspicion, and our object was to encourage voluntary self-restraint and willing reverence. The screen was, therefore, entirely removed, and never, for a moment, during the four years that have passed since its removal, has it seemed advisable to replace it.

He argued that a 'cellular arrangement in the chapel…forbids the feeling of <u>social</u> worship, and shuts out that contagious emotion which spreads through, and softens a congregation'.[10]

In the Preston prison chapel, the prisoners assembled 'like an ordinary congregation with scarcely any other restraint upon them than what is imposed by their own sense of propriety… An observant witness of their conduct in Chapel would also be struck with the simultaneous turning of the leaves of their Bibles and Prayer Books: an indication of real interest in the service'.[11] Upon nationalisation, the partitions in all prison chapels were removed with the work being completed by 1890.

ROMAN CATHOLIC MINISTERS

While the majority of prisons appointed Church of England chaplains, the Prison Ministers Act of 1863 and the Prison Act of 1865 allowed them to appoint chaplains other than those of the Established Church, and to determine their conditions of service.

The chapel at Newgate Prison and the 'Birdcage Walk', under which murderers were buried. (*Illustrated London News*, 29 December 1888)

Although Roman Catholic chaplains had been appointed in convict prisons from 1862, only nineteen local prisons had salaried Roman Catholic chaplains at the time of nationalisation. By 1888, this had increased to around forty such priests in fifty-nine prisons in use.[12]

There is evidence to suggest there was a real conflict between Anglican and Roman Catholic prison chaplains. The 1870 Select Committee heard of 'many acts of discourtesy, hostile discrimination and active harassment directed at Roman Catholic clergy and lay helpers'.[13] They also heard evidence of 'proselytizing by Anglican clergy' and of the inconsistency of salaries and rules in local prisons:

> In some prisons, a Roman Catholic prison minister is appointed with an adequate salary, and is placed on terms of equality with the Protestant chaplain; in others, a Roman Catholic prison minister is appointed with a salary, but is not permitted to assemble the Roman Catholic prisoners for Divine Service, being restricted to visiting them in their cells; in a third class, a Roman Catholic clergyman is permitted to visit the prisoners of his persuasion, and to assemble them for Divine Service, but is denied a salary; whilst in a fourth the visits of a Roman Catholic clergyman are only permitted at the express desire of a prisoner.[14]

VISITS BY THE CHAPLAIN

It has been argued that visits by the chaplain to the prisoners' cells 'permitted encounters so brief and infrequent that little information could be gained or imparted'.[15] Again, the calibre and dedication of the chaplain was paramount if the prisoners were to gain anything from these cell visits.

At the 1896 Committee on Prison Education, the Revd W.F. Stocken, who had been a chaplain at Pentonville for thirty years, explained how his visiting time was spent. He only had time to visit the long-term prisoners once every three months. In addition, he 'attended to those who sought confirmation or Holy Communion but considered religious exhortation to be wasted on the majority'.[16]

The Revd W.N. Truss, the chaplain of Knutsford Prison, had the pastoral care of 370 male prisoners and around twenty females. He believed that his cellular visits were 'sufficient moral instruction', but also pointed out that in a larger prison housing more than a thousand prisoners, there would need to be more than one chaplain for this system to work.[17]

The governor of Pentonville at the time, J.B. Manning, pointed out that 'prisoners get more moral, religious and secular instruction than the masses outside... Our chaplain is going round continually – our schoolmaster is attending to these people – they get much less attention outside'.[18]

11

EDUCATION

On admittance to prison, all prisoners and convicts were examined by the chaplain, or the schoolmaster under the chaplain's direction, to ascertain the standard of their education. This examination was rudimentary, partly because of a lack of time on the part of the staff and partly because little was required to determine the level of literacy of many prisoners. Jabez Balfour, a convict who was a former MP, described the examination as 'not a stiff one'. He 'read half-a-dozen lines from a school history of England, wrote a few sentences from dictation [and] successfully disposed of two or three sums in arithmetic…'[1] One Who Has Endured It, another well-educated convict, was simply asked to 'write a few verses of a Psalm on my slate, to see my handwriting…'[2]

Speaking of Lancashire, the Revd Clay, the chaplain at Preston, noted in 1854 that 'of the thousands imprisoned each year, in this county, only two in a hundred can read and write properly'.[3] The chaplain who succeeded the Revd Clay provided more detail in 1861 when he recorded some revealing information about the general education of the prisoners in the prison. 31.8 per cent were unable to read, 43.4 per cent could only read, 14.2 per cent could read but write imperfectly, 5 per cent could read and write well and only one prisoner had received a superior education. The prisoners' general knowledge was also recorded: 49.5 per cent were unable to name the months of the year, 40 per cent could not name the reigning sovereigns, 59 per cent were ignorant of the meaning of the words 'virtue' and 'vice' and 15 per cent could not count to one hundred. With regard to religious knowledge, 24.2 per cent could not repeat the Lord's Prayer, 57.8 per cent knew the Saviour's name, and were unable to repeat the Lord's Prayer more or less imperfectly, 13.4 per cent were acquainted with the elementary truths of religion, 8 per cent had adequate knowledge and just one was well instructed.[4]

SCHOOL INSTRUCTION

Under the terms of the 1865 Prison Act it was decreed that 'Provision shall be made in every Prison for the Instruction of Prisoners in Reading, Writing and Arithmetic during such Hours and to such extent as the Visiting Justices may seem expedient, provided that such Hours shall not be deducted from the Hours prescribed for Hard Labour'.[5]

At this time, cellular instruction was in place in the convict prisons but a mixture of cellular and classroom instruction was used in the local prisons, depending on the individual circumstances and preferences of the prison and its chaplain. The insistence of the central authorities that education should be provided in the form of cellular instruction attracted strong opinions on both sides.

The justices at Strangeways Prison in Manchester argued that 'the present system [of cellular instruction] is little better than a waste of time and money…no satisfactory result can be expected therefrom'.[6]

At the Leeds Borough District Gaol and House of Correction, cellular instruction was found to work well. The chaplain reported in 1851 that:

The criminal record of George Higgs from 1869-1906. (QGC 13-1 p.70, courtesy of Gloucestershire Archives)

The convict schoolmaster teaches from cell to cell, and those who are backward in education receive the largest share of attention. The progress which the prisoners make often fills me with surprise. It is no uncommon thing for a man who on his reception knew not a letter in the alphabet to be able to read and write very tolerably within the short period of three months.

He added that: 'The borough prisoners are assembled in school and receive about 3 hours instruction in the week. Their improvement is represented as being by no means as satisfactory as that of the convicts'.[7]

The Warwick Visiting Committee was in favour of class instruction:

The time now allowed for instruction is one hour and three quarters each evening, in which space of time an average of about seventeen cells have to be visited by the schoolmaster, the occupant of each cell therefore can have but six minutes of the master's personal attention and this only once in each week. The Committee would compare this with the class system as pursued under old regulations. Instruction was given twice daily in school. The time allowed for each attendance of the master being one hour and a half; prisoners were allowed to attend twice weekly consequently were enabled each to obtain three hours instruction weekly in lieu of six minutes.

They added that 'the class system bringing a feeling of emulation to bear afforded great assistance to the schoolmaster in imparting instruction - irrespective of the much longer time that each prisoner would have of the master's attention'.[8]

After a trial period in twenty-two local prisons between 1879 and 1884, a scheme was adopted to be followed in all English prisons, for which the employment of extra staff was sanctioned by the Home Office. On arrival in prison, all prisoners with sentences of four months or more were to be tested by the chaplain and classified as follows:

Class I – to include those who could not read Standard I of the National Society's reading book
Class II – those who could read Standard I, but who had not reached Standard III
Class III – those who had reached Standard III (which children aged 10 to 11 were expected to reach in primary schools)

Prisoners in Classes I and II were to receive instruction unless they were over forty years of age. If they were above this age limit, they could only receive instruction on the recommendations of the chaplain and approval of the governor. This also applied to prisoners who had already reached Class III.

All those prisoners who were believed to have no capacity for learning could be excluded. Any prisoners reported as idle during instruction could be excluded temporarily. Those with previous convictions could also be excluded.

Class I prisoners were taught reading in classes of not more than fifteen. These took place twice a week for half an hour at a time. All other teaching was to be in the form of cellular instruction 'for not less than two quarter-hour lessons per week'.[9] Juvenile offenders under the age of sixteen were to receive the most instruction: one hour's class instruction every day.

The educational standard the prisoners had reached affected other parts of prison life. Unless a prisoner could read Standard III fluently, he or she would not be entitled to have books from the library.[10]

CONVICT PRISONS

In convict prisons, the education of the convicts was an integral part of the weekly timetable. One Who Has Endured It described the scene on 'school night' at Dartmoor:

> Every cell door in the whole hall was open, and down in the hall itself were ranged rows of desks on trestles. I was told to take down my stool, slate and pencil. Together with others of the new arrivals I was marched up to the head schoolmaster's table, where he briefly examined each man. Those not requiring his instruction he bid return to their cells. The rest he allotted to such classes as they were capable of joining.[11]

He added:

> If a man cannot read or write, they do their best in one hour a week to teach him, and no man is allowed to enter the first class and enjoy its privileges until he can read or write…Three assistant schoolmasters were…each taking a separate class and the…head master walked about supervising the whole… The school orderly attended on them all, seeing to supplies of pens, books, ink, etc. One master was teaching writing; another was dictating; and a third, with a blackboard and a piece of chalk, was doing his best to drum some simple rule of arithmetic into the heads of those whose education had been evidently neglected.[12]

LOCAL PRISONS

In local prisons, the actual number of prisoners receiving instruction was small because prisoners serving sentences of less than four months were automatically excluded. In the three years up to 31 March 1895, 'only one-ninth of the average daily population of male prisoners was receiving education'.[13] In 1896, in the thirty-two local prisons that held females 'only nine had ten or more prisoners receiving education – the rest had seven or less'.[14]

Above: The exterior of a Victorian prison with its clock tower, possibly Wakefield.

Left: A prosecutor's bill of expenses for witnesses at the trial of Margaret Wilson, charged with obtaining money by false pretences, 4 January 1889. (QSP 4559/25, courtesy of Lancashire Record Office)

The seemingly ridiculous rule which excluded prisoners serving four months or less riled one member of the House of Lords. Lord Norton had arranged for the emigration of an orphan thief in Birmingham and had expected the prison authorities to use the time available 'to prepare him for colonial life'. However, as the boy's sentence was for less than four months, Lord Norton discovered 'he would be put in his cell, and pick oakum during the three months, but that they must studiously avoid giving him education or any of the moral influences I had hoped he would have before leaving this country for colonial life…It is really a rule so wholly absurd and utterly without reason, that we ought to do our utmost to break it down.'[15]

BOOKS, LIBRARIES AND READING

Prison libraries were developed from the middle of the nineteenth century onwards. The prison library was the responsibility of the chaplain who carefully chose the type of books he thought were best suited for the prisoners. In local prisons particularly, he could also set out rules which governed who could receive books.

As part of the punishment of convicted prisoners, no books were to be allowed them until three months of their sentence had passed. This did not include Bibles, prayer and hymn books. After this period, no prisoner could be allowed more than one devotional and one other book at the same time.[16]

At Worcester in 1863, the chaplain recorded in his journal: 'I gave directions to the Schoolmaster not to give Books except a Bible & Prayer Book to any prisoner who is not sentenced to six months imprisonment. Religious tracts to be given occasionally. No instruction in reading to be given to a Prisoner whose sentence of imprisonment is under six months'.[17]

In 1851 at the Preston House of Correction, the chaplain, the Revd John Clay, noted that: '…suitable books from a very extensive library, are supplied to all persons who can make a proper use of them. But every opportunity is taken to impress upon the minds we hope to improve, that to possess the ability to read and write is only possessing tools, which are of no value unless they are properly and regularly exercised'.[18]

The problem of handing out books to irresponsible prisoners was highlighted by the Revd Richard Appleton, the chaplain at the Kirkdale House of Correction. In 1842, he reported that 'I continue to furnish all those who can read, with Bibles, prayer and hymn books, cottage monthly visitors and tracts, of which many make a very good use. Others seriously abuse them by stripping off the backs, tearing at leaves…'[19]

For many literate convicts, books were vital. For the anonymous author of *Pentonville Prison From Within*, 'books stood alone like bright redeeming angels, between the prisoner and his dreary thoughts and insane impulses'.[20] For One Who Has Endured It, reading:

> was my great solace, and without it I fear I should have gone mad, for being so much by myself, my fearful position and fallen estate, and the ruin it had brought on those so dear to me, would rise up before me in condemnation. I believe that if the authorities were to take away the books a very large proportion of the convicts, and particularly the better class, those who have lost a good position, would become insane.[21]

12

RELEASE

When a prisoner or convict had reached the end of his or her sentence, he or she was officially discharged. The system of discharge varied across the country and arrangements in convict prisons were different from those in local prisons. In some cases, particularly where serious illness had occurred, a prisoner might receive a pardon before the end of his or her sentence, and be released early.

TICKET-OF-LEAVE

Convicts who had completed their term of penal servitude were released on licence, under a system known as 'ticket-of-leave'. This term originated in Australia where transported convicts could 'complete their sentences working as labourers outside prison, but subject to recall if they should break the terms of their conditional release'.[1] In England, as in Australia, 'ticket-of-leave' men and women were required to report periodically to their local police station for twelve months after their release. Some convicts had to report for longer periods as they had a certain number of years' police supervision attached to their sentence.

If a convict failed to report to the police station, this could mean a further spell in prison. This happened to John Penswick in 1889 who, four and a half years earlier, had been sentenced to five years' penal servitude and seven years' police supervision for 'stealing 25 sacks'. His punishment for failure to report was to forfeit his licence and to spend an extra calendar month's hard labour in prison 'at expiration of penal servitude'.[2] This implies that John had earned remission from his sentence for good behaviour and that by failing to report to the police, he had to serve out the remainder of the sentence.

DISCHARGE ASSISTANCE

Convicts were allowed to grow their hair before release, known in prison slang as 'growing one's feathers'. Short-term local prisoners did not have this luxury. Whichever type of prison the convict or prisoner had been in, the chaplain held a considerable amount of influence on how he or she was treated on discharge from prison. Certainly in smaller, local prisons, the chaplain had contacts within the business community and could recommend certain prisoners for employment or to charities.

Discharge assistance was considered extremely important by the Commissioners who argued: 'It cannot be doubted that judicious assistance given to discharged prisoners who are anxious to earn an honest livelihood but who have no friends to assist them, no means to provide tools, and no employer ready to give them work, may be the means of saving them from falling again into the criminal ranks…'[3]

Without such assistance, the released convict or prisoner had the odds stacked against him as argued by *The Times* in 1878:

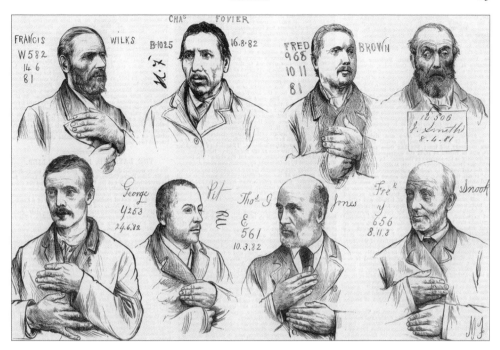

Sketches in Scotland Yard: Types of Habitual Criminals. (*Illustrated London News*, 29 September 1883)

> A man who has once committed a crime and been punished for it has all the chances against him. The occupation he once followed is gone, he has lost character and self-respect, he is thrown upon associates more depraved than himself…he is, perhaps, clothed in dress which is at once recognised as the mark of the prison, the police watch him with suspicion…and he is only too often thrust back into a life of crime from the sheer impossibility of gaining a livelihood by honest labour…'[4]

Anxieties about making a living outside prison were not confined to the working classes. A prison sentence left an indelible stain on every prisoner's reputation, especially if before conviction it had been spotless. As the time for his release approached, Jabez Balfour, a former MP sentenced to fourteen years' penal servitude, had 'inevitable doubts as to the possibility of finding creditable employment, and of earning an honourable livelihood'.[5]

When a prisoner was discharged, the Visiting Justices could order a sum of money 'not exceeding two pounds' to be paid out of monies under the control, and applicable to the payment of the expenses of the prison, by the governor to the prisoner himself or to the treasurer of a certified Prisoners' Aid Society. The Visiting Justices could also provide the discharged prisoner with the means of returning to his home or place of settlement 'by causing his fare to be paid by railway or in any other convenient manner'.[6]

DISCHARGE ARRANGEMENTS

The arrangements and system for the discharge of prisoners and convicts varied from prison to prison. Prisoners had several options when it came to being fitted out with an outfit of civilian clothes. They might be a member of a Prisoners' Aid Society which would purchase clothes for prisoners on their behalf or, in the late nineteenth century, they might have their 'own clothes, which have been sent…by…friends'.[7]

A third option was that prisoners could have an outfit provided by the prison. This would have been made by the prisoners and it was commented that, although the outfit would have been:

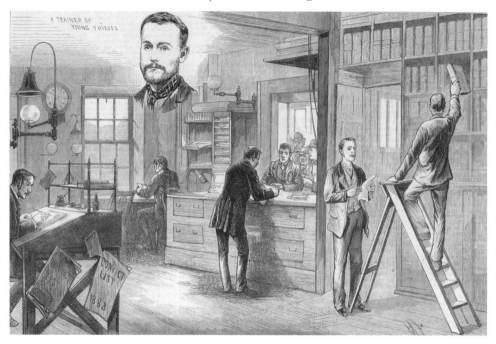

Sketches in Scotland Yard: The Convict Office for Ticket-of-Leave Men and Others Under Police Supervision. (*Illustrated London News*, 29 September 1883)

cut well, made well, and fitted well…every article…except the boots, bears upon it the unmistakable mark of the convict prison. A man may just as well wear his ticket-of-leave in the front of his hat as the clothes given to him on leaving prison. …they are made of a material so thoroughly well known as prison stuff that every policeman knows the wearer has just emerged from a convict establishment…the material is such utter trash that a fortnight's wear and one shower of rain reduce them to mere rags.[8]

One Who Has Endured It described the arrangements for release from Dartmoor, a convict prison:

A prisoner who has been convicted in the provinces does not go to London for discharge, but, on being rigged out in the clothes, …is taken down to the railway station at Horrabridge. …An officer goes with him, and at the station takes a *special* convict's ticket for him to his destination, whither he is bound, wherever he was convicted from, or his home in that county. It is not enough that the man has a suit of clothes that tells every official on the railway, and every policeman, and in fact everyone else that he is a discharged convict, but his very railway ticket confirms the fact.[9]

The arrangements were slightly different for those convicted in London:

He who is to be taken to London for discharge is manacled and handcuffed as if he were fresh caught. On arrival at Paddington, the warder takes his charge in a cab to the Queen's Bench Prison in the Borough… Men leave Dartmoor on Monday night, arriving at the Bench, or Queen's Prison on Tuesday morning, where they remain doing nothing till the day of their discharge, which takes place one day during the same week. …every prisoner is photographed prior to leaving Dartmoor, and his carte-de-visite supplied to the various police officers he has to go to for report. On the Wednesday all the prisoners for discharge that week have arrived at the Bench, and in the morning a number of detectives come and take stock of them all.[10]

Whenever a prisoner under the age of sixteen was to be discharged, the prison authorities had to inform any relatives and friends of the day and time of the discharge so 'that they may have the opportunity of attending to receive him'.[11]

DISCHARGED PRISONERS' SOCIETIES

The Commissioners urged every prison to set up a discharged prisoners' society so that 'by their aid and through their interest the prisoners whom it is desired to assist may be provided with employment, and in some measure watched over with friendly interest…'[12] By June 1884 every prison in the country, except Oxford, had established a discharged prisoners' society.

Arrangements for prisoners' applications for discharge assistance varied considerably from prison to prison. At Liverpool, the chaplain interviewed applicants in his capacity as secretary of the Aid Society. As one of the founders of the Manchester Prisoners' Aid Society, the governor of Strangeways, Captain C.W. Hill, acted as its agent. As he knew the prisoners, 'he could complete the Society's application form in a few minutes'. At York Castle, a recommendation from the chaplain and governor was a prerequisite for an interview with the society's agent.[13]

Aid offered to discharged prisoners could take the form of 'employment assistance, tools or accommodation'. The assistance could be as simple as starting prisoners off on their journey home by seeing them to the railway station, while the St Giles' Mission 'greeted every discharged prisoner at Wandsworth and other London prisons with an invitation to breakfast, and an interview with the Mission with a view to further help'.[14]

Charities might also offer medical assistance to convicts or prisoners whose health had deteriorated while in prison. In 1895, an experienced Salvation Army Officer raised awareness of the poor physical state of discharged convicts. He commented: '…we find a greater number of them incapable of pursuing any ordinary occupation. They are mentally weak and wasted, requiring careful treatment for months.'[15]

In his quarterly report of June 1872, the chaplain of Worcester recorded that: 'During the past three months, twelve prisoners received assistance from the Prisoners' Aid Society, at the expiration of their sentences. One female prisoner on her discharge received assistance to enable her to enter a Home or Refuge at Wakefield'.[16] By September 1872, three female prisoners had been sent to the Home at Wakefield. The chaplain recorded that 'On communication with the Chaplain [at Wakefield] I find one has been removed by her friends, the other two are conducting themselves satisfactorily and desire to express their gratitude for the opportunity afforded them of regaining their characters and obtaining honest employment.'[17]

The amount of discharge assistance available to a prisoner and his eligibility for aid from voluntary societies was inextricably linked to the stage he had reached in prison. After 1878 'in order to prevent a prisoner's gratuity being misapplied, its value, in whole or in part, might be given to him by the Commissioners in the form of some useful article'.[18]

AFTER RELEASE

The Revd John Clay, the chaplain at the Preston House of Correction, took a keen interest in the circumstances of released prisoners and what happened to them afterwards. His regular reports for the Visiting Justices frequently included appendices of letters about, or from, such prisoners.

In October 1847, thirty-four-year-old T.H. had completed a two-month sentence at Preston. The clergyman for his parish wrote to the Revd Clay stating that '…he seems in a fair way towards redeeming his character. His employers speak in high terms of him, as to his sobriety, steadiness, and attention to his work. He himself seems deeply grateful of your kindness, and the instruction which he received during his confinement; and a lasting impression for good, I trust, has been made on him'.[19]

'Innocence and Crime: A Scene in the Garden of the Convict Prison at Portland' drawn by Robert Barnes. The old convict's sentence has almost expired. (*The Graphic*, 14 October 1893)

A letter from a former prisoner, J.B., reveals that the Revd Clay recommended some men to Thomas Wright of Manchester, a prison philanthropist. He wrote: 'I take the liberty of informing you, of my gaining employment at the Leeds Railway; and it shall be my constant study to keep my place in an honest and sober manner as it is possible for a man to do. Sir, the kindness I have received from Mr Wright, I would be ungrateful if I did not state it. He exerted himself in all places to get me work, and also provided me with money to buy the necessaries of life...'[20]

Local prisons held newly convicted men and women until they could be moved to a convict prison. In 1854, the Revd Clay wrote that he had been visited by a ticket-of-leave man, a discharged convict, a man 'not belonging to this part of the country, but who had been under our care after his conviction at Lancaster, called upon me, on his way to Northumberland. His whole demeanour and language were such as to win confidence. Indeed, there was no possible motive for imposture or hypocrisy. Supposing he might need help in his journey, I offered it; but it was at once declined, with thanks. He had been supplied...on leaving Dartmoor, with sufficient means of reaching his destination.'[21]

One Who Has Endured It had prepared well for his release:

On obtaining my liberty I went as fast as a four-wheeler could carry me to where I had appointed decent clothes to be sent to me. These I put on, glad to get once more into the habits of civilisation. I then walked straight to the chief office in Whitehall Place – not the Scotland Yard entrance – reported myself and stated my intention to leave England. In a few days the Channel was crossed, and when my twelve months ticket was expired I had the satisfaction of tearing it up and dropping it overboard as I returned again to England to endeavour to resume my place among friends and society. A monthly report to the police in my case meant absolute ruin, and I took good care to avoid it.[22]

THIEVES AND PICKPOCKETS

LARCENY

Simple larceny, or theft, was one of the most common criminal offences dealt with by Petty Sessions in England. The reasons for such offences are not given in the criminal registers so it is not possible to distinguish between those, for example, who stole food or pawned illegally out of hunger or those who picked pockets or stole goods through greed or purely for financial gain. There is no doubt that a great many of the recorded simple larceny offences were committed by habitual offenders.

At first glance, Joseph Cordingley's sentence of five years' penal servitude and seven years' police supervision for stealing a roll of bacon appears exceedingly harsh. However, in September 1889, the thirty-six-year-old baker pleaded guilty to the charge of simple larceny after a previous conviction of felony. Joseph did not use aliases and he had four previous convictions. His first criminal offence in 1880 of burglary and stealing four coats earned him twelve calendar months' hard labour at Lancaster Prison. Two years later, Joseph was convicted at Preston of 'shop breaking and stealing 2s and 4 bottles of quinine wine' for which he was sentenced to eighteen calendar months' hard labour and seven years' police supervision at Strangeways Prison.[1]

There followed a minor offence of being drunk and disorderly before Joseph's first sentence of penal servitude. In July 1885, he was convicted at the Preston Sessions of shop breaking and stealing five pairs of clogs and one pair of boots. The sentence was five years' penal servitude and seven years' police supervision. Stealing the roll of bacon in 1889 earned Joseph an identical sentence and, at the time of the 1891 census, he was at the public works prison in Portland.

Joseph's career as a thief continued after his release in around 1894. Surprisingly, in October 1895, although his previous convictions were taken into account, at the Liverpool Assizes he was only handed two sentences of one day's hard labour which were to run concurrently. This was a punishment for 'stealing three pairs of drawers and one chemise, the property of Elizabeth Grime'.[2] It is possible this was a case of 'snow-dropping' – the practice of stealing washing from unguarded clothes lines.

Two years later, a conviction for stealing two tame hens resulted in six calendar months' hard labour for Joseph.[3] In 1898 and 1900, he served two separate sentences of nine calendar months' hard labour for stealing one pair of trousers and two rice cakes.

George Beasley, a thirty-four-year-old brick maker from Birmingham, was convicted in December 1857 at the Warwick Winter Assizes of stealing lead fixed to a building, after a previous conviction. His sentence was four years' penal servitude. Married with three children, George had four previous convictions for aiding and abetting a manslaughter, assault, stealing fowls and assault and criminal damage. After his conviction at Warwick, George spent eight months in the prison there before being sent to Millbank for one month. In October 1858, he was transferred to Pentonville to start the solitary confinement part of his penal servitude. Here, he spent five months and twenty-five days and his character was described as 'good'. In April 1859, when he arrived at Portland from Pentonville, he was a first class prisoner and had made good progress in school. George spent twenty-three months at Portland and was released in March 1861, after serving three years and three months of his sentence of four years' penal servitude. He had earned nine months' remission from his sentence for good behaviour.[4]

Uriah Smith, photographed 1892 (see page 72). (Cambridgeshire County Gaol, photographic register of prisoners 1882-1905, courtesy of the County Record Office Cambridge)

THEFT FROM THE PERSON

Pickpockets had their own social hierarchy and crimes were often committed by highly organised gangs, each member playing their part. Henry Mayhew termed the pickpocket a 'mobsman' who took his name from 'the gregarious habits of the class to which he belongs, it being necessary for the successful picking of pockets that the work be done in small gangs or mobs, so as to "cover" the operator'. The 'mobsman' usually dresses in the same elaborate style of fashion as a Jew on a Saturday… and "mixes" generally in the "best of company", frequenting for the purposes of business, all the places of public entertainment, and often being a regular attendant at church, and the more elegant chapels – especially during charity sermons'.[5]

Organised gangs, particularly of children, might also be used to 'draw the damper' in shops – the practice of stealing from the shop till. While one or two children distracted the shopkeeper, another carried out the theft.

Theft from the person, especially if it was committed with violence, was usually punished more severely than simple larceny. In January 1865, Edward Draper, aged nineteen, and Oliver Smith, alias 'Shaw', both gypsies, were charged with assaulting and stealing from the person of James Randall the sum of 18s 6d, a purse and a handkerchief at the Horse and Jockey public house in Luton in October 1864. Edward Draper pleaded not guilty while Oliver Smith admitted to the offence. However, both men were found guilty and Edward was sentenced to nine months' hard labour while Oliver got twelve months', having pleaded guilty to a previous conviction at Hertford. Edward was the son of a locally famous fiddler gypsy, Samuel Draper, who was painted and photographed by a number of artists.[6]

BURGLARY AND HOUSEBREAKING

In the Victorian period, a distinction was drawn between burglary and housebreaking. Burglary was defined as breaking and entering a dwelling house between 9 p.m. and 6 a.m., with intent

Cornelius Smith, photographed 1892 (see page
72). (Cambridgeshire County Gaol, photographic
register of prisoners 1882-1905, courtesy of
County Record Office Cambridge)

to commit a felony, or the breaking out after having committed one inside, or after having
gone in with the intention of committing one.[7] Housebreaking, on the other hand, was not
dependent on the felony being committed between defined hours and it was not confined to
dwelling houses alone but extended to out-houses, shops, school houses etc.

Shop-breaking was part of Charles Brierley's repertoire of illegal activities. His first criminal
offence was committed in April 1867 in Manchester when he stole a hen. At the time, he
was a twenty-three-year-old iron moulder from Lancashire and his punishment was three
calendar months' hard labour in Manchester Prison. Charles served his sentence under the first
of his aliases – Andrew McFadlen. Two years later came two separate offences in March and
November 1869 of stealing a pair of trousers and 'apparel'. Charles was given sentences of one
calendar month and two calendar months' hard labour. Again, the sentences were served in
Manchester Prison so why were the sentences so lenient, considering Charles had committed
three criminal offences?

The answer is that he used another alias: John Harrington. Before 1870, photographs of
prisoners were not routinely taken. Prisons had to rely on the eagle eyes of their chief staff in
recognising previous 'customers'. There are frequent references in prison records to expenses
paid to warders to visit neighbouring prisons to view identity parades of prisoners.

Charles Brierley progressed to stealing money for his next criminal offence in January 1871, again
as John Harrington. Manchester Prison was the venue again for a much longer sentence – eighteen
calendar months' hard labour and seven years' police supervision. Following his release, Charles
must have travelled to Ireland, as in March 1875 he was convicted at Mullingar Sessions of larceny
as John Harrington. This time, a more serious sentence was passed: five years' penal servitude.

It was in October 1879 that Charles got his first taste of English penal servitude. At the
Manchester Assizes, he was convicted of burglary under his third alias: John Snowan. He was
sentenced to ten years' penal servitude. After sentencing, Charles would have been sent to
Pentonville or Millbank to undertake nine months of separate confinement before being sent
to one of the public works prisons, such as Chatham or Portland, to serve out the remainder
of his sentence.

No.	NAME.	Age	TRADE.	Degree of Instruction.	Name and Address of Committing Magistrate.	Date of Warrant.	When received into Custody.
14₃	Joseph Cordingley... Lancaster Assizes, 5th July, 1880, burglary and stealing 4 coats, &c., 12 calendar months hard labour, as Joseph Cordingley, Lancaster Prison. Preston Sessions, 18th October, 1882, shopbreaking and stealing 2s. and 4 bottles of quinine wine, 18 calendar months hard labour and 7 years police supervision, as Joseph Cordingley, Preston and Strangeways Prisons. Burnley (County), 8th June, 1885, drunk and disorderly, 7 days hard labour, as Joseph Cordingley, Preston Prison. Preston Sessions, 1st July, 1885, shopbreaking and stealing 5 pairs of clogs and one pair of boots, 5 years penal servitude and 7 years police supervision, as Joseph Cordingly.	36	Baker	Imp.	J. Greenwood, Esq., Burnley.	11th Sept...	11th Sept...
	12						

The criminal record of Joseph Cordingley, prior to being convicted of stealing a roll of bacon, 1889. (QJC 13, courtesy of Lancashire Record Office)

Shortly after his release, there followed two minor offences for which Charles was sentenced to one month and three months' hard labour in Lancaster Prison. Again, these sentences appear lenient as the authorities at Lancaster do not seem to have been aware of Charles's previous convictions. He was charged and committed for these offences under a fourth alias: Thomas Moore.

In August 1889, Charles Brierley, now aged forty-five, was charged at Accrington with:

Being in the shop of one Illingworth Baxter and another did steal 116 watches, 304 rings, 3 gold chains, 22 silver chains, 61 common chains, 4 silver nutcrackers, 2 silver bracelets, 2 suits of clothes, 2 shirts, 1 pair of trousers, one vest, two boots, 9 silk handkerchiefs, 2 metal spoons, one pocket knife, and 1s. 5 ½ d. in money, the monies and property of the said Illingworth Baxter and another, and feloniously did break out of the said shop, at Accrington 3rd August 1889.

Charles pleaded guilty to shop breaking and larceny after a previous conviction of felony. He was sentenced to ten years' penal servitude and seven years' police supervision. While he may have gained some remission from his first ten-year sentence, there was probably only a short break of less than a year between sentences.[8] It is known that during this second sentence of penal servitude, Charles was sent to the public works prison at Portland as he was listed there at the time of the 1891 census. It is not known if he reoffended after his release in 1899.

THEFT FROM AN EMPLOYER

Sometimes a man's profession provided him with opportunities to steal high-quality items. In 1852, James White Hinds, a 'young man of respectable appearance' was charged with stealing three watches and other articles, to the value of £110, from his master William Jackson at Clerkenwell.[9] James had been employed by William Jackson as a journeyman watchmaker for a year 'during which time property to a considerable amount was missed, but no suspicion was entertained of the prisoner, in whom much confidence was reposed'.[10]

William Jackson contacted the police and Inspector Brennan carried out extensive enquiries. This led him to believe that 'all was not right on the part of the prisoner'. At the same time, the

No.	NAME	Age.	TRADE.	Degree of Instruction.	Name and Address of Committing Magistrate.	Date of Warrant.	When received into Custody.
22	Charles Brierley .... Manchester, 1st April, 1867, stealing a hen, 3 calendar months hard labour, as Andrew Mc Fadlen, Manchester Prison. Manchester, 25th March, 1869, stealing 1 pair of trousers, 1 calendar month hard labour, as John Harrington, Manchester Prison. Manchester, 15th Nov., 1869, stealing apparel, 2 calendar months hard labour, as John Harrington, Manchester Prison. Manchester Sessions, Jan., 1871, stealing money, 18 calendar months hard labour and 7 years police supervision, as John Harrington, Manchester Prison. Mullingar Sessions (Ireland), 3rd March, 1875, larceny, 5 years penal servitude, as John Harrington. Manchester Assizes, 31st Oct., 1879, burglary, 10 years penal servitude, as John Snowan. Barrow-in-Furness, 21st Jan., 1889, stealing 1 shirt and 1 singlet, 1 month hard labour, as Thomas Moore, Lancaster Prison. Barrow-in-Furness, 25th March, 1889, frequenting, 3 months hard labour, as Thomas Moore, Lancaster Prison. 13 times in Manchester Prison for drunkenness, frequenting, &c.	45	Iron Moulder	Imp.	W. Ratcliffe, Esq., Accrington.	1889 12th Aug....	1889 12th Aug....

The criminal record of Charles Brierley, prior to being convicted of shop-breaking, 1889 (see pages 69-70). (QJC 13, courtesy of Lancashire Record Office)

Superintendent of Luton contacted Inspector Brennan to inform him that a man had offered a gold and silver watch for sale and that it was one of the items stolen from William Jackson. The man was taken into custody and gave his name as Ezra Hinds, brother of James White Hinds.

Ezra Hinds was already a convicted thief, having previously stolen a tarpaulin, and on being locked up at the station house in Luton, he attempted to cut his throat using a razor. He recovered and was charged with receiving the stolen watch. At the brothers' trial in December 1852, James pleaded guilty. Both brothers were sentenced to twelve months' hard labour in the Clerkenwell House of Correction.

This was not to be the brothers' last criminal offence as James and Ezra were later charged on separate counts with other cases of theft. In March 1861, Ezra was charged with 'feloniously steal[ing] one [gold breast] pin of the value of 15/ the property of the said Richard Harvey from his person'.[11] The offence was alleged to have been committed at the Opera Tavern in the Haymarket. He was found guilty and sentenced to six months in Coldbath Fields Prison. Nothing is known of him after this time.

James was also to spend more time in prison with a much harsher sentence than his brother. In May 1866, he was found guilty of stealing watches and jewellery at Huddersfield and was sentenced to seven years' penal servitude.[12] James served the latter part of his sentence at Dartmoor.

THEFT IN RURAL AREAS

George Higgs, an agricultural labourer, was born in rural Gloucestershire in about 1839. His impressive list of over thirty-five criminal offences spanning almost forty years is typical for a rural area. They include illegal poaching and fishing, stealing turnips and mushrooms, drunkenness and sleeping out. While these offences may not appear to be of a serious nature, two of them earned George two separate sentences of seven years' penal servitude. The first, in January 1869, was for 'stealing tame rabbits'. George must have had a previous conviction to be sentenced to penal servitude for this offence. He served out his sentence at Woking Invalid Convict Prison which meant that his health was not strong enough to serve at a public works prison. In August 1881, George was again sentenced to seven years' penal servitude for 'stealing ducks'.[13]

It is possible that George was a vagrant but gypsies were also commonly charged with the offence of 'sleeping out'. This law was designed to clamp down on and reduce the number of vagrants but it did not distinguish between vagrants and gypsies. Gypsies, by their very nature and way of life, frequently slept out in the open. Cornelius and Uriah Smith were gypsy brothers in rural Cambridgeshire. They appear regularly in the county gaol records of the 1880s for such offences as 'wandering abroad', 'lodging in the open air', 'game trespass' and being 'drunk and disorderly'. For the offence of wandering abroad or lodging in the open air, Cornelius and Uriah were usually punished with seven days' hard labour.

Convictions for theft carried longer prison sentences. Both Cornelius and Uriah were convicted of 'stealing three rabbit traps' in June 1886. Cornelius served one month's hard labour while Uriah was sentenced to two months. In May 1888, Cornelius stole a hoe valued at 1s 2d and had to undertake one month's hard labour for his crime. When Uriah was convicted of 'stealing 4 stone of mutton' in April 1887, he was sentenced to nine months' hard labour.[14]

Sentences for theft in rural areas can seem extremely harsh. In the late 1860s, One Who Has Endured It met a man in the association room at Dartmoor who was sentenced to seven years' penal servitude 'for stealing twelve eggs from under a duck'. He had a previous conviction from three years earlier for stealing a pound of butter, for which he was punished with two months' imprisonment in the county gaol. This man was a farm labourer earning eleven shillings a week to support and provide for a wife and four children. There was sickness in his house and he 'was driven by his children's wants to take twelve eggs from under a duck that had just begun to sit in a hedge near the farmyard pond'. He told One Who Has Endured It that 'he worked far harder for his eleven shillings a week than ever he had at stone-quarrying or anything else in prison'. When at home he seldom, if ever, had meat of any sort, and when he did it was 'only fat bacon'. He considered the living in prison luxurious compared to what he had at home and he said 'he never slept so comfortably in his life, and should sadly miss it when he returned home'. The irony was that the parish had to provide for his wife and children while he was in prison. The family was allowed half a crown a week plus four quartern loaves. This expense would have been minimal had the man been sentenced to a few months' hard labour instead of a long sentence of penal servitude.[15]

HABITUAL THIEVES

Many men and women, once set on the path of a career in theft, could not break the cycle of criminal convictions and prison sentences. Such was the life of William Anderson, a labourer from Lancashire, whose first criminal offence was committed in 1852 when he was aged just fifteen. He was convicted at the Manchester Petty Sessions of stealing one window racket and was sentenced to three calendar months' hard labour.

William's criminal career spanned over fifty years. He used multiple aliases including Thomas Johnson, James McGuinness, William Pearson, William Edwards, William Robson and William Evans. His offences ranged from stealing clothing and umbrellas through to attempted theft and receiving stolen property. William's sentences ranged from fourteen days' hard labour to twelve years' penal servitude. When all his sentences are added together, between 1852 and 1904 William Anderson spent forty-six and a half years in prison. Of these forty-six and a half years, thirty-five years consisted of five separate sentences of penal servitude.[16]

14

MURDERERS AND VIOLENT OFFENDERS

MURDER

Until the 1820s, there were some 400 criminal offences which carried the death penalty including 'picking someone's pocket of anything worth one shilling (5p) or more and stealing anything worth £2.00'.[1] The number of capital offences were gradually reduced by successive governments until 1861 when the Offences Against the Persons Act specified that only wilful murder and treason were punishable by death.

From the middle of the nineteenth century, even when the death sentence was passed on a convicted murderer, there was still a chance that he or she could be reprieved and instead spend the rest of his or her life in penal servitude. In such cases, the prisoner might have to wait several weeks to know whether he or she was to live or die.

Murder by means of poison appears to have been a common occurrence in Victorian times because of the ready availability of chemicals for medicinal purposes. In 1889, Charles Parton, an eighteen-year-old labourer, boxer and convicted jewellery thief, progressed to using chloral (chloral hydrate) 'a stupefying drug' to drug his victims before stealing from them. At his trial in March 1889 at the Liverpool Assizes, he was charged with administering chloral to John Parkey in December 1888 and 'stealing one watch, one chain and 18s 6d' and with administering chloral to Samuel Oldfield in Manchester in January 1889 and stealing 'one watch and guard of the value of £10, and certain moneys' from him.[2]

Charles was also charged with a more serious offence, that in February 1889 he 'feloniously, wilfully, and of his malice aforethought, did kill and murder one John Fletcher…and unlawfully and feloniously administered to the said John Fletcher…chloral…and feloniously stole from the said John Fletcher one watch and guard, and certain moneys…' At the time, John Fletcher, who was a wealthy paper manufacturer, was travelling in a cab. It was alleged that Charles had drugged John Fletcher while they were drinking in a public house, that he got in the cab with him and robbed him before fleeing the scene.[3] It is not clear whether Charles had accidentally administered a higher dose of chloral than to his previous victims or whether it was a pre-meditated case of murder. Whatever the motive, Charles was found guilty of murder and sentenced to death. However, Charles must have received a reprieve as, at the times of the 1891 and 1901 censuses, he was listed as a convict at Portland and Kingston upon Hull Prisons respectively.

PUBLIC EXECUTIONS

Public executions were real spectacles, attracting hundreds, sometimes thousands, of people. On 27 May 1856, Dr William Palmer was convicted of the murder of John Parsons Cook by the administering of strychnine. The twelve-day trial took place at the Central Criminal Court in London because 'it was felt that local prejudice against him was very strong' in Rugeley, Staffordshire, where the crime was committed.[4] Dr Palmer's execution was scheduled to take place on Saturday 14 June outside Stafford Prison. Huge crowds were expected to witness the execution as the trial had attracted a great deal of public interest. *The Times* reported that:

Balconies and platforms were erected on several of the housetops and in almost every imaginable place commanding a view of the spectacle and the windows of the houses in the front and near the scaffold had their full complement of eager spectators. The express train and others from London on Friday night brought down a great number of well-dressed persons…the crowds…kept constantly arriving during the night by railway and other means of conveyance from the adjacent towns for 50 miles around, including the Pottery districts, Birmingham, Wolverhampton, Walsall, Tipton and the rest of what is called 'the black country'. The great bulk of the people were young men and lads, labourers and artisans, thousands of whom had left their ordinary occupations and travelled many miles to witness the spectacle…[5]

A public execution took place at Worcester on 2 January 1863 when William Ockold was executed for the murder of his wife.[6] William was sentenced to death on 13 December 1862, and from this day onwards until the execution, he was visited in the condemned cell, morning and night, by the prison chaplain, the Revd John Adlington.

William Ockold was seventy years old at the time of his execution and he and his wife had been married for almost fifty years. During their marriage, they 'had had many wrangles together, and they frequently fought, the old woman being as often the assailant as her husband'. His wife was found lying dead on the floor, 'death having apparently been caused by violent blows inflicted by a broken mopstick. There was a good deal of blood in the room and on the stairs, which had flowed from the deceased's nose and face'.

William 'persisted to the last that he did not kill his wife, and declared he only struck her in the mouth, which had caused the flow of blood'. It was thought that because of the circumstances of William's previous life with his wife and his advanced age that the capital sentence would not be carried out. However, no reprieve was forthcoming and it was reported that he listened closely to the ministrations of the Revd Adlington who was 'most assiduous in his attention to the condemned man'.[7]

On 2 January 1863, the Revd Adlington recorded in his journal, 'Visited W. Ockold early in the Morning and accompanied him to the Scaffold'.[8] It was said that William's appearance 'with his blanched face and white hair flying in the breeze, was pitiable in the eyes of the crowd'.[9] William Ockold was to be the last man executed publicly at Worcester.

PRIVATE EXECUTIONS

The last public execution in England took place in 1868. After this date, executions took place in private behind closed doors in prison. Crowds still gathered in large numbers outside to see the black flag hoisted above the prison which was a sign that the sentence had been successfully carried out.

RAPE AND SEXUAL ASSAULT

Punishments for prisoners found guilty of rape or sexual assault seem lenient compared with those given for theft or larceny. In April 1870, Alfred Woodhurst, a forty-two-year-old hatter from Bethnal Green, was charged on two counts of indecent assault and of 'carnally knowing a girl under the age of 12 years'. The girl in question was none other than his daughter, Elizabeth Eliza. The offence was committed on 15 October 1868 when Elizabeth was ten years and three months old. Until 1875, it was legal for girls above the age of twelve to have sexual intercourse. It is not known why there was such a long period of time between the offence and the trial.[10]

The chief witnesses at the trial were Elizabeth herself, her brother Arthur Alfred, her father's common law wife Mary Ann Eldridge plus a surgeon and police officer. The trial records do not mention that Alfred was Elizabeth's father or that incest had allegedly been committed. Newspaper reports from *The Times* revealed this fact, and also that Alfred was living in a state of concubinage, 'his wife having left him and since lived with his brother in adultery'.[11]

Samuel Holding, convicted of unlawful wounding in 1901
(see page 76). (Courtesy of Rita Richardson)

On passing sentence, the judge said the evidence had 'disclosed a horrible state of immorality'. Alfred was convicted of the lesser offence of indecent assault and sentenced to twelve months' hard labour in Clerkenwell House of Correction. At the time of the 1871 census, he was in Nottingham Prison, presumably because there was insufficient cell accommodation at Clerkenwell.

The case is a particularly sad one as Elizabeth and Arthur were deeply affected by what had happened. Their mother had left home to bigamously marry their father's brother in 1862. When Alfred was sent to prison, there was apparently no family member able or willing to look after them. Both Elizabeth and Arthur spent time under the care of the Bethnal Green Union, Elizabeth at the Bethnal Green Union Workhouse school and Arthur at the Bethnal Green Union Workhouse itself.[12]

Henry Francis Burholt, a forty-four-year-old baker from Islington, was not at home on the night of the census in April 1881 because he was on the run from the police. A warrant for his arrest had been issued on 6 January for the rape of Harriet Stump, his fourteen-year-old servant. Henry's baker's shop in Andover Road, Islington, was put up for sale after he disappeared. He was finally arrested at his other shop in Clerkenwell on 17 May. It is not known where Henry was living for the intervening four months.

Perhaps Henry believed enough time had passed for any evidence to be null and void. He was mistaken and was charged on 18 May that 'he on the Eleventh Day of December last past at Islington in the said County and District, and with the Jurisdiction Of the Central Criminal Court did feloniously and Violently assault the said Harriet Stump and then Violently and against her will feloniously did Ravish and carnally hurt her the said Harriet Stump...'[13]

The alleged offence was committed in the parlour while Henry's wife and daughters were out of the house. In her deposition, Harriet Stump claimed that she immediately told Henry's wife what had happened and that 'she jawed him and he hit her with his hat'. Henry's wife persuaded Harriet not to tell her mother who lived opposite as she did not want a 'disgrace' and she did not let Harriet go home for a fortnight. After Harriet finally told her mother, it was another ten days before she left the service of the Burholts. This was approximately three weeks after the alleged offence had been committed.[14]

It was Harriet's mother who lodged the complaint against Henry with the police. She claimed that as soon as she had fetched her daughter home, Henry came round to her house. It was alleged that he said 'It's no use for you to interfere in it, it's too long ago...No doctor would be able to tell...you had better settle it and I'll give you any recompense you want.'[15]

In what must have been a very traumatic time for Harriet, the lengthy depositions reveal that she was repeatedly questioned about her truthfulness and whether she had had 'connection' with anyone else. In his deposition, Henry pleaded not guilty, but sadly no evidence remains to tell his side of the story.[16]

However, at his trial at the Central Criminal Court in June 1881, Henry pleaded guilty to the lesser charge of attempted rape and was sentenced to twelve months' hard labour in Clerkenwell Prison.[17] Henry died in prison just two months later of tuberculosis.[18]

ATTEMPTED MURDER

In some cases, sentences for other violent offences could also be surprisingly lenient. In April 1901, Samuel Holding, a fifty-year-old draper from Stoke Newington, was charged with attempting to murder his son Morton. Although Morton was seventeen at the time, he had hardly ever attended school because he had always been of low intelligence. In addition, Morton had suffered with consumption since the age of ten and required a great deal of nursing and medical attention.

During Samuel's trial at the Old Bailey, witnesses told how he was found in the kitchen in the basement of his home with Morton. There were pools of blood on the floor and the boy had eight serious wounds to his head. Nearby was an axe with wet blood on the blade and handle. Samuel was 'to a certain extent under the influence of drink'.[19]

When arrested, Samuel admitted assaulting Morton saying 'I have thought about it for the past eight months. This morning I meant to kill him. He is consumptive and has caused a lot of trouble at home. I thought he was best out of his misery, poor boy.'[20] It appears that Samuel had been worried about his drapery business which had been affected by local competition. Morton 'had seen him crying several times, and it was then that he took to drink'.[21]

There is evidence to suggest that Samuel intended to commit suicide after killing Morton as he borrowed a sharp knife from a neighbouring butcher's shop prior to the attack. He also mentioned to a police officer that if anything happened to him, he could not leave the boy to be a burden to his mother.[22] In the event, Morton recovered quickly from his injuries and was a witness at his father's trial.

Despite the seriousness of the crime, the jury seems to have been influenced by evidence given as to Samuel's previous good character. He was described as a 'kind and affectionate father'[23] and 'of a genial and even gentle and harmless disposition'.[24] The jury returned a verdict of unlawful wounding and the judge noted that he was 'sure in his sober moments, prisoner would not have thought of doing it…'[25] The judge added that he 'did not think it a case for a severe punishment and hoped that prisoner's enforced abstention from drink would have a beneficial effect'. Samuel was sentenced to just four months' imprisonment in the second division. He served his sentence in Pentonville which, by this time, had been reclassified as a local prison and no longer took convicts.

After Samuel went to prison, the lease on his drapery business in High Street, Stoke Newington, was sold and the stock was disposed of by public tender. Samuel's wife Charlotte moved back to her home town of Northampton with Morton and her younger children. Sadly, although Samuel followed them after his release from prison, they lived apart from then on. When Charlotte died in 1910, Morton became more disturbed and after threatening to kill his father, he was admitted to Berrywood Lunatic Asylum in December 1910. Samuel's troubled life came to an abrupt end a month later when he drowned himself in the canal at Blisworth.[26]

MANSLAUGHTER

When wilful murder could not be proved, the accused was usually convicted of the lesser charge of manslaughter. In February 1889, John Fenton, a twenty-eight-year-old joiner, and Elizabeth Porter, a twenty-four-year-old servant, were charged with feloniously killing and slaying a male child at Liverpool. They were also charged with unlawfully abandoning and exposing a certain male child 'being under the age of two years, whereby the life of such child was endangered' in Manchester and Liverpool on 26 and 27 January.

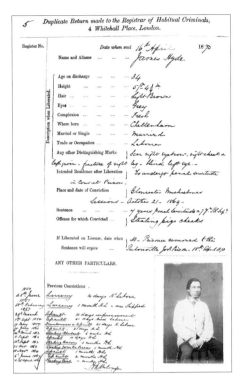

Above left: The criminal record of James Hyde, convicted in 1869 of stealing pigs' cheeks. His previous convictions included assault. (QGC 10-1 p6, courtesy of Gloucestershire Archives)

Above right: James Hyde, photographed before being sent to Pentonville to start a seven-year sentence of penal servitude. (QGC 10-1 p6, courtesy of Gloucestershire Archives)

Neither John or Elizabeth had a previous conviction and they were both found guilty of the lesser charge of manslaughter. Elizabeth was sent to prison for eight calendar months of hard labour while John was sentenced to five years' penal servitude.[27]

HOMOSEXUALITY

In the nineteenth century, homosexuality was considered to be a violent, heinous crime which sometimes carried a sentence of penal servitude. In December 1889, George Porter, a forty-two-year-old well-educated artist, was charged in Lancaster on two charges. The first charge was of 'unlawfully assaulting at Lancaster, on the 30th day of November 1889, one Charles McLaughlin, with intent, feloniously, wickedly, and against the order of nature to carnally know the said Charles McLaughlin, and with him to commit and perpetrate the abominable crime of buggery'. The second charge was of 'unlawfully assaulting at Lancaster, on the 9th day of November 1889, one Luke Kearns, and with him to commit and perpetrate the abominable crime of buggery'.

George Porter was found guilty of the first charge and sentenced to seven years' penal servitude. He had previously been acquitted in May of the same year of a similar 'abominable offence' at the Central Criminal Court in London. At the time of the 1891 census, George was serving out his sentence at Parkhurst. In 1901 he was living in Birmingham and working as a glass painter.[28]

Another man charged with offences relating to homosexuality was Oscar Wilde. In 1895, he was charged with 'unlawfully committing certain acts with Charles Parker and Alfred Wood, and with certain persons whose names were unknown'.[29] He was found guilty of the lesser charge of 'committing acts of gross indecency' and received a far lighter sentence than George Porter: two years' hard labour.

ATTEMPTED SUICIDE

One form of violent assault, that of attempted suicide, was also considered to be a serious indictable offence. Prison sentences of several months, usually with hard labour, were the punishment for those who had unsuccessfully sought to end their own lives. Despite such prisoners' fragile mental states, they were rarely sent to an asylum. One can only imagine the effect of such a prison sentence on someone who had attempted suicide. Whilst a sentence with hard labour would have kept the mind (and body) occupied during the day, being locked in a cell during the night would have given perhaps too much time for reflection. However, prisoners who were known to have attempted suicide would have been watched carefully by prison staff to prevent further attempts. A prison sentence was seen as a way to protect the prisoner from harming him or herself again.

In July 1888, Joseph Gill, a sixty-eight-year-old blacksmith, was tried at Preston on the charge that he did 'unlawfully…cut and wound himself with a certain razor, with intent to kill and murder himself, at Haslingden'. This was not the first time Joseph had attempted to commit suicide. Six years earlier in Blackburn, he was charged with the same offence but was discharged, 'his friend promising to look after him'. Joseph was found guilty and sentenced to four months' hard labour.[30]

PROCURING AN ABORTION

For many desperate women with already large families, an abortion could provide a way out of having another mouth to feed. However, anyone convicted of procuring an abortion for a woman, by using an instrument or chemical substances, could face a sentence of penal servitude.

Robert Johnson, a herbalist originally from Dumfries, was charged in March 1886 in Preston with 'using instruments and administering drugs to procure abortion'. He had no previous convictions. Robert was found guilty and sent to Strangeways Prison.[31] At this time, penal servitude sentences for first offences were for a minimum of five years. By the time of the 1891 census, Robert Johnson was back home in Preston with his wife and nine children so he had obviously earned remission from his sentence.

In May 1884, a visitor to Pentonville Prison:

> had some lengthened conversation with two prisoners in their own cells quite alone. They were both men of superior education and of a very different class. …The first of these prisoners has been a surgeon in Birmingham. He was now under sentence of penal servitude for life for causing death by procuring abortion and although of good address and superior education, evidently an old rascal…He had been four years in penal servitude and therefore had had experience of 'public works life', as well as separate confinement. He said he thought there was very little if any fault to find with their treatment generally…[32]

Cases of procuring an abortion often came to light if a woman died as a result. In December 1895, Sarah Ann Eden, a midwife from Warwickshire, was convicted of the murder of Rebecca Simister, a mother of six children who could not face a seventh confinement. Rebecca died after begging the midwife to bring about a miscarriage. The post-mortem revealed she had died from blood poisoning 'arising from punctures by an instrument'. Sarah Ann was convicted of murder and the death sentence was passed upon her, although this was later commuted to penal servitude for life.[33] In 1901, Sarah was serving out her sentence at Aylesbury Prison.

15

FRAUDSTERS AND EMBEZZLERS

Nicknamed 'gentlemen prisoners' by prison staff, fraudsters and embezzlers had a good education and came from a higher social class than the majority of prisoners and convicts.

OBTAINING MONEY BY FALSE PRETENCES

Francis Henry Atkins was the author of *The Devil Tree of Eldorado* and *A Queen of Atlantis*, writing under the pen name of Frank Aubrey. In November 1900, he and the Revd Frederick Holmes Carlisle were jointly charged with 'conspiring to obtain money from persons whom they engaged as clerks or secretaries in connexion with a limited company called the Charity Aid Publishing Society'.[1] Francis had formed the Society to publish a magazine, the profits of which he proposed to give to London hospitals. Sums of money amounting to £575 were obtained from several gentlemen as 'qualifying fees', on the promise of employment with the Society. However, the magazine was never started and no money had been returned to any of the gentlemen, who, 'in most instances, had parted with the whole of their savings'.[2] The examinations of the remanded prisoners, which had commenced early in October, took six weeks until their actual trial on 24 November. Both prisoners were granted bail although after one hearing, bail for Francis was refused on the grounds that 'if he was liberated he would be arrested for a similar offence alleged to have been committed in 1891'.[3]

At the trial, both prisoners pleaded guilty 'on the advice of their counsel…to certain counts of the indictment'. Francis was sentenced to nine months' hard labour in Pentonville and the Revd Carlisle to six months' imprisonment in the second division. Francis' criminal record does not seem to have harmed his literary career as he went on to write a further seven novels, half a dozen serials and short stories up to his death in 1927.[4]

EMBEZZLEMENT

Charges of embezzlement could arise if a person looking after the finances of a society, for example, had made a mistake and could not account for missing money. This happened to Jabez Steane in July 1857 when he was called to answer a summons before the local magistrates, charged with 'withholding money the property of the Loyal Ivy Lodge'. Jabez appears to have been in charge of the cash book for the society and the treasurer, G. Pickett, gave evidence to explain how much cash was owing to the society. Jabez was ordered to pay the whole amount of £43 16s 6d plus 40s penalty and 10s costs or, in default, spend six weeks' hard labour in prison.

Jabez could not afford to pay the fine. He was taken into custody by the police the day after he attended the magistrates and 'was marched off to prison'. He kept a journal for 1857, including the period he spent in Abingdon Gaol. Only two days after arriving in prison, Jabez was placed on the sick list 'with a severe cold headache'. This was treated with 'a mustard plaster on the back of the neck and feet in hot water for half an hour at bedtime (4 o'clock) by order of the Surgeon (Bowcher) was better the next day able to work again'.

Jabez was a prisoner of the third class as he was 'sentenced to hard labour for any time more than 21 days but not exceeding 6 weeks…' He noted in his diary that misdemeanants at Abingdon were clothed in a yellow dress while felons wore a part-coloured black and yellow dress.

On 10 September, the day of his release, Jabez recorded the routine:

> …after dinner called out of cell and taken to schoolroom to sign the book in which were entered every article of clothing, cash 6¼ &c taken from me on entering the prison and which were all returned to me exactly as they were taken from me having changed my dress and given up the one I had been wearing I was then allowed to leave time 2 o'clock PM.[5]

The role of a parish relieving officer involved handling money, so he was 'subject to constant temptation…'[6] Richard Hartill, a Relieving Officer for the Dudley district in the Dudley Union, was to succumb to this temptation. He was appointed in 1853 at a salary of £120 per annum.[7] Ten years later, the guardians informed the central authorities that Richard had been found guilty of embezzlement and that he had 'been committed to the House of Correction for the space of nine months, with hard labour'.[8]

SWINDLING

Aliases were a valuable tool to swindlers. In August 1889, a man calling himself Ernest Norton Rolfe was arrested in Blackpool for uttering a forged bill of exchange and defrauding John Harling, a confectioner. As his trial approached, more details emerged about the man with multiple aliases who soon came to be known as the 'Prince of Swindlers'. The case in Blackpool was outrageous in its audacity. Ernest told everyone he met that he was Mr Bennett Burleigh, a war correspondent for the *Daily Telegraph* who was writing an article for the newspaper on the evolution of the torpedo fleet, which was then cruising in the neighbourhood. When he arrived in Blackpool, he had a letter with him which purported to be a letter of introduction from the well-known writer, Mr George Augustus Sala. He showed this letter to Mr Holland, manager of the Winter Gardens, who the following day introduced Ernest to Mr Harling. Ernest made himself so agreeable that he was able to obtain £21 in cash from Mr Harling on a forged bill of exchange.[9]

As soon as he had the money, Ernest absconded and was apprehended in Lincolnshire. In his possession there were found 'a large number of similar bills of exchange in blank', and the prosecution suggested that the prisoner intended to use these in swindling other persons who might become his dupes. At the time of his apprehension warrants without end were out against him.

When news of Ernest's arrest broke out, the newspapers devoted many column inches to his exploits. Ernest Norton Rolfe or Ross Raymond was born in New South Wales, Australia, in 1851 and he developed a remarkable ability for languages at school. After graduating, he was engaged as a teacher at the Naval School, being proficient in French, German, Italian, Spanish and 'Hindoo'. It was believed that he had served in the Navy and the India service before arriving in America in around 1877.[10]

Ernest's aliases included Austen Chamberlain, Captain Rathburn, Melton Prior, Major Rhodes, Captain Rexford and Ross Raymond, the name which the American authorities knew him by. The Chief Constable of Blackpool sent a portrait of Ernest to the New York police. The inspector there replied with a telegram stating that 'there was not the least doubt that the face was the deceptive and confidence-winning physiognomy of the great and only Raymond, who was one of the ablest *chevaliers d'industrie* the police of New York have had to deal with'. He concurred with the Chief Constable's opinion that Raymond or Ernest Norton Rolfe was 'one of a gang of American swindlers, that came to this country in the autumn of last year…'[11]

It was claimed that he 'found no difficulty in securing a good position as a journalist…but he was not content with earning twice an ordinary salary'. He stole a coat worth £10 from the

An aerial view of Dartmoor Invalid Convict Prison where One Who Has Endured It completed his sentence of penal servitude.

A group of chained convicts leaving the prison at Princetown, Dartmoor, for a day's work outside.

Prison officers at the prison gate, Princetown, Dartmoor.

Fifth Avenue Hotel in New York and was sentenced to Sing Sing Penitentiary. After his release, he obtained a position as a night editor on a daily newspaper in Baltimore. Ernest/Ross was described as:

> a born journalist, and even with an ordinary amount of rascality he could easily hold a position on prominent journals…He was one of your typical, well-built, jaunty fellows, always neatly dressed, and with a frank, engaging manner. He won confidence, and was a favourite in society and public circles. No one seemed to know of his prison record, and all went well with him, until he took to sending in false vouchers to his publishers…no one apparently cared to prosecute him until he began a system of drawing forged cheques on journals with which he had been connected. Then he was forced to leave America.[12]

Ernest/Ross had a wife in New York but it was said he had 'slaughtered many a heart' with many temporary 'widows' mourning his absence. Well-written billets-doux were received at the prison from 'a lady of refinement and culture' in Blackpool and it was known that he had an actress companion in London whom he called wife.[13]

When summing up at Ernest's trial at the Manchester Assizes in November 1889, the judge doubted 'whether a more veteran swindler ever stood at the bar of a court of justice'. He went on to comment: 'It is not too much to say that there is scarcely a town that you have visited during the last few years of your life in which you have not either perpetrated or attempted to perpetrate some gross fraud or other'. As well as offences committed in Britain, Ernest had two previous convictions in New York.

For his crime, Ernest was sentenced to ten years' penal servitude. Immediately after the trial, Ernest spent time at Strangeways Prison before being transferred to Stafford in January 1890.[14] At the time of the 1891 census, he was at Portland, a convict public works prison. His prison record describes him as being of superior education.[15]

FRAUD

One Who Has Endured It was the *nom de plume* for Edward Bannister Callow, a gentleman convicted of fraud in 1867. He wrote about his experiences in prison in *Five Years' Penal Servitude* which was published in 1877. This book is a valuable source of information about life as a convict in Newgate, Millbank and Dartmoor. He briefly described the circumstances which led him to be convicted:

> …after over twenty years of commercial life in more than one large English city, I found myself in the year 186-, drawn into the meshes of a man who was too clever for me and for the law, and who, crossing the seas to a place of safety, left me to meet a charge to which in his absence I had really no defence. I was sentenced to five years' penal servitude…[16]

At the time of the 1871 census, Edward was serving his sentence at Dartmoor. His previous occupation is listed as 'Secretary of a Railway Company'. According to *The Times*, on 8 July 1868 Edward Callow, secretary of the Elham Valley Railway Company, pleaded guilty to 'forging and uttering six checks, by which the company was defrauded to the extent of 637*l*'.[17] He told the Court that 'the money was not applied to any private matters of his own, but in furtherance of a project for making a harbour at Seabrook, which would be connected with the railway, and which undoubtedly would be a means of benefiting the company'. He added that he 'felt his position very acutely, and that no amount of punishment which could be awarded him would be equal to the mental anxiety he had experienced and the degradation he had felt since his apprehension and confinement in prison'.[18]

Unlike some convicts, One Who Has Endured It was heartened by his sentence of five years' penal servitude:

Until the sentence was pronounced it seemed a long way off, but now it was too terribly near. Five long years; yet mine was the lightest sentence of any that session…When my judge said five years I could have hugged him in gratitude…Five years would soon slip by. I looked back and saw how quickly the last five years had passed and took courage. I thought how soon five years would pass, and I had hopes. I was still a young man. I should barely be middle-aged at the end of my time.[19]

Nevertheless, the stigma of someone from a good social class becoming a convict was hard to bear. One Who Has Endured It was transferred from Newgate to Millbank to start his sentence of penal servitude and '…was handcuffed. This was my first acquaintance with the 'Darbies', the first time I had ever been deprived of the free use of my hands, and it was with some difficulty I kept down the swelling lump in my throat. A mingled feeling of shame, rage, and indignation came over me'.[20] Perhaps as a consequence of this shame, after his conviction, he never 'saw either wife or child of mine till I met them as a free man'.[21]

For One Who Has Endured It, the ability to gain remission from his sentence by gaining marks spurred him on:

When I went to Dartmoor I calculated exactly how many days I had to serve to complete my time. Reckoning upon obtaining all my marks, and losing none, every evening when I went in there was the satisfaction of reducing the number. I well remember the joy I felt when I first reduced the figures from four to three – 999 days seemed ever so much shorter than 1,000. Each time the leading figure was altered, and the hundreds were reduced, home seemed growing nearer. …the day I reduced it to two figures – actually less than 100 – and I got permission to let my hair and beard grow, which every man does three months before his time expires, my joy knew no bounds…There were two occasions when I had to alter my figures the wrong way. I was twice fined forty-eight marks, and until the week was out, and I regained the old figures, my 'slate' used to look quite disgusting to me.[22]

FORGERY

Forging signatures to obtain money was another criminal offence committed by the 'gentleman' prisoner. On 31 March 1858, Dennis Trenfield, a fifty-four-year-old attorney at law, was convicted of forgery at the Gloucester Assizes. He was charged with 'forging the signatures to a bond for 200*l*, and also with uttering the same, knowing it to be forged, with the intent to defraud'.[23] Dennis was a solicitor, who had been in practice at Winchcombe for thirty years. Although he had no previous convictions, he was sentenced to ten years' penal servitude. Described as a tall and stout respectable-looking man with grey hair, Dennis had a superior education and was married with one child.

Dennis's prison record reveals that on the right side of his neck he carried a severe injury caused by a 'pistol shot attempting self-destruction'.[24] He had attempted to blow out his brains with a pistol loaded with two bullets. One of his jaws was broken and, though one of the bullets had been extracted, 'the other still remained in the back of the neck'.[25] Dennis spent time in Millbank, Lewes Prison and the *Defence* prison hulk before being transferred to Dartmoor to complete his sentence.[26]

TRANSPORTED CONVICTS AND EXILES

Until 1868, convicts sentenced to penal servitude could be transported to a penal colony on the other side of the world as a punishment for their crimes. Before the War of Independence started in 1775, English convicts had been transported to American colonies. After 1775, the destinations included Bermuda, Gibraltar and Australia. The very first fleet of transported convicts to Australia arrived in Botany Bay in 1788 and transportation continued to Van Diemen's Land (Tasmania) until 1853. After this date, Western Australia became a penal colony and only those sentenced to fourteen years' transportation or more were actually transported. The last ship carrying transported convicts to Australia left England in 1867.

CONDITIONS ON THE CONVICT SHIPS

Once the convict had undertaken a period of separate confinement, he or she would be put on a list for embarkation on the next convict ship to leave England. Before a convict could board the ship which was to transport him or her to a penal colony, he or she had to have a certificate provided by a medical officer from the shore authorities. This was necessary because 'many of the convicts had been in custody in fever-ridden gaols or hulks for months…'[1] Only those medically fit to survive the long journey were supposed to be passed for embarkation. However, countless surgeons' journals record many instances of 'both men and women concealing illness or injury for fear they would be left to rot in prison or aboard the hulks'.[2]

Once on board, the convict faced a long and difficult journey. The clothing provided was rarely sufficient to combat the 'cold of the high southern latitude when the ships were running down their easting'. As late as the 1840s, spare clothing was not supplied to replace worn-out items or those lost overboard during squalls and 'surgeons had to cut up sheets and blankets to make extra shirts, trousers and caps'.[3] Although the convict ships could be damp and dank, when in the tropics, the heat made them stifling and oppressive.

Conditions slowly improved and from 1844, each convict was given a separate sleeping berth.[4] The later convict ships 'were better, or at least no worse, than the early emigrant ships'.[5]

TRANSPORTATION FOR THEFT

Convicts could often be transported for seemingly trivial offences but this was usually because they had previous convictions. In July 1845, Henry Excell, a thirty-four-year-old carrier from Maidstone in Kent, was sentenced to ten years' transportation for 'stealing 307 use poles, value £9, the property of Frederick Terry, at Teston'.[6] Henry's wife Avis had died the previous year, leaving him with six children to look after and provide for. He had found a buyer for the coppice-owner's poles and proceeded to sell them to other tradesmen, or use them as a form of barter to settle some of his debts. It appears that he hoped that the remainder of the unsold poles could be sold at a high enough price for the coppice-owner to be paid.

Henry had a second offence on the charge sheet, namely 'Stealing a silver watch, a seal, and a chain, value £3, the property of Daniel Norley, from his person, at Offham'. However, he was not tried for this offence. Unfortunately for Henry, he had a previous conviction from five years earlier. In 1840, he had been tried and convicted at the Maidstone Quarter Sessions of 'feloniously receiving... seventy-five pounds weight of hay of the value of one shilling...knowing the said goods to have been feloniously stolen'. Whether Henry simply took the hay as a favour to the thief or he actually paid for the hay made no difference. Receiving stolen goods was a serious offence and Henry was sentenced to be 'kept to hard labour in the House of Correction' for three calendar months.

This earlier conviction meant that transportation was the only sentence the judge could give. On 17 July 1845, Henry was transferred from Maidstone Gaol to Millbank Penitentiary in London where he was held in ward C, cell 4. Here, he would have been kept in solitary confinement. His prison records state that he could neither read nor write, and that there were six references to him in the Misconduct Book and Governor's Journal. Sadly, neither document has survived so it is not possible to ascertain the manner of his 'misconduct'.[7]

Almost five months later on 11 December, Henry left Millbank. He 'is likely to have been chained and marched through the tunnel to the gate on the river bank where the barge was waiting to take him and many of his fellow prisoners to Woolwich'.[8] At Woolwich, he embarked on the *Joseph Somes* with 249 other convicts. The ship was bound for Van Diemen's Land and the long journey was not without difficulty.

The surgeon on board the *Joseph Somes* recorded in his journal that three days after leaving Woolwich on 22 December, they had to anchor in the Downs because of 'foul winds'. When the ship finally left the Downs on 14 January, they 'encountered a succession of foul winds for a month'. The surgeon advised putting into Teneriffe for water and refreshments including 'a quantity of oranges which were highly refreshing to the prisoners'. On 18 February, the ship left Teneriffe and anchored off Hobart, Van Diemen's Land, on 19 May 1846. This was more than five months after Henry had embarked at Woolwich.

Despite the hardships of the journey and imprisonment, Henry's transportation offered the chance of a new start, without the burden of a large family to provide for. Life for Henry's six children left behind in Maidstone was considerably more difficult. The four youngest children were in Linton Workhouse near Maidstone at the time of the 1851 census. Sadly, admission and discharge registers have not survived to provide further details about their time as inmates or to clarify whether the two older children also spent time in the workhouse.[9]

SERVING A SENTENCE ON THE 'HULKS'

Not all convicts sentenced to transportation were actually banished to the colonies. Old and infirm convicts could expect to serve out their sentences in the hulks while young men might be offered the chance to join the army or navy instead.[10] The 'hulks' were decommissioned naval vessels moored in the Thames Estuary and on the South Coast.

In May 1846, John Devereux, a forty-year-old widowed labourer from Tewkesbury, was charged and found guilty of 'stealing a casting net'. While this was a serious offence in itself, because it deprived the owner of the net from making his living, this was not John's first brush with the law. In 1838, he had been convicted of 'stealing a silk handkerchief, the property of Mr Henry Insall in town'. He was sentenced to two months' hard labour in the House of Correction. Two years later, John was charged and found guilty of 'breaking into a cellar of Mr William Browell senior of this parish with the intent to steal and carry away the goods and chattels of the said William Browell'. For this offence, he was sent to the House of Correction for one year. In April 1845, John was brought to the attention of the law again when he was charged with 'forging a certain paper purporting to be an order for delivery of certain grocery goods with intent to defraud one Mr Stephen Stone, a grocer of the borough of Tewkesbury'. At his trial, he was found not guilty.[11]

When John was found guilty of stealing the casting net in 1846, the judge took his previous convictions into account and sentenced him to seven years' transportation. From 1837, it was

The convicts returning to the hulks after a day's work. (From Mayhew & Binny)

general practice for 'convicts sentenced to seven years or less transportation to serve out their sentences in government prisons or on the English hulks instead of being transported'.[12] This was to be John's fate. He was sent first to Millbank for two years and then transferred to the *Warrior* prison hulk at Woolwich. Two years later in March 1850, John was granted a free pardon and released early from prison. This was possibly because of ill health.[13]

EXILES

Not all convicts sentenced to penal servitude were to serve out their sentences in prison. On 11 September 1843, James Brake, a twenty-nine-year-old attorney's clerk from Somerset, was convicted of embezzlement of £27 and upwards from his employer at the Stoke Newington Quarter Sessions. He was sentenced to seven years' penal servitude but was given the opportunity of a conditional pardon if he went to Australia. James agreed and with fifty other 'exiles', he sailed on the *Stratheden*.[14] An 'exile' was 'a prisoner who had served part of his sentence in Britain before being transported to New South Wales, Moreton Bay, Van Diemen's Land or Port Phillip' before 1852.[15]

James arrived in Williamstown, a suburb of Melbourne, in 1845. As an 'exile' with a conditional pardon, he would only have had to report to a police magistrate periodically. He would have been granted a full pardon after the term of his sentence had expired. After marrying, James became the first head teacher at Wannon National School. He died suddenly in June 1854.[16]

TRANSPORTATION FOR MANSLAUGHTER

By the time the final batch of convicts arrived in Western Australia, the flow of convicts 'had dwindled to an annual selection of some 600 suitable long-sentence prisoners'.[17] Solomon Stenton was one of the last convicts to be transported to Western Australia, sailing on the *Corona* in 1866. Aged just twenty-one when convicted of the manslaughter of his grandmother, Solomon was a labourer or fetler at the Thorncliffe Ironworks in Yorkshire. He was in good physical health of 'middling stout build' and therefore ideal for selection to be sent to the colonies.

Her Majesty's Prison at Lewes, Sussex.

It was Solomon's liking for drink which led to his downfall and to the fatal assault on his grandmother, Eliza Drabble. He had been brought up by Eliza in Chapeltown near Sheffield and lived with her from an early age after the death of his parents. On 24 March 1865, Solomon was at the Coach and Horses public house in Ecclesfield and although he was not considered to be drunk, he appeared to be 'a little in liquor'.[18] This was probably 'just sufficient to rouse his violent passions'.[19] Just after midnight, Eliza came to fetch her grandson to take him home. It was said at the trial that she was in the habit of going to him for that purpose 'in order to prevent him from spending the whole of his wages'.[20]

Solomon reluctantly left the Coach and Horses with his grandmother and another man named William Hanson, and as soon as they were on the road home, he attacked Eliza, kicking and beating her brutally. He repeated this on five separate occasions with Hanson intervening to protect Eliza. Further along the road, Solomon renewed his assault on his grandmother.

> He knocked her down and abused her very much, but Hanson interfered and pulled him away. The prisoner was quiet for a short time, but he recommenced his violence, knocked the old woman down upon the road, and rendered her insensible. Hanson again interfered, and upon the deceased reviving a little she said that the prisoner had given her her death blow. With Hanson's aid she managed to get up, and walked on for a short time, but the prisoner again attacked her in a very determined manner, and when Hanson again came up and interfered the deceased was either dying or dead.[21]

Solomon left the scene apparently unconcerned and, when arrested at home, he said 'I have been in many scrapes but this is the worst of them all.' He immediately realised the implications of his actions and on the way to the lock-up in Chapeltown, he asked the constable to hang him at once.[22] Solomon was known to the police as he had 'frequently been brought before the magistrates on charges of poaching and assaults'.[23] Eliza's murder created 'a great sensation' in the small village of Chapeltown. She was a quiet, inoffensive old woman and it was known that Solomon had frequently ill-used her in the past.

Given that Solomon was originally charged with wilful murder, the judge convicted him of the lesser charge of manslaughter and sentenced him to twenty years' penal servitude. This 'took everyone by surprise – nobody more so than the prisoner, who…had been warned by his learned counsel that there could only be one termination to a case so clear'.[24]

Solomon became convict no. 9305. His records describe him as being single, 5ft 5¼in tall with light brown hair, hazel eyes, an oval face and a sallow complexion. He had a cut under his left eye and the first joint of his middle finger on his right hand was smashed. From Leeds, he would have been sent to Millbank or Pentonville for his nine months of separate confinement. After this period, he was transferred to Portland convict prison, a public works prison designed to toughen up the transported convicts. From here, Solomon and 303 other convicts boarded the *Corona* on 16 October 1866, bound for the Swan River Colony in Western Australia.[25]

The journey took sixty-seven days, the fastest the crossing had ever been made.[26] On arrival on 22 December 1866, Solomon started serving his twenty-year sentence in Fremantle Prison. He must have been well behaved in prison as he obtained his ticket-of-leave on 10 February 1877, after serving just over ten years of his sentence. After leaving prison, Solomon would have had to carry his ticket-of-leave with him at all times and report twice a year to the authorities. He would not have been able to marry or leave the district without permission but was free to move around the district to find work. Solomon's transportation records reveal that he worked as a sawyer, farm servant, wood cutter and labourer before being rewarded with his Certificate of Freedom on 1 April 1885. This was calculated from his original trial date.

As a free man, Solomon decided to move to Tasmania and left the Swan River Colony on 26 April 1885. By now he was a middle-aged man of forty-two, so he had spent almost half of his life in prison – all because of a quick temper and a liking for drink.[27]

JUVENILE OFFENDERS

The problem of how to deal with juvenile offenders was an issue which perplexed the Victorians as much as it does us today and there were frequent debates about the treatment of such young criminals.

PRISON SENTENCES FOR JUVENILE OFFENDERS

A 'juvenile offender' was anyone under the age of fourteen at the time the offence was committed. However, much younger children found themselves in prison. At Millbank Prison, an old warder recalled 'a little boy six years and a half old sentenced to transportation; and the sentence carried into effect, too, though the poor child couldn't speak plain'.[1] The governor of Stafford Gaol reported in 1863 that 'I have had them really so small and so tender that I have been obliged to put them in the female hospital to play with the kitten; that is an absolute fact…'[2]

Prison could be an intimidating, often terrifying, place for the first offender. Imagine, then, how much worse it was for a mere child. There were no special facilities for juveniles in prison. They occupied cells designed for adults, were expected to undertake a certain amount of work and, until the 1890s, slept on a hard, plank bed.

While imprisoned at Reading in the 1890s, Oscar Wilde described seeing two warders ('not unkindly men') talking sternly to a child on remand whose face 'was like a white wedge of sheer terror. There was in his eyes the terror of a hunted animal. The next morning I heard him at breakfast-time crying, and calling to be let out. His cry was for his parents.' Wilde believed that 'The cruelty that is practised day and night on children in English prisons is incredible except to those who have witnessed it and are aware of the brutality of the system.'[3] At Stafford, the governor reported that 'I have had three or four boys in whose cases we have been obliged to light their gas, and leave the door of their cells open by night'.[4]

At Preston in 1842, the Revd John Clay, the influential chaplain at the Preston House of Correction, reported that a 'poor child of seven years old' was committed to prison for illegally pawning. The Revd Clay was at pains to point out that the child's mother had encouraged him to break the law: 'He had stolen a shirt exposed to dry, and then pledged it, having been taught how to pawn by his mother, who a short time previous, had sent him to pledge a pair of his own trowsers, which she had obtained from charity'.[5] The chaplain had very strong views about the imprisonment of juvenile offenders. He argued that, 'I feel assured that if a child's first offence were immediately punished by solitary imprisonment for some period not exceeding a month, the best results would follow'.[6]

To many other prison chaplains, the imprisonment of juveniles was ineffective and pointless. Two successive chaplains of Worcester County Prison highlighted the futility of prison sentences for young offenders. The Revd John Adlington argued in his quarterly report of December 1868 that, 'a sound whipping out of Prison would be more effective to deter from crime, with this class of criminals, than imprisonment in Gaol'.[7] He attributed the high numbers of juvenile offenders in Worcester County Prison to 'parental neglect and bad example'.[8]

The Revd Adlington's successor, the Revd George Cresswell Salt, was of the same opinion. In December 1870, he wrote:

> It seems to me that the committal of young children under the age of twelve for a first offence tends rather to degrade than to deter them from crime, and that it is possible a better effect might be produced if such offenders were whipped by the Police, and then discharged without being branded, at such an age, with the lasting disgrace of imprisonment.[9]

William Walker, the governor at Banbury writing in 1849, had the following opinion of punishment for juvenile offenders:

> Having myself had 15 years experience in prison discipline I can venture to say that the new [separate] system is the best that has ever been adopted for adult criminals, although not so well adopted for juvenile offenders, wanting at the expiration of their sentences, some Asylums resembling that at Mettray near Tours in France, in order that they may be never allowed to return to the scene of their former exploits; or I would rather Magistrates had the power to send, at once to such an asylum, without committing to prison at all…[10]

For some juveniles, the experience of prison was a pleasant one compared with life at home. Edwin Witheford was the chief warder in charge at Dorchester Prison. He reported to the Gladstone Committee that a boy under the age of twelve had recently been sentenced to seven days' imprisonment at Dorchester, and added that prison had not had the desired effect on the child: 'That boy we sent out of prison last week was perfectly delighted with the treatment he got in prison. There is nothing to deter that boy from coming again. He was treated with utmost kindness: the boy was quite pleased. He was treated kinder in prison than he would be in his own home'.[11]

OFFENCES COMMITTED BY JUVENILE OFFENDERS

Visitors to Victorian prisons frequently commented on the inappropriate imprisonment of juvenile offenders for petty offences, many of whom were young children. At Stafford Gaol, children were imprisoned for stealing 'gooseberries, apples and the like, and trespassing in fields in pursuit of birds' nests'[12] and at Worcester County Prison, juvenile offences included 'cruelty to animals, gambling, vagrancy and theft'.[13]

Sentences for juvenile offenders were less harsh from the middle of the nineteenth century, but punishment for a petty offence could still be a prison sentence. Juveniles could be committed for short prison sentences combined with corporal punishment, such as a whipping. Girls, however, could not be subjected to corporal punishment.

Perhaps one of the youngest prisoners at Gloucester Prison was seven-year-old Edgar Leopold Kilminster. In June 1870, he and his nine-year-old brother, Joseph William, were charged at the Stroud Petty Sessions with 'stealing sweetmeats'. At just 3ft 10¼in tall, Edgar stood behind a chair when his photograph was taken for his prison record and is only slightly taller than the chair rail. Whatever the motive for the theft, whether from hunger or for a dare, Edgar and Joseph were both found guilty of the offence and were sentenced to seven days' hard labour. Both boys were also to receive twelve strokes with a rod. It is not clear why the two boys were imprisoned for so long as no previous convictions are listed. From Chalford in Gloucestershire, Edgar and Leopold were the eldest sons of a cordwainer.[14] It would appear that this short, sharp shock worked in deterring Edgar and Joseph from a life of crime. The Kilminster brothers do not appear again in the Gloucester Prison records.

The great majority of offences committed by juveniles appear to have been cases of theft. The motives for committing such crimes may have stemmed from poverty, greed, bravado or from parental neglect. The availability of ready money was too much of a temptation for some children sent into service or to be apprenticed for the first time. This was especially true for those who had known nothing but poverty like Richard Hughes, a thirteen-year-old boy sent from Dudley Union Workhouse into the employment of a man named J.H. Baker. On 30 December 1870, the guardians of the Dudley Union recorded that Richard had 'been convicted as a juvenile offender and is now in gaol at Stafford'.[15]

Richard's offence was the stealing of money on 26 December 1870, presumably from his employer. For his crime, he was sentenced to one calendar month's imprisonment at Stafford Gaol. Richard was not sent to a reformatory at the end of his sentence, presumably because this was his first offence. After his release on 22 January 1871, Richard was sent back to the Dudley Union Workhouse as he had no home or family to go to. At the time of the 1871 census, he was again recorded as an inmate of Dudley. Richard's criminal record would undoubtedly have made it more difficult for the guardians of the Dudley Union to find a suitable apprenticeship for him.

The appearance of a wide-eyed juvenile could be deceptive and some undoubtedly deserved to be in prison. While on remand at Newgate in the 1860s, One Who Has Endured It recalled:

> There were also two very decent-looking and respectably-dressed lads, who should have been at some ordinary boarding-school, but instead of studying Euclid and Delectus, their readings had been of the 'Jack Sheppard' and 'Claude Duval' style of literature in the penny dreadfuls, and they were now in Newgate awaiting their trial for burglary and half-murdering an old housekeeper in some City offices. …All London pictured to itself one or more terrible ruffians of the Bill Sikes stamp, men who were first-class adepts at their unlawful profession, and had graduated under scientific teaching in either Seven Dials or Whitechapel. Great was the public astonishment to find the perpetrators were two schoolboys in their teens.[16]

PUNISHMENTS FOR YOUNG OFFENDERS IN PRISON

While in prison, juvenile offenders could be punished for misbehaviour in a number of different ways. On visiting the Liverpool Borough Gaol in 1850, Mary Carpenter discovered that 'solitary confinement and a bread and water diet' was usually sufficient but flogging was 'resorted to very rarely for insubordination'.[17]

At Easter 1846 in the Gloucester Gaol and Penitentiary, it was reported that two prisoners named Thomas Lacey aged thirteen and Simon Tew aged eleven were causing disruption in the prison. They had been sentenced to transportation but the sentence had been commuted to eighteen calendar months' imprisonment in the penitentiary. They were considered 'mischievous and unfit for Treadwheel labour'. It was ordered that 'besides Schooling and the instructions from the Chaplain…that each of them be taught some useful Trade or Employ and also be subject to hard labour during their Imprisonment suitable to the several ages such as breaking stone or gravel'.[18]

Some prisons were found to use punishments of children too readily. At Birmingham in 1854, investigations revealed numerous illegal punishments of adults and juvenile offenders. One such punishment highlighted by the Commissioners involved 'a sentence of whipping, imposed upon two boys who had been guilty of repeated acts of disobedience, [which] was carried out continuously day by day, twelve lashes being dealt on one day, and six more the next *and so on until the boy became obedient*'.[19]

TREATMENT OF JUVENILE OFFENDERS IN PRISON

Juvenile offenders committed to prison were supposed to be kept separate from the adult prisoners to avoid corruption. However, the architecture of many prisons made this basic

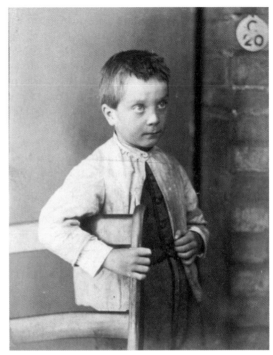

Above left: The criminal record of Edgar Leopold Kilminster, convicted of stealing sweetmeats in 1870 (see page 90). (QGC 10-1 p268, courtesy of Gloucestershire Archives)

Above right: Edgar Leopold Kilminster who was just seven years old when sentenced to seven days' hard labour and twelve strokes with a rod. (QGC 10-1 p268, courtesy of Gloucestershire Archives)

requirement impossible, especially when juveniles were on remand awaiting trial. Here, young boys would mix daily with hardened criminals who had been in and out of prison, listening to their stories, 'the cleverness of which they can readily perceive, whilst their minds are not sufficiently cultivated to feel the immorality…'[20] It was this moral corruption which was most objected to by countless prison chaplains who had to report regularly on the juveniles in their care.

It was not until 1896 that prisons were required to completely separate juveniles from adults. Those serving a month or more were to be housed in a prison where there was a separate section for juveniles. Those serving under a month could be accommodated in a prison 'completely separated from the adult prisoners'.[21]

At this time, juveniles were no longer subjected to the plank bed and could have extra library books, in addition to educational books, and did not have to earn marks to have them. They could work in association with other juveniles in workshops and at outdoor labour and were to be instructed in a trade 'as far as possible'. If certified medically fit by the medical officer, the juvenile was to participate in 'daily physical drill instead of, or in addition to, the usual walking exercise with a view to his physical development'.[22]

PARKHURST

Parkhurst Gaol on the Isle of Wight opened in 1838 as a prison exclusively for boys awaiting transportation. However, 'there were always more criminal children sentenced to transportation than there were places at Parkhurst' so the remainder were sent to Millbank. One such boy was thirteen-year-old Thomas Groves who on 2 January 1845 was convicted of stealing wearing apparel at the Maidstone Quarter Sessions. He was sentenced to seven years and, fifteen days later, he was transferred to Millbank. Thomas's record reveals that when he was an infant, he was left at the door of a house in Whitechapel. It is likely, therefore, that he spent much of his childhood in the workhouse. It was stated that he was 'supposed to have lived in crime about five years' and that he had been imprisoned once before for 'having lodged in an outhouse'. On 25 February, Thomas was removed once more, this time to Parkhurst on the Isle of Wight. Some four and a half years later in August 1849, he was sent on to Van Diemen's Land.[23]

After transportation ceased as a punishment in 1852, Parkhurst continued as a juvenile prison for boys to serve out their sentences. If their sentences had not been completed by the time they reached the age of seventeen, they were transferred to other prisons such as Dartmoor, Portsmouth and Portland.[24] Parkhurst continued as a prison for juveniles until 1864 when the boys' section was closed down.

Mary Carpenter, the penal reformer, argued in her book *Reformatory Schools* that Parkhurst was an inappropriate place for children:

> With such a state of feeling, with nothing to exercise and give free vent to their restless and adventurous spirit, with no direct and sufficiently powered stimulus in the way of remuneration for work efficiently done, their pent-up energies should break out into frequent acts of disrespect to the officers, violence, wanton damage to property, and even theft, as well as disorder and prohibited talking, for which an average of 445 boys incurred in 1844, 4105 separate punishments (among them 165 whippings), making an average of above ten per diem![25]

REFORMATORIES

After the passing of the Youthful Offenders' Act in 1854, a short prison sentence for juveniles could be followed by a period of between two and five years at a reformatory.[26] This did not apply for a first offence but was immediately carried out if a subsequent offence was committed. By 1858, there were fifty such reformatory schools and this had increased to sixty-five by the end of 1865.[27] These institutions were considered preferable to prison as juveniles could usually be kept there until the age of sixteen and they were far removed from the contaminating influences of adult criminals. There were separate reformatories for boys and girls and many of them were run by religious organisations. The parents of juveniles sent to reformatories were 'compelled by law to contribute, if they were able, up to 5 shillings a week'.[28]

In 1865, the Visiting Justices of the Gloucester Gaol and Penitentiary decided to send girls from their prison to the Red Lodge Reformatory School near Bristol run by Miss Carpenter. In return for the clothing, maintenance and care of each girl, they had to pay an entrance fee of £1 plus 2s per week.[29] Opened in 1854, Red Lodge was run and managed by Mary Carpenter, the penal reformer who had started her charitable work by setting up the first ragged school in Bristol. In her influential book *Reformatory Schools for the Children of the Perishing and Dangerous Classes, and for Juvenile Offenders*, Mary Carpenter argued that juvenile offenders should be treated as children and stated that love 'draws with…cords far stronger than chains of iron'.[30]

By 1866, the New Bailey Prison in Salford was using no less than seven different reformatories as the destinations for ten boys and girls convicted of criminal offences. Only one, Blackley in Manchester, was in the same county as the New Bailey Prison, indicating that there were no places available at other Lancashire reformatories for children of a particular religious persuasion and that the use of these institutions was widespread at this time as a means of dealing with juvenile offenders. The other six reformatories were in Leicestershire, Cheshire, Bedfordshire, Northamptonshire, Liverpool and Birmingham.[31]

The kind of children sent to reformatory schools was highlighted in March 1869 by the chaplain at Worcester Prison. He reported that:

The convict nursery at Brixton Prison.
(From Mayhew & Binny)

…we have had twenty-one boys from the respective ages of 9 to 14 as criminals in the Prison. Of these boys seven at one time have been waiting, after a short imprisonment, to be sent to a Reformatory. The history of these boys is a sad but common one, showing neglected education, early depravity, and an opposition to all legal and moral restraint. Some of them have been several times in Prison, one, only eleven years of age, was justly suspected of larcenies in the City of Worcester before he was committed a second time for felony. Prison discipline seems to have little or no beneficial effect on such criminals.[32]

Nine-year-old Patrick Canney from Barrow-in-Furness was a typical candidate for a reformatory. In September 1889, he was convicted of being 'found in [a] dwelling house with intent to steal'. His punishment was ten days in prison and five years at a reformatory. As he was a Roman Catholic, Patrick was sent to the Roman Catholic Reformatory School at Holme in Yorkshire.[33]

In his quarterly report of December 1871, the Revd George Cresswell Salt reported that: 'Of juvenile offenders…three have been sent during the quarter to Reformatories. It occurs to me to suggest that it might be desirable, occasionally, to send some of the boys to training ships, and so entirely isolate them from their associates, and put them in the way of beginning a new course of life, apart from their surroundings.'[34]

The treatment of juvenile offenders bound for reformatories after an initial period of imprisonment varied from prison to prison, but it was supposed to be the same as for juveniles only sentenced to imprisonment. In the 1880s at Manchester, children were given instruction and school books while at Kirkdale, they could sleep in beds and 'were not required to perform the same amount of work as other prisoners'. The governor of Westminster reported that the juvenile offenders were 'placed under the charge of the most experienced, careful and kindly officers'.[35]

It was believed that girls especially could 'be exposed to peculiar dangers' by communicating with adult criminals. For this reason, in 1884 it was suggested that their imprisonment prior to being sent to a reformatory should be in solitary confinement.[36]

In order to ascertain their treatment of juvenile offenders, the Royal Commission used a representative sample of seven prisons. They were Coldbath Fields, Kirkdale, Manchester, Preston, Strangeways, Wakefield and Westminster. In the majority of these prisons, it was found that the juveniles and the adult prisoners met at chapel or exercise so were never completely separated.[37]

18

WOMEN

The Victorians' 'idealised view of womanhood'[1] was greatly at odds with the kind of women who became criminals in English prisons. A contemporary source described criminal women to be 'more degraded than the slave, less true to all natural and womanly instincts than the untutored squaw of a North American Indian tribe'.[2] One convict prison director described the language of the penal class women as 'fouler than anyone who had not heard it could possibly imagine. Nothing but the gag can restrain the abominations they utter'.[3]

HABITUAL OFFENDERS

Were female prisoners really so fearsome and shocking? For most of the second half of the nineteenth century, women 'outnumbered men in the class of those who had ten or more previous convictions – the "hardened habituals", making up well over two-thirds of those who had been imprisoned more than ten times'.[4]

It has been argued that desperate or sick women 'saw the local prison as a place of asylum…[and] as a somewhat unlikely benefactor in times of need'.[5] For many women who were 'regulars' to prison, they preferred it to their own homes. Others had no home to go to and viewed prison more favourably than the workhouse. Elizabeth Little, the matron of Strangeways, commented that the women '…would rather remain there than go out…They get perfectly comfortable inside and it is not so bad as they thought even as first offenders'.[6] Similar sentiments were expressed at Liverpool where the matron reported that the women '…like coming back; they say they come home again. Many of them, have no other home'.[7]

Female prisoners who had regularly been in prison for short periods knew the routines and did not fear imprisonment. Knowing they would be released in days or weeks meant they were unlikely to be swayed by the influences of the warders or the chaplain. In 1877, of the women entering Tothill Fields House of Correction in London, 'over half were sentenced to terms of less than fourteen days, three-quarters to less than one month, and well below one-tenth to more than six months…'[8]

ADMITTANCE TO PRISON

Separate prisons for male and female prisoners were preferred as they prevented 'the embarrassment of prison pregnancies and…minimised corruption'.[9] Where there was no female prison in the area, the ideal was a completely separate, detached building from the men's prison. When a detached building for females was opened at Wakefield Prison, it was commented that the prisoners were '…a great deal easier to manage when removed to a distance from the men. The spirit of reckless stubbornness and bravado dies within them when they know that they are out of sight, hearing, and notice of their fellows of the other sex'.[10]

The hair of female prisoners could not be cut without their permission unless it was verminous and cropping was necessary to maintain good hygiene. Speaking of those women who had to submit to have their hair cropped, a prison matron at Millbank reported that, 'Women whose hearts have not quailed, perhaps, at the murder of their infants, or the poisoning of their husbands, clasp their hands in horror at this sacrifice of this natural adornment…it is one of the most painful tasks of the prison'.[11]

KEEPING A DISORDERLY HOUSE

While the prostitute was 'the typical woman prisoner of the late nineteenth century'[12], prostitution itself was not a criminal offence. However, keeping a disorderly house was and this was the offence Louisa Dent, a thirty-seven-year-old single woman, was charged with in December 1899. She pleaded guilty to the charge and was fined £10 with 8 shillings costs or two months' imprisonment. As she could not afford to pay the fine, she was sent to Wakefield Gaol.

Her three youngest children were sent to Huddersfield Union Workhouse as there were evidently no family members to look after them. This must have been a traumatic time for the children as they spent twenty months in the workhouse before being transferred to the newly built Children's Home at Outlane near Huddersfield in August 1901. At the time, Louisa had a baby girl, Elizabeth, just a few months old, who went into prison with her.

On the 1901 census, Louisa was recorded as a 'waste sorter', living in Leymoor, a suburb of Huddersfield, with Elizabeth and her sixteen-year-old son Gilbert, who became a soldier. She also had two male boarders living with her. Louisa's troubled life came to an abrupt end in January 1909. She had gone missing from her home on 3 January and was described as being depressed.[13] She was 'between forty-five and fifty years of age, has a dark complexion, is of spare build, and is supposed to be dressed in grey shawl, black skirt and boots'. Ten days later, Louisa's body was found in the River Colne near Ramsden Mill, Golcar. At the inquest, the cause of death was 'having drowned herself whilst of unsound mind'.[14]

DRUNKENNESS

The Howard Association's annual report for 1880 declared, 'It is well known that the least hopeful subjects of moral influence are habitual criminals, and most of all, criminal and debased women'. These habitual criminals were usually petty offenders sentenced for petty theft and public order offences, 'outcasts incapable of surviving in outside society'.[15] Repeated prison sentences for such drunken and mentally deficient women was both 'inappropriate and unproductive'. The chaplain of Brixton Prison argued that, 'It does seem important that women of this class should be treated in a special manner and in a *special place*, and that they should be placed under medical treatment, as their presence among other prisoners operates most injuriously upon those around them, and constitutes one of the chief difficulties in carrying out the discipline of the prison'.[16]

It was not until 1898 that the Inebriates Act finally removed alcoholics from prison and into 'certified' and state-run reformatories. Habitual drunkards and those who had committed serious crimes while drunk could be held in these organisations for up to three years. By 1904, 91 per cent of those held in these local reformatories were women.[17]

THEFT AND DECEPTION

Many women made a career out of being a criminal, spending almost concurrent sentences in various prisons around the country. In January 1899, forty-one-year-old factory operative Margaret Wilson was convicted at the Preston Quarter Sessions of obtaining £1 by false pretences from William Schofield 'with intent to cheat and defraud, at Chorley on 29

December 1898'.[18] At her trial, she pleaded guilty to the charge 'after a previous conviction of misdemeanour'. She was sentenced to three years' penal servitude and in 1901 was serving out her sentence at Aylesbury Convict Prison. Here, she was described as a widow, born in Salford and a cotton spinner before being convicted.

The routine at a convict prison would have been very familiar to Margaret as three years earlier, in October 1896, she was convicted of obtaining ten shillings by false pretences and sentenced to three years' penal servitude. Margaret could have earned up to one-sixth remission off her sentence and so could have been released after two years and six months. However, there cannot have been a very long period of time between the offence at Oldham and the one at Chorley. This meant she would have served two sentences of between two and a half and three years almost concurrently.

Margaret's prison record reveals numerous previous offences, all involving theft or deception. Before she was sentenced to her first three years' penal servitude at Oldham, Margaret had been convicted of eleven previous offences with sentences ranging from fourteen days' hard labour up to twelve calendar months with hard labour plus three years' police supervision. She was a prisoner at a number of different prisons including Preston, Strangeways, Knutsford and Liverpool and also used the aliases of Margaret Renshaw and Margaret Schott. In Margaret's case, long periods in prison do not appear to have deterred her from a life of crime.[19]

INFANTICIDE

Infanticide was a criminal offence normally associated with women, who were usually unmarried and driven to commit this horrendous act out of desperation. In some cases, members of the woman's family might be accomplices in the crime. In August 1844, twenty-year-old Eliza Daley, thirty-year-old James Daley and sixty-six-year-old Elizabeth Daley were all prosecuted for 'having at Manchester, feloniously attempted to suffocate a new-born male child, by throwing it into an ash-pit, with intent then and there to commit the crime of murder'.[20] It is not known if Eliza and James were brother and sister or husband and wife, or if Elizabeth was the mother or grandmother of James and Eliza. However, all three were acquitted of the attempt to suffocate the baby but were remanded to the next assizes for concealing the birth. This ancient offence is still in existence today. At the December assizes, James was acquitted but both Eliza and Elizabeth were sentenced to twelve months in prison. [21]

MURDER

In July 1869 at the Summer Assizes in Worcester, Fanny Frances Maria Oliver, a twenty-six-year-old milliner from Dudley, was put on trial charged with the wilful murder of her husband James on 16 May. It was alleged that James was murdered by the administering of arsenic which Fanny had bought 'for the purpose of cleaning bonnets'. It appeared that Fanny had recently renewed acquaintance with the man to whom she was engaged before marrying James and this was the motive the prosecution put forward for the crime.[22] She was convicted and a sentence of execution was passed upon her but afterwards she received a reprieve.

The chaplain at Worcester County Prison where Fanny Oliver was held prior to her trial and immediately after the death sentence was passed on her, recalled the character of the woman:

> …I daily attended this woman in her cell after her condemnation, and though I always found her respectful in her manner and attentive to my admonitions and instructions, she persisted in denying any guilty knowledge of her husband's death. From what she stated to me, it seems she and her husband had lived very irreligious lives, had neglected the public means of grace and had generally passed the Sunday in worldly pleasures and amusement. Though an intelligent woman, she could scarcely read when she was admitted to the Prison.[23]

'Female Convict Life at Woking – Convicts at Work in the Laundry' drawn by Paul Renouard. (*The Graphic*, 7 September 1889)

Soon after her reprieve, Fanny would have been transferred to Millbank. After a period of separate confinement, she was sent to Woking District Female Convict Prison to serve out her sentence of penal servitude for life.

PUNISHMENT OF REFRACTORY WOMEN

The phenomenon of 'breaking out', which was peculiar to female convict prisons, increased in the 1850s and 1860s after the ending of transportation. 'Breaking out' was a form of riotous behaviour by women 'amounting almost to a frenzy, smashing their windows, tearing up their clothes, destroying every useful article within their reach, generally yelling, shouting or singing as if they were maniacs'.[24] In one year at Millbank, 154 such cases of breaking out were recorded.[25]

Unlike male prisoners, females, considered to be the 'weaker sex' could not be punished by corporal punishment nor were physical restraints often used. Instead, the most common form of punishment for refractory female prisoners was close confinement in a 'dark cell' for a short period. As the women knew that this was the only punishment available, it was not feared and did not serve as a deterrent. This undoubtedly made life extremely difficult for the female prison staff. G.L. Chesterton, a prison governor, noted in his *Revelations of Prison Life* (1856) that 'The female attendants, in the extremity of their disgust and horror, used to exclaim what a blessing it would be, if we could employ some stout-armed woman to give them the rod!'[26]

Arthur Griffiths, the deputy-governor of Millbank, reported this observation of female prisoners. He claimed: 'When given to misconduct they are far more persistent in their evil ways, more outrageously violent, less amenable to reason or reproof'.[27] Despite such accounts of refractory behaviour, 'in 1880-1, 91 per cent of women completed their sentences without punishment'. By 1895-6 this had risen to 96 per cent.[28]

Restriction of diet was one kind of punishment prisons could enforce. However, Miles Walker, the governor of Liverpool Prison, reported that 'The women, as a rule, are a low class, and I do not think they can stand much dietary punishment. They feed badly outside, and some of them are not in the best of health, and therefore I do not think you ought to punish them too much'.[29]

THE STRONGEST CONVICTS AT FIRE PUMP DRILL

'Female Convict Life at Woking – The Strongest Convicts at Fire Pump Drill' drawn by Paul Renouard. (*The Graphic*, 7 September 1889)

Elizabeth Little, for twenty years the matron at Strangeways, was not in favour of dietary punishments either as she did not like to see prisoners 'lowered too much'. She preferred withdrawal from associated labour as a punishment and took time to build positive relationships with her charges: 'I think they like me…I have got at their hearts somehow or other, and I think they would be sorry to offend me. I ought not to say it, but I feel they like me. They trust me, and would be sorry to offend me.'[30]

WORK TASKS

Women were not allowed to work on the treadwheel, the heavy crank or at stone-breaking. Instead, first class hard labour for female prisoners might include the unpicking of one pound of unbeaten oakum, without the assistance of a tool, heavy work in the laundry or working in the kitchens. Even mothers with babies were expected to pick oakum but 'were not required to pick a quota'.[31]

In his evidence to the Gladstone Committee, Evelyn Ruggles-Brise highlighted the fact that the work options for women prisoners 'has been to a certain extent neglected. It has been taken for granted that women are only good for laundry work and needle work, and it is difficult to extend it much beyond those boundaries'.[32] There was a never-ending amount of laundry work available in all prisons, especially in local prisons where there was such a high turnover of prisoners requiring clean clothing.[33]

At the Kirkdale House of Correction, female prisoners sentenced to second class hard labour were expected to undertake a wide range of work tasks. These might include washing and laundry work, sewing, knitting, winding bobbins for weavers and wool-bordered mat-makers, making heald mats by hand and cleaning and arranging yards, passages, rooms and cells. Some female prisoners also acted as nurses in the female hospital, under the direction and supervision of the hospital warder. Female prisoners not sentenced to hard labour might undertake any of the work duties assigned for hard labour except for washing and laundry work.[34]

In some prisons, discipline was so lax that the female prisoners were able to neglect their work. At Lancaster, the gaoler wrote in his journal: 'The female crown prisoners reported for having returned their cotton unpicked. I am quite sure this is the result, not only of idleness, but of misapplication of time, for when I yesterday visited the penitentiary, the women were playing at blindman's buff in one shop, while those in the other were dancing'.[35]

THE NURSERY IN FEMALE PRISONS

A special and affecting feature of female prisons was the nursery for babies and infants of female prisoners. Women who gave birth in prison could keep their babies with them, providing they were breastfeeding, sometimes until the end of their sentences. Inevitably, the discipline of the prison could not be strictly enforced in the nursery as 'rules and regulations had to be waived in the interests of the children'.[36] This could arouse the envy of other inmates and where the requirements for work were waived, 'prison mothers often found themselves in a far easier position than women outside prison who were struggling to earn enough to support their offspring'.[37] Children were rarely kept in prison above the age of twelve months, except in special circumstances.[38]

In the 1860s, when Henry Mayhew visited Brixton Prison, the chaplain explained the rules about infants in the prison:

> If the child be born here it is to stay with the mother but if born in jail before the mother comes here, it is to be sent to the Union immediately she is ordered to be removed to this prison. We never had a child older than four years, but at Millbank one little thing had been kept so long incarcerated, that on going out of the prison it called a horse a cat.[39]

In some cases, children might be kept with their mother in prison for a much longer period of time. Henry Mayhew met 'a flaxen-haired, fair-faced little boy, who held fast hold of the matron's hand, and clung closer to her skirts at the sight of a strange man' at Coldbath Fields Prison. The matron explained:

> He's the son of one of the prisoners…His mother has got four years' penal servitude, and was sent away to Millbank; but they wouldn't receive her there on account of the child, since they had no nursery at that place. The mother and the boy have been here two years now, sir, and he comes to us every day to learn his prayers and letters. His name is Tommy.

Tommy was four years old.[40]

The first crèche for prison babies was at Holloway Castle prison where babies born in the prison and those under three months old at the time of their mothers' conviction were cared for. Under this system, a baby slept in a cot in its mother's cell and was taken to the day-nursery at 8.30 a.m. It was the duty of the wardresses to bathe and feed each baby before putting it to bed again. If the conduct of the baby's mother had been satisfactory, she might be allowed to see her baby at lunchtime or even to take it with her when she was at exercise in the prison yard. In fine weather, after lunch the baby spent most of the day with a prison nurse in a special tent in the garden. By 1900, 'all babies had to leave the prison at nine months'.[41]

Concerns were raised about the children in convict prison nurseries, especially when kept there for long periods. The contaminating influence of the criminal mothers on their children, it was feared, would mean the children themselves would be tempted into a life of crime.

If a criminal mother had older children, and no family to look after them, the poor law union where the mother had her settlement would be expected to take care of them. This meant that the children became inmates of the workhouse for the length of the mother's prison sentence. From 1866, under the provisions of the Industrial Schools Act, children of mothers

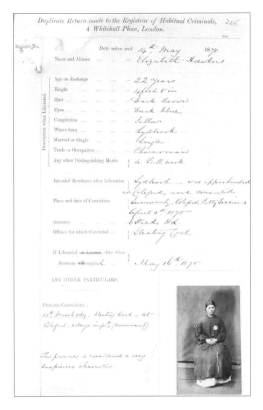

Above left: The criminal record of Elizabeth Hawkins, convicted of stealing coal in 1870. Her record notes she is 'a very suspicious character'. (QGC 10-1 p226, courtesy of Gloucestershire Archives)

Above right: Elizabeth Hawkins photographed in 1870 before starting a sentence of six weeks' hard labour. Notice the number on her uniform. (QGC 10-1 p226, courtesy of Gloucestershire Archives)

who had two previous convictions and who were under the age of fourteen were removed to an industrial school instead of the workhouse. This was extended from 1871 to include children of mothers with one previous conviction. While an industrial school may have provided a more stable environment for such children, the mother-child relationship would have been irreparably damaged forever.

In September 1857, Mary Ann Eynon (also known as Fortley), a twenty-three-year-old laundress, was found guilty of 'cheating' and unlawfully obtaining money by false pretences. She was sentenced to three months' hard labour at the Wandsworth House of Correction. At the time, Mary Ann was seven and a half months pregnant.

The indictment papers state that Mary Ann:

unlawfully and knowingly did falsely pretend unto Mary the wife of James Wastie Green that a certain paper writing and letter which she the said Mary Ann Fortley then produced and showed to the said Mary Green was written by one Elizabeth Scott (a person well known to the said James Wastie Green and the laundress of the said James Wastie Green) and that the husband of the said Elizabeth Scott had met with an accident and that the said Elizabeth Scott wanted a sovereign to take the husband of the said Elizabeth Scott to the hospital.[42]

Mary Ann served her three-month sentence at the Wandsworth House of Correction where her daughter Agnes was born in November 1857. When Mary Ann was released, Agnes was around six weeks old. The child was brought up by William Brett and Mary Ann Frances Brett (*née* Fautley). Mary Ann Brett is believed to have been the sister of William Fautley, the father of Agnes named on her birth certificate.[43]

At the time of her conviction at Devizes, thirty-year-old Sarah Coleman was around six months pregnant. In July 1850, she was charged with 'feloniously stealing £20, linen and blanket, the property of Mary Packer at Purton'. She was found guilty and sentenced to seven years' transportation. It is likely that the severity of the sentence was because Sarah had at least one previous conviction. On 3 September 1850 at Fisherton Anger Gaol, the matron reported that Sarah Coleman 'was confined with a Female child at quarter past 7 o'clock'. The following day 'The Surgeon saw Coleman, and the child, who are going on well, ordered her a Feather-bed, tea, sugar and butter'. On 7 October, Sarah Coleman's baby was named Mary Ann by the chaplain and two days later, Sarah and Mary Ann were transferred to Millbank.

Sarah was destined to be transported to Van Diemen's Land (now known as Tasmania). She and Mary Ann sailed on the *Aurora II* from London, arriving at their destination on 10 August 1851. The journey took 106 days. Nothing is known of either Sarah or Mary Ann's fate in Tasmania.[44]

EDUCATION

As with the male prisoners, only a small minority of females were eligible for instruction. In 1893 there were thirty-two prisons for women. In these prisons in the three years ending on 31 March 1893, twenty-five 'had educational groups of an average daily size of only ten or less'. If the daily average of women eligible for instruction was less than eight, education was not to be provided 'unless it was voluntarily undertaken by the matron or other officer'. This restriction was removed in 1898 when an extra £5 per annum was provided to pay for an officer to instruct small numbers of female prisoners.[45]

PRISON VISITORS

Unlike male prisoners, females could be granted the special privilege of seeing a prison visitor. These lady visitors were generally from the middle and upper classes of society and undertook the work for religious reasons. Some lady visitors had special interests in other forms of social work such as reforming prostitutes or promoting temperance.[46]

Supervised by the chaplain, the lady visitors saw the prisoners in private in special rooms set aside for the purpose. The visits were encouraged by the authorities as many of the lady visitors had links with the local discharged Prisoners' Aid Society. While not every female prison had lady visitors, by 1894 there were lady visitors 'in twenty-nine out of the fifty-four prisons in England in which women were confined'.[47]

RELEASE

Concerns about the fate of discharged convicts prompted numerous charities to set up refuges and shelters specifically for women, under the auspices of the Discharged Prisoners' Aid Societies. There were also three government-run refuges: the Carlisle Memorial Refuge for Protestant Women, the Winchester Memorial Refuge and the Eagle House Refuge for Catholic women. In the 1870s, a state-run scheme was introduced which targeted women 'whose conduct and character' justified 'the hope of complete amendment'. Such women could be released on license nine months before the end of their sentence into the care of either a voluntary or state refuge. A woman would forfeit her license and be returned to prison if she persistently misbehaved or tried to escape from the refuge.[48]

LUNATICS

LUNATICS IN PRISONS

Official prison returns reveal the shocking statistic that during 1883, 621 people had been sent to prison 'under suspicion of insanity'.[1] It can be safely assumed that the figure was similar in previous years. The Commissioners continued to stress that prisons were unsuitable for people of unsound mind: '…a prison is not a proper place for persons such as these. The care and management of lunatics is claimed and admitted to require special experience, and those who are so affected require peculiar treatment, and it cannot be expected that such experience should be available in prisons, more particularly in the small prisons which forms the large majority'.[2]

PROBLEMS WITH DIAGNOSIS

The identification of the truly insane depended on the skill of the medical officer in making a correct diagnosis. It was his duty to examine all remanded prisoners to check they were free from any infectious disease, and 'in sufficient bodily health to take their trials'. In 1874, the surgeon of the Salford Hundred County Prison certified that thirty-six-year-old Abraham Royle and fifty-eight-year-old Ann Fielding were of unsound mind and not fit to plead. They would have been sent to an asylum instead of staying in prison.[3]

While some prisoners were clearly insane making a diagnosis straightforward, the majority of prisoners with suspected insanity were more difficult to diagnose. This was compounded by the time constraints faced by the medical officer in examining the large numbers of prisoners in his care. When compared with the time taken in an asylum to examine and make notes on a potential lunatic patient, it is hardly surprising that misdiagnoses were regularly made by medical officers. Dr David Nicolson, the Superintendent of Broadmoor Criminal Asylum, had served in convict prisons for over ten years. At Broadmoor, he took 'between an hour and two and a half hours' to interview a patient for a report. He believed it was unjust for a prison medical officer to be pushed by any pressure of work 'to slur that most particular kind of work over hurriedly….'[4]

Malingerers often tried to feign insanity, making the medical officer's job even more difficult. It has been argued that prison administrators who were unable to distinguish feigned insanity from real 'preferred to err on the side of skepticism'.[5] In 1843, Ann Ray, a prisoner at Lancaster who was known for her refractory behaviour, assaulted a fellow prisoner, 'beating her severely about the head and trying to kill her'. She was brought before a visiting justice and 'behaved most violently' when he sentenced her to twenty-five days' solitary confinement. A few days later, it was reported that she had refused to eat for three or four days and that 'whenever I have visited her…I have found her singing wildly, and in other respects acting like a maniac'. The justices and two doctors came to see her but decided that she was not truly insane. Other members of staff at the prison did not agree and believed if this was the case, 'she is acting her part very skilfully'. Four days later, Ann Ray was in the hospital and was forced to wear a strait-jacket as she and another prisoner were so violent they had broken four panels of glass. Was this another case of 'breaking out'? It is not known what happened to Ann Ray and whether she truly was insane.[6]

It was not just a lack of time which made diagnoses of lunacy difficult. Prison medical officers rarely had any experience or training in treating or diagnosing mental illness. For this reason, the Superintendent of Wakefield Asylum argued that they would benefit greatly from spending six months attached to a large county asylum since 'The difficulties of diagnosis are very great, and it is requisite that they should have very fair training in insanity'.[7]

A need for training in lunacy practice was also stressed by Dr Nicolson of Broadmoor who told the Gladstone Committee: 'The mode of approaching and questioning a lunatic is somewhat different from one's mode of approaching and questioning a criminal or an ordinary prisoner'.[8]

When the prison medical officer was unavailable, the chaplain might be called upon to visit a prisoner who was suspected of being insane. In November 1860, the chaplain at Worcester Prison reported that:

> After the Afternoon Service, I was called by the Chief Warder at the request of the Governor to see a prisoner named Rowland Nock. I found him suffering in mind under a delusion that he had in some way made himself liable to punishment. I expressed an opinion that the door of his cell should be kept open, under the inspection of a warder, until the Surgeon could see him.[9]

The consequences of a delayed diagnosis or complete misdiagnosis of lunacy could be catastrophic for the prisoner. At the end of the nineteenth century in Pentonville, there was

> a bank clerk, a man of about forty years…who kept us awake at night, with a rigmarole about the Prince of Wales and the King, whom he expected as visitors on the morrow. For three entire nights and days…this man slept not a wink, but continued steadily, and with great perseverance, in the face of much opposition from those he was disturbing, his rambling conversations. Then, at last, he was taken up out of his poisonous cell into the light and air of the big hospital ward. But kindness had been deferred too late, and he was soon certified insane, and he went off to a lunatic asylum.[10]

DIAGNOSIS OF INSANITY

Even when the medical officer diagnosed a prisoner as insane, the magistrates could still 'decline to give the certificate necessary for his removal to a lunatic asylum' on the basis of cost, leading to questions about whether the prisoner should not simply be discharged.[11] The situation improved slightly with the passing of the Criminal Lunatics Act of 1884, under which prisons could obtain certification for criminal lunatics and have them transferred to asylums. In order to reduce the number of refusals for certificates for criminal lunatics, maintenance charges were to be paid by the Treasury during the period of their prison sentence.[12]

Despite the passing of the 1884 Act, insane people were still being sent to prison. During 1889-90, ninety-three sentenced prisoners 'were found to be insane on reception'.[13] In his report for 1893, Dr Robert Gover, the Medical Inspector of Prisons, referred to these insane prisoners: 'All were unfit for prison discipline, and many must have been unable to understand why they were placed upon their trial, or the meaning of any of the legal proceedings taken. The insanity was very obvious in most cases'.[14]

ASYLUMS

The Broadmoor Criminal Lunatic Asylum in Berkshire was opened in 1863 and was the first purpose-built asylum for the criminally insane. The first patients were ninety-five females and

Convicts proceeding to work
at Princetown, Dartmoor.

the male section of the asylum opened the following year. Criminally insane patients from Bethlem were transferred to Broadmoor when it opened. The patients at Broadmoor were most likely to have committed the most serious crime of murder.

Prisoners who had committed lesser crimes, and who were found on admittance to be insane, were usually sent to other asylums, not necessarily in the local area. On 28 March 1868, the Visitors of Worcester Prison recorded in their quarterly report that Thomas Futerill, who was committed from the Worcester City Police Court on 6 January, had been removed under a Secretary of State's warrant to the Fisherton Asylum.[15] Between 1850 and 1872, Fisherton House Asylum accommodated a number of 'harmless criminal lunatics from Bethlem and from asylums in other parts of the country' in special wards.[16]

One man destined for Broadmoor was Police Constable Alfred Bligh. In 1885 he was awarded the badge of merit in recognition of the gallant conduct displayed when arresting a man in Kirkham. A 'large crowd of roughs' set upon PC Bligh and kicked him very severely but he still kept a hold of the arrested man. By the following year in May 1886, PC Bligh found himself on the wrong side of the law when he was charged with the wilful murder of his three children Lillie Ada, Gertrude Maria and Sarah Eleanor at Kirkham.

The tragedy unfolded after PC Bligh was widowed in 1884 and his sister-in-law, Annie Turner, became his housekeeper. The relationship became more serious and Annie found herself pregnant. She left his employment and, after giving birth in November 1885, she started asking for money to help maintain the child. PC Bligh already had three children to support and on 15 May he told his new housekeeper that he had received a letter from Annie Turner with a summons to affiliate the child. This would mean that he would have become financially responsible for the child in law.

A more serious implication of the affiliation order was that the matter had been reported to police headquarters and on the very afternoon of the murders, PC Bligh was heard in conversation outside the house with his commanding officer Superintendent Stafford. It is unclear whether PC Bligh had been dismissed from the police service but the housekeeper stated when he came back into the house, he exclaimed: 'It's "domino" with me: my bread is

Above: The jail at Peterborough.

Left: Female convicts at work on the landings under the silent system in Brixton Prison. (From Mayhew & Binny)

taken out of my mouth and I have three little children, and nothing in my pocket.' 'Domino' was a slang term for signifying the end of a situation.

After putting the eldest two children to bed, the housekeeper saw PC Bligh seal four letters. He then persuaded her to go to the circus which was in Kirkham at the time, and where he had spent the afternoon with two of his children. The housekeeper went out to the circus and on returning to the house after ten o'clock, she found PC Bligh lying on his bed with his throat cut. Shortly afterwards, she discovered that the three children were all lying on the same bed with 'their skulls fractured, the deed having no doubt been done by an axe which was found near Bligh'.

PC Bligh's attempted suicide was unsuccessful and when he found he was in the hands of the police, he 'deliberately jumped through the window into the yard, and sustained some very serious injuries to himself'.

He was sentenced to death but received a reprieve and was ordered to be confined during Her Majesty's Pleasure. He was removed to Wormwood Scrubs and afterwards to Broadmoor Asylum. Here, it was reported that he was allowed considerable liberty in the way of correspondence with his friends and among his most constant correspondents were the Staffords, the family of PC Bligh's superintendent. In his letters, PC Bligh never referred to the tragedy but he seemed to be 'possessed with hallucinations on other subjects'. At the time of the 1891 census, Alfred Bligh was still a patient at Broadmoor Asylum.[17]

RECOVERY

Even when a lunatic prisoner had been committed to an asylum, it was still possible, in time, for him or her to recover. Edward Abbott, a fifty-one-year-old stonemason from Somerset, was discharged from Broadmoor on 30 May 1883 after ten years' treatment. He was classed as 'recovered'. He had been admitted after being tried at Wells Assizes for the murder of one of his children aged about three years old. After being found guilty, he was sentenced to death but was later certified as insane.

When he was admitted to Broadmoor, Edward was diagnosed with acute melancholia. He had been in a depressed state of mind at home since the death of three of his children from diphtheria. This had led to several unsuccessful attempts to take his own life until he decided to try again.

> Fearing that in case of his death his youngest and favourite child would be left unprovided for, he thought it would be better that she should die with him. He therefore killed her by cutting her throat with a razor, and, at the same time, he attempted to take his own life in the same manner. The wound that he inflicted upon himself, although severe, did not, however, prove fatal.

After ten years at Broadmoor, Edward appeared to be 'sane…rational, cheerful, coherent in his conversation, and free from delusion or other indication of insanity'. He was released into the care of his wife 'in order to support her and the surviving children'.[18]

SEPARATE PRISONS FOR FEEBLE-MINDED CONVICTS

Although it had been recommended back in 1879, it was not until 1897 that feeble-minded convicts begin to be segregated at Parkhurst Prison on the Isle of Wight.[19] These were men and women who did not require treatment in an asylum but whose imprisonment in a standard convict prison was inappropriate.

DEBTORS

In the nineteenth century, men and women could be imprisoned for owing money. Outside London, these debtors were kept apart from the criminal prisoners, living in their own section of the prison. In London, there were separate prisons exclusively for debtors. As with other aspects of prison life, before 1877 the treatment of debtors varied from prison to prison.

RULES AND REGULATIONS

Under prison regulations, debtors were allowed to maintain themselves and 'to procure or receive at proper hours food, wine, malt liquor, clothing, bedding, or other necessaries'. If a debtor could not provide himself with such necessaries as food and bedding, he was entitled to receive the normal prison allowance. Debtors could also work and follow their respective trades and professions 'provided their employment does not interfere with the regulations of the prison'. They were allowed to take daily exercise in the open air.[1]

Although prison life was more relaxed for debtors, they still had to adhere to certain prison rules and regulations. Debtors had to clean their cells, passages, staircases, day-rooms, yards, furniture and utensils. They were locked up at night immediately after the other prisoners, and unlocked in the morning in the same way. Debtors were expected to attend divine service and gambling or games of any description were strictly prohibited.

Debtors were allowed to talk freely in association and in their yard or day-rooms but 'anything approaching to disorder or improper noise, as well as talking in their bed-cells after being locked up' was strictly forbidden. They were permitted to see their friends and relatives twice a week and could write to and receive letters from relatives and friends. However, no newspapers or books were permitted to be brought in by or be sent to any debtor, although they could borrow books from the prison library.[2] Debtors were not to be placed in separate confinement or to be clothed in prison dress but were to be strictly confined to their own wards and airing yards.

There were a number of prison offences for which debtors could be punished. These included disobeying prison rules, assaulting a prison officer, debtor or another prisoner, profane cursing and swearing, any indecent behaviour and any irreverent behaviour in chapel or using insulting or threatening language to a prison officer, debtor or any other prisoner. Such offences could be punished by keeping the offender in close confinement and on bread and water only, for any term not exceeding three days.[3]

PRISONS FOR DEBTORS IN LONDON

There were five debtors' prisons in London, one of which was the Queen's Bench Prison in Southwark. It had 225 rooms, eight of which were 'state rooms' which were 'set apart for the better class of prisoners'. In the 1840s, prisoners paid half a crown a week to rent these larger rooms. For the other rooms, rent of one shilling per week was paid. Poor prisoners could occupy one of the back rooms free of charge. Debtors had to provide their own furniture and rooms could be shared to minimise the cost of rent.[4]

There was also 'a sort of street, within the walls, [which] contained shops for the purchase of meat, vegetables, coals and candles, groceries, tobacco, stationery, and other commodities, two licensed taverns or wine-shops, a coffee-house, and other conveniences for those who had money to spend, or whose friends chose to treat them'.[5]

If debtor prisoners paid a stipulated fee 'varying in the way of percentage on the amount of their debt' they could obtain leave to go out for the day 'and walk about freely within the local "rules" or "liberties" which extended to nearly all the Borough of Southwark'. However, they had to return to the prison at night and be locked up. According to *The Illustrated London News*, many wives, children and sometimes servants lived with the debtors at the prison and there were between 800 or 1,000 inmates.[6]

As a result of the 'anxiety of the poorer class of prisoners to save a few shillings a week', as many as six or eight people lived together in 'a dark, dirty apartment, measuring only sixteen by nineteen feet or slept on the benches in the tap-room, without any other covering than their clothes'.[7] It was said that 'the imprisonment of the poorer classes in the Queen's Bench proves, in many cases, the pathway to a premature grave; and that, in others, the constitution receives a shock from which it never afterwards recovers'.[8] Debtors who had committed criminal acts in the Queen's Bench Prison were confined to the strong-room for a fortnight's or month's solitary confinement.

In 1851, John Robinson, an upholsterer, was sent to Queen's Bench Prison in Southwark for one year. He owned a ship which he inherited from his father and was charged with:

the unshipping of certain foreign goods of great value the Duties of Customs for which had not been paid or secured that is to say divers towit Five thousand pounds in weight of foreign unmanufactured Tobacco of great value to wit of the value of Six hundred and eighty pounds of lawful Money of Great Britain the said Goods being then and there Goods liable to the payment of Duties of Customs to her said Majesty on the Importation thereof into the United Kingdom and which had been imported into the United Kingdom from parts beyond the Seas to wit at Ratcliff...

The Treasury charged John three times the value of the tobacco he had smuggled into England. As there were several similar offences committed over a number of years, John owed the Treasury a total of £6,220 in fines. A year later, the debt was paid, John was released and he went on to buy another ship.[9]

PRISONS FOR DEBTORS OUTSIDE LONDON

Outside London, there were separate sections for debtors in county prisons. At Lancaster Castle, there were thirty-two rooms for debtors altogether, with two set aside for women. The Constables room was a large room for the poorest debtors. Some of the larger, and more expensive, rooms to rent, accommodated only eight prisoners each. A guide of 1843 described the Constables room:

in one of the windows is perched an industrious cobbler...in another an unfortunate tailor. Over a fire of no ordinary dimensions, about half a dozen are leaning; in different parts of the room are groups in earnest conversation; here and there a few lie at full length on their bedsteads;...a party in a corner are exceedingly busy at a draught board; and...the room is nearly filled with tobacco smoke, emanating from a small knot of furious politicians.[10]

Each room was run by a 'room's man' who 'filled a role similar to that of a landlady of a boardinghouse'.[11] In the 1860s the Quakers, a large room in the Lungess Tower, was the most

Sketches of the Queen's Bench Prison – Front of Prison & Racquet Court. (*Illustrated London News*, 17 January 1880)

Sketches of the Queen's Bench Prison – Large Room and Poor Debtors' side of prison. (*Illustrated London News*, 17 January 1880)

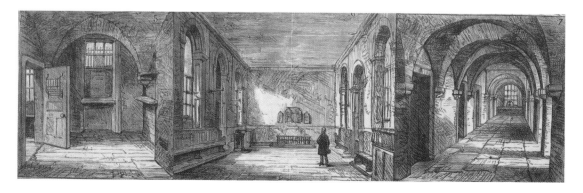

Sketches of the Queen's Bench Prison – Chapel and Corridor. (*Illustrated London News*, 17 January 1880)

popular 'because its enterprising room's man (who spent thirty-two years in the Castle) had furnished it in style with "easy chairs, sofas, a piano, and every thing to make the room look comfortable".'[12] A market was held within the Castle where debtors could buy meat, vegetables and fish.[13]

On visiting the debtors prison at Lancaster Castle, an inspector complained that 'Instead of being a place of rigid economy and sober reflection, [it] is like a somewhat noisy tavern and tea-garden; the prisoners idling about, smoking, drinking, talking in a loud voice, and playing at skittles and pitch-farthing'.[14] As the debtors were not clothed in prison dress, many still wore rags, with 'care-worn and haggard visages which express all the horrors of a withering poverty'.[15]

CHANGES TO IMPRISONMENT FOR DEBT

The 1869 Debtors Act was intended to abolish imprisonment for debt once and for all. The majority of those with small debts were no longer imprisoned. However, under the terms of the 1869 legislation, there were still 'a number of circumstances in which the court could commit to prison for up to six weeks [a debtor] provided that it was satisfied that the debtor had means to pay but had neglected or refused to do so'.[16]

By the 1890s, the number of debtors in prison had been considerably reduced. At Wandsworth 'there were generally no more than nine or ten debtors out of the daily population of around 1,100'.[17] These debtors were kept separate from the criminal prisoners and had their own day room.

After 1898, the special privileges enjoyed by debtors were reduced. While they were still kept separate from the criminal prisoners and were allowed to wear their own clothes, they were no longer entitled to procure their food from outside. They were also required to work at their own trade or profession or 'alternatively, at productive labour set by the prison, and were entitled to receive the whole of their earnings, subject to a deduction for maintenance and tools'.[18] Perhaps the most stringent new regulation was that they no longer had access to day-rooms and 'except when at chapel or exercise debtors were to be confined to their cells'.[19]

GOVERNORS

The governor had overall responsibility for the prison and therefore had the highest status of all the prison officers. This high status was signified by the fact that, unlike the other officers, the governor did not wear a uniform.[1]

RECRUITMENT

Although governors of prisons were traditionally recruited from the ex-members of the armed forces, before 1877 this was not always the case in local prisons. In 1841, twenty-nine-year-old Benjamin Lovett Stable was the clerk of Worcester County Gaol. Born in Bermondsey, Surrey, he had previously been a clerk in a merchant's office. By 1845, he had been appointed as governor to the gaol.[2] Benjamin continued as governor of Worcester for at least twenty-six years as he was listed there on the 1871 census.

George Pinson, the governor of Norwich Castle Gaol, started his career as a turnkey there before moving on to become the master of Gressenhall Workhouse in March 1837. His wife was the matron and his daughter was the schoolmistress. After gaining management experience as a workhouse master, he was appointed as governor of the Norwich Castle Gaol in December 1843.[3]

The ultimate promotion from warder to governor was still possible before nationalisation. William Linton was a warder at Pentonville before moving to Buckinghamshire County Gaol. From there, he was appointed the keeper of the Horsley House of Correction and then promoted to the governorship of Nottingham Gaol. He went on to be the governor of West Sussex County Gaol at Petworth from January 1857. When Petworth closed in 1878, he was posted back to Nottingham.[4]

Miles Joseph Walker had been a warder at Coldbath Fields Prison in London before being appointed as deputy governor at Worcester in 1872. He was obviously prepared to move around the country to further his career in the prison service and he used this post as a stepping stone to obtain a post as a governor. Here, he would have gained ample experience of running a prison in the absence of the governor and this must have stood him in good stead when he started to apply for governorships.[5] Subsequent censuses reveal he was governor of Leicester County Prison in 1881 and of Preston in 1891.

With regard to recruiting governors, by 1895 the Gladstone Committee stated that 'Military and naval training undoubtedly develops capacities for organisation and the maintenance of discipline, but we do not consider it to be by any means essential to the qualifications of a prison governor'.[6]

DUTIES

The governorship of a prison was a live-in post. Apartments were provided within the prison or, more usually, there was a separate house to accommodate the governor and his family. He

'A Prisoner Taken Before the Governor for a Breach of Discipline' – Convict Life at Wormwood Scrubs Prison drawn by Paul Renouard. (*The Graphic*, 5 October 1889)

was not allowed to be an under sheriff or bailiff and could not be concerned in any other employment whilst fulfilling the role of governor, as he was expected to devote the whole of his time to his prison duties. If he wanted leave of absence for even one night, he had to request it in writing from the Visiting Justices.[7]

A key responsibility of the governor was to visit the whole of the prison and see every male prisoner 'once at least in every twenty-four hours' and at least once in the week go through the prison 'at an uncertain hour of the night'. When visiting the female prison, he was always attended by the matron or other senior female prison officer.

Visiting the prisoners daily meant that the governor could adhere to yet another regulation: that of notifying the medical officer of any prisoner 'whose state of mind or body appears to require attention'. He also had to provide the medical officer with a daily list of prisoners complaining of illness, those removed to the infirmary, those who were confined to their cell by illness and those who were confined in punishment cells. The chaplain was also to receive this latter list.[8]

Prison governors had to be organised and sufficiently well educated to enable them to keep the bewildering array of records and accounts required of them. Given the fact that most governors had a military background, book-keeping was not a natural skill for most of them, so it is unsurprising to find that irregularities in the books were not uncommon. The books included:

A journal
A nominal record of all prisoners committed to his charge
A punishment book
A visitors' book

A record of articles taken from prisoners

A record of the employment of prisoners sentenced to hard labour and the manner in which they have been so employed

The register required by the Prison Ministers Act, 1863 to be kept of the church or religious persuasion to which every prisoner belongs

A list of books and documents committed to his care

An inventory of all the furniture and moveable property belonging to the prison

An account of all prison receipts and disbursements[9]

The governor was required to produce quarterly reports recording the daily average of the number of prisoners and the movement of prisoners to convict prisons, lunatic asylums and reformatories. These statistics from the New Bailey Prison in Salford dated April 1866 illustrate the level of detail required. The governor recorded that the daily average number of prisoners was 557. In that particular quarter, fifteen male and four female convicts were sent to Millbank Prison and ten male and four female convicts were removed to Wakefield Prison. One female prisoner, who was found to be insane on arraignment, was sent to Fisherton Criminal Lunatic Asylum in Salisbury. Another twelve females were sent to Lancaster Castle and thirty males to the City Gaol in Manchester while one female prisoner was sent to the Prestwich Lunatic Asylum.[10]

It was expected that the governor should 'exercise his authority with firmness and humanity, and shall enforce similar conduct on the other officers'.[11] This responsibility meant that the governor held a supremely powerful position within the prison. In any case of misconduct by a subordinate officer, he could suspend him or her immediately.

The governor had to be ready to receive any complaints or applications from prisoners at all times, so he needed excellent interpersonal skills. One Who Has Endured It reported it was during the dinner hour that 'the Governor tries those men who are brought before him on "reports" by the warders for misconduct, and also gives audience to such men as wish to see him to make any request, and have put their names down in the morning for that purpose'.[12]

On admission to the prison, the governor had to read, or cause to be read to the prisoners the prison rules and regulations. For long-term prisoners and convicts, this had to be repeated once in two months. The governor was also responsible for ensuring that the distribution of food according to the prescribed scales of diet was correct and that, if requested by a prisoner, any article of food could be weighed or measured in front of him.[13]

When the governor was absent from the prison, for whatever reason, the deputy governor undertook all his duties. It has been argued that, in small to medium-sized prisons, the governor's post was not a taxing one[14] because responsibilities could be devolved to the deputy governor or chief warder. One prison governor claimed that 'From about 9 a.m. until noon is about all the actual time necessary…to perform the purely routine duties of his office. A look round in the afternoon, with perhaps another in the evening'.[15]

One Who Has Endured It believed that the governor of Dartmoor in the late 1860s was 'but a popinjay in office'. He claimed he 'had as much to do with the management of the prison as a Russian cavalry colonel has to do with the navigation of the man-of-war he is, through Court interest, appointed to the command of'. Here, the chief warder, a soldier and strict disciplinarian, 'was everything here and was a man quite capable of ruling all under this charge'. Although many of the men disliked the chief warder, especially many of the officers, 'yet everyone respected him'.[16]

Just before the chief warder left, a new governor was appointed 'who needed no one to rule for him, but was as efficient a man as the chief….It was not long before every man in the prison, officers and men, had a very wholesome respect for …the new governor'.[17]

Sketches of the Queen's Bench Prison – Entrance Gateway to Governor's House. (*Illustrated London News*, 17 January 1880)

ACCOMMODATION FOR GOVERNORS

As the highest-ranking prison officer, a governor could expect the highest standard of accommodation within the prison. However, his quarters varied greatly from prison to prison, particularly before 1877 in the local prisons. In 1836, the Gloucester County Gaol and Penitentiary advertised for a new governor in the *Cheltenham Journal*, *The Times* and the *Morning Herald & Sun*. In a letter to one of the potential candidates, the clerk wrote:

> The Duties of the Office are to take the Charge of the prisoners, to see their sentences carried into effect, & to see that the Rules & Discipline of the Prison be observed which you will conclude requires steadiness and firmness coupled with humanity & unremitting application. The Governor's Appartments are within the Gaol – there is a good Parlour which is used as a Committee Room, a Kitchen, Cellar & requisite Offices, two large Bed Rooms & a Lobby or Passage Room which as it is without a Fire Place can only be used as a Room in Summer – On the whole the House Appartments I consider inadequate accommodation for a family, but sufficient for a Man & Wife.

He went on to comment:

> 'There are at this early period several applicants for the situation of Governor – One the present Keeper of the Gaol at Bedford whose Testimonials are such as to warrant him in expecting the Appointment having held his present situation nearly 20 years & seeks the Office by reason of the increase of salary. A Captn. Mason of Gloucester a Gentmn. from Family Connections, with the leading Men of the County has I am told flattering promises of support – The Head Turnkey at Coldbath Fields Prison comes likewise well recommended & two Gentmn. of considerable rank & standing in the Army are candidates & tell me they intend producing most satisfactory Testimonials'.[18]

This method of recruiting governors into the prison service through the canvassing of magistrates ended after the nationalisation of prisons in 1877.

By 1864, the governor at Gloucester had a new purpose-built house with a small stable, coach house and 7ft-high walls to form a garden. This must have been of a far higher standard than the previous accommodation and the Visiting Justices ordered that ten sets of Venetian blinds be procured for the house.[19]

Stone cutting by machine at Portland.

SUCCESSFUL GOVERNORS

Major William Fulford was the governor of Stafford County Gaol from October 1849 until his death on 5 June 1886. After being commissioned into the Royal Artillery in 1831 and serving in Corfu and Jamaica, he was invalided home to become a recruiting officer in Exeter.[20]

Major Fulford had strong views about the reformatory and moral effects of prison which he reported to a committee in 1863. He believed efforts to reform receivers, habitual thieves, vagrants, passers of counterfeit coins and those who had been convicted more than twice were a waste of time. He was convinced that the chaplain had very little moral effect on the prisoners, 'a proportion of one in 500 cases, at best. These were persons who came to prison from an otherwise blameless life…they are accidental offenders, and are of a totally different class from thieves or vagrants, and all other classes of criminals. They come to prison because it is the accident of their life, just as in the case of a man hunting who breaks his collar-bone…it is the accident of their lives, and a very disagreeable one to come to gaol'.[21]

With regard to the hard labour prisoners were expected to undertake, Major Fulford argued that, 'If I had the means of giving every man who is sentenced to hard labour in Stafford prison the full amount of discipline that I am empowered to do by Act of Parliament, for two years, no man alive could bear it; it would kill the strongest man in England'.[22]

Major Fulford favoured shorter sentences with a low diet and hard work as he believed 'a man could survive up to three months on such a regime'.[23]

The governor at Gloucester from 1862 was Captain Henry Edmund Cartwright who was appointed at an annual salary of £340 'with Residence, Fuel and Light, and also the plain Washing for himself and Household to be performed by the Prisoners'. At the time, there was a huge gulf between the salary of the governor and the deputy governor. Compared with the governor's salary, the deputy governor's salary was increased from £100 to £105 per annum.[24] A similarly wide disparity between the most senior members of prison staff was in evidence at many other prisons and this served to heighten the governor's special status.

Captain Cartwright remained the governor at Gloucester until October 1869 when he resigned 'on account of his failing health'. His successor was Henry Kenneth Wilson who was appointed on a salary of £400 per annum. Henry Wilson used his post at Gloucester as a stepping stone towards gaining a post in a larger prison and moved to Maidstone Gaol as governor five years later.[25]

COMPLAINTS

Investigations at Birmingham Prison in 1854 into alleged cruelties revealed that the governor, Lieutenant Austin, had frequently used a special punishment jacket as a punishment for all kinds of offences and it had become, 'in the Commissioners' words an "engine of positive torture".' A case of suicide in 1853, which had prompted the investigation, occurred after 'prolonged periods of solitary confinement during which the punishment jacket was repeatedly applied'. The Commissioners ruled that the suicide was a 'deliberate act of self-destruction, committed by the prisoner to relieve himself from bodily and mental suffering…' They went on to state that Lieutenant Austin had been entirely culpable in the matter: 'We are of opinion, that by the order and with the knowledge of the governor, he was punished illegally and cruelly, and was driven thereby to the commission of suicide'.[26]

It was judged that Lieutenant Austin:

appears almost from the first to have adopted the notion, that the principle of strict separation, combined with hard labour, was to be effectually maintained by no other means than by the instant infliction of punishment for every infraction of the discipline or failure in the labour; … he introduced of his own authority another, not only utterly illegal, but most objectionable from its painful, cruel, and exasperating character, which he practiced with a frequency distressing to hear of, for offences often too trivial to call for any severity of punishment at all, and upon offenders quite unfit to be subjected to it, combining with it also other inflictions and privations, and directing and witnessing their application with a lamentable indifference to human suffering, until the penal system of the gaol became almost a uniform system of the application of pain and terror… For the punishment of the strait jacket, Lieut. Austin never obtained or asked the sanction of the magistrates; he never made it known to the inspector of prisons; and he discouraged as much as he could all remonstrance against or interference with it on the part of the officers of the prison.[27]

Both the governor and the surgeon were forced to resign and were criminally proceeded against, and found guilty. Lieutenant Austin was sentenced to three months imprisonment, 'which…he was allowed to serve as a first-class misdemeanant'.[28]

The extreme nature of the complaints about the governor at Birmingham was rare. More common failings of prison governors related to irregularities in book-keeping or in maintaining good working relationships with the staff under their leadership. At Gloucester in 1845, the matron resigned and the under female officer was dismissed for employing prisoners. At the same time, it came to light that the governor, Captain George Henry Mason, and the several officers of the prison had employed prisoners 'for the washing of the Clothes of the Governor, of his Wife, Family and Servants and the Clothes of the several Officers of the Prison'.

The governor did not suffer the same fate as the matron and the Visiting Justices simply admonished him 'to be careful in conforming to the Regulations in future'.[29] In the following year, it was agreed that 'the necessary Washing and mending of the Clothes of the several officers of the County Prison and House of Correction may in future be performed by the Female Prisoners under the direction of the several Matrons of the said prison'.[30]

In 1854, during investigations into the alleged drunkenness of the under matron at Gloucester, the Visiting Justices were highly critical of the role played by Captain Mason who was still the governor of the prison there. They recorded that,

It is upon him that the first and gravest responsibility rests for every transaction in breach of Discipline or Regulations of the Prison occurring within its walls. It was his duty to investigate

Convicts at work in
the quarries at Portland.

and report every case of misconduct which might come to his knowledge whereas he is chargeable with a serious omission in his journal...He has exhibited a laxity of proceedings quite incompatible with the due appreciation of the duties of his office...he has ignored the whole case and has consented to join with others in concealing it. Such conduct must have the effect of weakening the confidence which this Board should repose in the first Officer of so large an Establishment, and tend to impair his authority in the eyes of his Subordinates.[31]

Again, Captain Mason did not lose his position.

Captain Mason's prison career finally came to an end in December 1861 when he resigned from his post. In his letter of resignation, he wrote: 'I do so with great regret after having served the County more than 24 years, I trust with zeal and fidelity – The confinement involved in the due discharge of my Office, in addition to my advancing years, have suggested to me the propriety of the course I now adopt...' Captain Mason was rewarded for his long service, despite the two irregularities already mentioned, with an annuity of £120 per annum.[32]

Captain Mason was described by a prisoner as '...bland, imperturbable, civil and firm, he was never weak and never rude...he governed the gaol like a drawing room, excepting that the *desserts* were not quite the same. I saw rude men baffled, they could not make out how'. The same prisoner commented that, 'As blandly and courteously as he wished me good morning, he would have conducted me to the gallows, had instruction to that effect reached him...'[33]

PRISON WARDERS

After 1877, the Victorian English prison was staffed according to a pyramidal 'para-military structure' with a strict hierarchy of command.[1] At the top, with overall responsibility for the running of the prison, was the governor. Under him was the deputy governor and then the chief warder. In a large prison, there might be more than one chief warder. Under the chief warder there were three other grades of prison officer: first, the principal warder, then the warder and finally at the bottom was the assistant warder.

This staff structure had been in operation in the convict prisons since around 1850. Prior to 1877 in the local prisons, a similar structure was in operation but job titles differed from prison to prison.

RECRUITMENT

While the highest-ranking prison officers such as governor and deputy governor usually came from the army or navy, lower-ranking warders were often recruited locally and therefore had a variety of previous occupations. In around 1866 at the age of thirty-nine, John Blainey took up a post as a warder at Portland Prison. Born in Renfrew, Scotland, John had previously worked as a shoemaker in St Helier, Jersey, and as a musician in Devon. It is not known why John moved to Dorset but his wife was born in the Portland area so they may have moved to be closer to her family. It is possible that John's shoemaking skills helped him to secure his prison warder position. In other convict prisons, industrial trades such as shoemaking or tailoring were taught to prisoners so that they could undertake them as work tasks.

As a prison warder, John Blainey lived with his wife and the four youngest of his seven children in prison accommodation in Grove Road, Portland. Here, a row of terraced houses was built specifically for the prison officers, not long after the prison opened. There were quarters for married warders and smaller homes for bachelor staff. In 1872, John died in hospital in Exeter. His family would have been expected to leave the house at Grove Road straight away. Nothing is known of John Blainey's service record as a prison warder.[2]

From the middle of the nineteenth century, governors and inspectors alike voiced concerns about the required character and qualifications of potential prison warders. Writing about local prisons, William Walker, the governor at Banbury, wrote a personal reply to Gloucester about the attributes and qualities required of warders, and the importance of selecting the right one: 'I would most respectfully submit, that the subordinate officers should be chosen from a Class of men entirely different from the Old Turnkey, Firm but kind in their leaning towards Convicts, so much depending on them'.[3]

The difficulty of recruiting warders with the right character was not restricted to the local prisons. In the early 1850s, there were similar concerns about the staff working for the rapidly expanding convict service. Captain Gambier was the first governor of Dartmoor, a public works prison. In his first report from 1850–51, he commented that:

> Many of the warders on their appointment had no conception of the kind of duties they
> undertook to perform, and others were quite unaccustomed to either exercise authority or

submit to discipline – many have resigned or have been dismissed and now a body of zealous, active and trustworthy men are established here, there are a few who I fear will not be able, satisfactorily, to discharge their duties.[4]

Captain Gambier asserted that the required attributes of prison warders for closed prisons and public works prisons were different. He argued that in a public works prison, the prison warder:

should exercise the utmost vigilance, activity and intelligence in seeing that his men are properly distributed at their work, and in taking care to keep them all in view at all times. The class of men who are best qualified for such duties are pensioned NCOs, because from their previous habits they not only exercise a watchful vigilance over their different gangs, but they are also obedient to any instruction they may receive.[5]

One Who Has Endured It believed that:

…old soldiers are the best warders, and…the discipline of the prison would be much better conducted if the warders were all taken from the ranks of discharged soldiers. The generality of men who enter the convict service as assistant warders are of a very poor type. They take to it as a last resource, except in some instances such as where whole families – father and sons – are in it, and are to a certain extent born and bred in it. A man generally comes there with hardly a rag to his back or a shoe to his foot; has never had the least authority over another man in his life, and is suddenly placed with very great power and authority over a lot of men who are for the time being slaves to his orders, whims and fancies. Very few become efficient officers; most of them are perfect tyrants. They soon find out that any accusation they make against a man is listened to, and the prisoner's word is under no circumstances believed.[6]

One man whose previous occupation made him ideally suited to life as a prison warder was Sergeant Edward Beer. Born in Whitechapel in 1805, he joined the 95th Regiment in December 1823. Almost immediately, he was sent to Malta to guard the garrison there. His next posting was to Corfu where between 1829 and 1835 he was the castle guard. From there he was transferred to Carrickfergus Castle in Ireland. He ended his career in the army as a recruiting NCO in Halifax with his discharge in February 1823. On his retirement, Edward received a year's gratuity.

On 16 June 1845, Sergeant Edward Beer joined the staff of Millbank Prison in London as a warder. His experience as a soldier would have been invaluable in his new career. At the time of the 1851 census, Edward was listed as a 'soldier' at the prison while his wife Mary Ann was recorded at a private address. This could indicate that Edward was on night duty at the time. Edward continued as a warder at Millbank until the mid-1860s. By the time of the 1871 census, Edward and Mary Ann had moved to Kent and Edward was described as a 'pensioner'. No record of an army pension has been found so it is likely that the pension was awarded when Edward left the prison service. Having served over twenty years at Millbank, such a pension would prove that he was considered to be a valued and trustworthy employee.[7]

There was nothing military about James Derbyshire's background when he was appointed assistant taskmaster at the County Prison, Cheetham, Manchester (Strangeways). Like so many children in the industrial north, at the age of thirteen James was working as a cotton factory worker. By the time of the 1871 census at the age of twenty-three, he had joined the staff of Strangeways. His previous occupation was given as 'salesman', so it is perhaps unsurprising that James's career in the prison service was short-lived. When he married in 1877, James was a book-keeper in Cheshire so he seems to have acquired some education along the way. He went on to have a number of different occupations including cashier in a cotton mill, manager of a cotton factory and an agent for the Calico Company Estate. At the time of his death in 1911, James was a Justice of the Peace.[8]

FAMILY CONNECTIONS

In some cases, a career in the prison service ran in families. Although little detail is known about their working lives, three generations of the Marsh family were prison warders. In 1839, Robert Marsh, who had been a sergeant in the Royal Artillery, joined the newly opened Juvenile Prison at Parkhurst on the Isle of Wight as one of the taskmasters. He continued in the service until at least 1851. Robert's son, George, also served as a prison warder at Parkhurst, having married Elizabeth Bull, the daughter of the Parkhurst farm bailiff James Bull. Elizabeth's sister, Fanny, also married a Parkhurst warder, William Palmer.

At some point in the 1860s, the Marsh family moved to Nottingham where the third generation, George Marsh junior (son of George), joined the prison service and worked with his father there.[9]

Another family with a tradition of working in the prison service was the Scott family. William Scott Snr was a warder at Portsmouth by 1849 and remained in the service until the 1870s, by which time he had reached the rank of principal warder at Woking. William Scott Snr had at least four sons, three of whom chose a career in the prison service. It is highly likely that family recommendations would have been invaluable to each son in obtaining their first posts.

The eldest son, William Scott Jnr, followed his father into the service when he became an assistant warder at Portsmouth in November 1854. At the time, William was twenty-one years old and had returned from eight or nine years at sea as an ordinary seaman. He was to be paid £52 per annum to include lodgings and meals. By 1862, William was promoted to the post of warder. During William's prison career at Portsmouth, he supervised the transfer of convicts on at least two convict ships, the *Adelaide* and the *Clara*.

In around 1870, William was transferred to Parkhurst on the Isle of Wight and was promoted to the post of principal warder at the same time. He retained this post until he retired from the service in 1883. On retirement, he was granted a superannuation allowance which was a 'special retired allowance of annual amount of £93 - 4 - 6 which is calculated at 46/60th of his pay and emoluments instead of the 28/60ths which would otherwise have been his due'.

William Snr's second eldest son, John, started his working life as a carpenter/joiner but by 1871 he had joined his brother William as a warder at Parkhurst, where he remained until the 1890s. Meanwhile, by 1871, William Snr's third son, Richard, had become a warder at Woking, serving there at the same time as his principal warder father.[10]

ACCOMMODATION AND SALARY

The majority of the convict prisons provided accommodation for their prison staff. However, prior to 1877, not all local prisons provided such accommodation.

Between 1849 and 1854, the clerk of Gloucester Prison wrote to a number of large local prisons, enquiring about the salaries and accommodation offered to their staff. The replies reveal just how different each local prison was. In 1847 at Maidstone, the governor had a residence in the prison with fuel and candles, the deputy governor had apartments in the prison plus fuel, candles and a small garden while the chaplain had his own house and small garden. The gatekeeper and the turnkeys received a weekly wage and no other allowances. In addition, the authorities at Maidstone stated: 'The Officers do not wear Uniform, nor have they any Rations found them…'

At Reading in 1849, the governor, chaplain, deputy governor and storekeeper all had houses while the matron had an apartment with rations and washing. The subordinate staff had a better deal than those at Maidstone as the principal warder, female warder and warders 1, 2, 3 and 4 all had apartments, rations and washing.

The officers at Stafford were all 'allowed Coal, Candles and Oil for Lamps, when on Duty'. The governor, deputy chief officer, matron, head turnkey and the top four turnkeys all had a house, coal and candles. There were eighteen lower-ranked turnkeys who had no extra allowances or accommodation. The hospital warder had a lodging room, coal and candles while the three female turnkeys had washing, coal and candles but no accommodation.

Above left: An unidentified convict prison warder.

Above right: William Scott, a convict warder at Portsmouth and Parkhurst, probably photographed shortly before his retirement in 1883 (see page 121). (Courtesy of Kenneth Scott)

Prison warders' houses at Portland.

The Salop County Prison was less generous to its staff. The governor and taskmaster had a house, lights and fuel while the matron and the female turnkey had a residence, lights and fuel. To encourage loyalty, the prison offered the male turnkeys on their first appointment 18s per week. After two years' service, this rose to 20s and after five years, to 22s per week. They also had a 'Uniform, Cap, Coat and a pair of trousers annually'.[11]

After nationalisation, in order to improve recruitment and retention of prison officers, steps were taken to 'provide some or all officers with quarters near the prisons'. This was introduced slowly because of the high cost, but by 1883 prisons were reporting increased expenditure on staff quarters. Such quarters were built for staff especially where rents were high and where they were 'likely to be thrown into undesirable contact with a certain class of the population in their search for lodgings'.[12]

Before the availability of such housing, staff in metropolitan areas had found it difficult to find affordable and respectable accommodation. There had been noticeable resignations among newly appointed staff in Holloway because 'houses and lodgings in this part of London are difficult to obtain and very expensive'.[13] Enlargements and reconstruction at prisons continued throughout the 1880s, along with developments in staff quarters.

In around 1890, a report about local prisons listed staff quarters, purchased, rented, or built. There were ten quarters for superior officers, ten for chief warders, nine for principal warders and 136 for warders. As with all other aspects of prison life, the provision of accommodation differed significantly from prison to prison. At Bodmin all the staff had quarters but at Newcastle, the chief warder was the only member of staff with quarters. Prison staff complained that where quarters were provided, they were too small because the entitlement for a warder was two bedrooms. This was clearly insufficient for a warder with a large family. The staff complained further 'that the rent allowance was quite insufficient to get a house away from the "certain class"'. Newcastle, as in all other respects, seemed to suffer as much as any: 'in the vicinity of the prison it literally swarms with brothels'.[14] By the late 1890s, there was sufficient accommodation for it to be decided to quarter officers or to give them a rent allowance in lieu.[15]

UNIFORM AND WEAPONS

The uniform of each prison warder depended on his rank. Different insignia was used on convict warders' uniforms with the crown symbol on their hats and tunic buttons.[16] The type of weapon carried by a warder also depended on his rank. Convict warders and assistant warders who were on duty outside at a public works prison were armed with bayonets and short rifles. When working inside the prison, they carried a truncheon which was carried in cases worn at the side. Chief warders and principal warders carried a cutlass.[17] In addition to their weapons, warders carried their keys in a small cartouche-box or pouch, which was attached to their belt,[18] and a whistle-chain for emergencies.[19]

DUTIES

Working in the prison service was undoubtedly difficult and there was 'a real sense that officers were themselves prisoners both inside and outside the walls, for much of their off-duty life was also supervised, including their housing'.[20] The lack of an adequate warder-prisoner ratio made the job even harder. In 1865 there were 'only about one thousand wardens to cope with an average prison population of eighteen thousand'.[21]

Prison officers were expected to 'exercise their authority with firmness, temper and humanity, and abstain from irritating language, at the same time avoid the least approach to familiarity of conversation on any subject whatever'.[22] In addition to this firmness of character, prison officers were expected to work extremely long hours. Convict prison warders were usually on duty at six in the morning, and with the exception of meal-times, were with the prisoners until nine at night. They were off duty every alternate Sunday. Similar hours were worked at local prisons.

A photograph taken from the Marsh family album dating from the 1870s/1880s (see page 121). (Courtesy of Dominic Pinto)

There was little respite at mealtimes either. At Dartmoor in the late 1860s, all the warders had their breakfasts and teas in the officers' mess-room in the prison. At dinner time, the married officers were allowed to 'go outside to their own homes in the barracks or cottages at Princestown to dinner', but the single men had to eat their dinner in the mess-room.[23]

Warders could not be absent without leave from the governor, and before leaving the prison, they had to leave their keys, instruction book and report book in the governor's office. All subordinate officers were required to regularly examine 'the state of the cells, bedding, locks, bolts &c, and shall seize all prohibited articles' and deliver them to the governor.

Prison officers could not have any interest, direct or indirect, in any contract for the supply of the prison. They were also forbidden from accepting money, fees or gratuities of any kind for the admission of visitors to the prison or prisoners.

One regulation which was rigorously enforced was that prison officers were forbidden from selling or letting articles to any prisoners. Given the low wages of some of the subordinate warders, it must have been a strong temptation to sell items such as tobacco to prisoners.[24]

One Who Has Endured It described the life of the convict prison warder as '...very little better than the prisoners'...A convict warder is a man continually in a tiger's cage. With few exceptions, the men he is placed over are scoundrels, with but few redeeming qualities, who hate the warders placed over them, regarding every one of the prison authorities as their natural enemies'.[25]

It has been argued that prison staff developed 'a symbiotic relationship...with prisoners, for each could make the life of the other either easier or more difficult'.[26] A former convict, Ticket-of-leave Man wrote in 1879:

James Derbyshire, photographed
with his family, who was
an assistant taskmaster at
Strangeways in the 1870s (see
page 120). (Courtesy of Lyn and
Jim Owers)

There is a tacit understanding between all 'second-timers' and old thieves, and the officers who have charge of them. If the officer is caught in any dereliction of duty he is liable to a fine; these old thieves act as his spies, and take care that he is *not* caught. In return he allows the thieves to fetch what they call an easy lagging.[27]

The life of a prison warder, especially in a public works prison, could be a dangerous one. This was because the convicts had to use tools in their work which could be used as weapons. In the 1860s, there were several instances of warders being attacked and even murdered by convicts while at work outside the prison. In September 1866, James Boyle, a warder at the Chatham Convict Prison was attacked and killed by a convict named James Fletcher 'with the hammer used by him in breaking stones'.[28]

PROMOTION

One had to be patient to gain promotion within the convict prison service. Robert Langshaw Smith had been a mariner before being appointed to the service in October 1866 at the age of twenty-five. He joined Portland Prison as an assistant warder on a salary of £51 per annum. Born in Melcombe Regis, Robert was local to the area. He had married two years earlier and may simply have wanted a secure job on land, rather than at sea.

Robert had to wait eight years for his first promotion to warder in 1874 and another ten years before he was finally promoted to principal warder. Unlike some other convict prison warders, Robert only served at Portland. If he had been prepared to transfer to another prison, it is possible he would have been promoted earlier.

By June 1887, after twenty years of service, Robert was forced to retire due to ill health. He received a superannuation allowance of £40 10s 8d. After retiring, he became the landlord of the Adelaide Arms in Weymouth.[29]

There was a defined hierarchy within the prison ranks. In the local prisons, once a man had secured a post as a prison warder, it was possible for him to work his way up the ranks with loyal, efficient service. In November 1858, Giles Cambridge was appointed as 'Treadwheel Officer No. 2' at Gloucester Prison. By March 1860 he had been promoted to 'Treadwheel Officer No. 1' and the following year, he became 'Head Officer of the Gaol'. Five years later, Giles was appointed 'Warder 2nd Class – Gaol and Penitentiary'. He finally became Principal Warder in November 1871.

In October 1874, Giles Cambridge was attacked and assaulted by a prisoner named Charles Cooke. The circumstances are unclear but it was reported that 'assistance [was] rendered by a Prisoner named Walter George Tredwell' to him and 'Her Majesty had been advised to remit two months of Tredwell's imprisonment'.[30]

From 1870, another career path was opened up to warders when it was decided they could become clerks or schoolmasters within the prison.[31]

SUCCESSFUL PRISON OFFICERS

Charles Corby, an ex-police officer, joined the prison service as a warder in 1877. On his retirement in 1912, several local newspapers interviewed Charles and the information he provided about his thirty-five years in the service gives a valuable insight into the working life of prison officers. Before being appointed a warder at Wakefield Prison in 1877, Charles had been a police officer with the Wakefield Borough Police Force 'in a rough district'. While this would have given him experience in dealing with criminals, his first three months as a warder at Wakefield must have been a real baptism of fire.

The *Cambridgeshire Weekly News* reported that:

> The prison population at Wakefield at that time was extraordinarily high, and extra officers were required to cope with the rush. The average number in [the] prison at one time was 1700, and 1735 prisoners were there one Christmas Day. It was nothing very unusual to have 100 admissions and 120 discharges in one morning. As there was not sufficient cell accommodation, a large number of prisoners had to be held in dormitories 30 and 40 in a room.

Charles was put on night duty from 6 p.m. to 6 a.m. and had charge of one of the dormitories which held thirty prisoners. Beds were arranged on either side of the room and he 'was instructed not to allow the men the slightest communication with each other'. To prove he was attending to his duties all night, every fifteen minutes he had to peg a so-called 'tell-tale' clock. Charles was visited occasionally during the night by the deputy governor and the principal warder in charge of the night officers.

After three months of this onerous night duty, Charles applied for a day duty post and was 'placed in charge of prisoners in a ward, whose employment was chiefly mat-making'. When the government took control of all English prisons in 1878, Charles volunteered to be transferred to Leicester North. Here, there were military prisoners which he thought were 'some of the best he has had to deal with' as they were 'clean and amenable to discipline'. After about ten months, the prison closed and Charles was transferred to the county prison of Leicester South where he instructed the prisoners in the making of mats and brushes.

Three years later, Charles was transferred to Cambridge Prison where he was to spend the remainder of his prison service. It was reported that Charles 'never had a prisoner who gave him the slightest difficulty. I always found that by using a little tact that I could get on with the worst prisoner'. He was promoted to principal warder in March 1901 and again to chief warder in November 1903. In 1913, Charles was rewarded with the Imperial Service Medal in recognition of his 'long and meritous service'.[32]

Robert Langshaw Smith, a convict warder at Portland for twenty years, photographed in full prison dress with his sword (see pages 125-126). (Courtesy of Brian Wollaston)

David Crosbie, the deputy gaoler at Worcester Prison, tendered his resignation on 26 August 1871 after thirty-five years' service. He was first appointed as a warder in June 1836 at a weekly wage of 21 shillings. At the Midsummer Sessions of 1854 he was promoted to chief warder and again at the Easter Sessions in 1861 to the rank of deputy gaoler at an annual salary of £80. After the amalgamation of the County and City Prisons, this salary was increased to £100 per annum. In addition to this salary, he received '£10 per annum for length of service pay, according to a long established usage in the prison, with house, coals, gas and uniform'.

When he resigned, David Crosbie was sixty-five years old. The Visiting Justices argued that 'if long and faithful services combined with uniform exemplary conduct, entitle an officer to a superannuation allowance, Mr Crosbie is deserving of one on the most liberal scale'. The Visitors recommended 'pursuant to the 15th section of The Prison Act of 1865 that one be granted on that basis: this may be an annuity not exceeding two-thirds of his salary and emoluments'.[33]

COMPLAINTS

There were serious consequences for any warder who flouted the rules or shirked his duties. Punishment might include docking of wages, suspension from duty, demotion or even dismissal. If dismissed, the warder would be expected to vacate the prison accommodation immediately which, if he had a family, would adversely affect them too.

Irregularities at Gloucester were discovered in October 1861 when it was found that books had been lent by an officer to a prisoner without the permission of a Visiting Justice or the chaplain. More seriously:

> prisoners had been let out of their Cells, to go to the Water Closet, and been allowed to return by themselves to their Cells, the Officer in charge being satisfied with hearing the doors of such Cells slam without personally ascertaining that they had thus become fastened – that two Prisoners by preventing the bolt of the lock from fastening the door, had been thus enabled to visit each other in their Cells…

On investigation, the Board decided that Principal Warder Ursell was most to blame in the matter and recommended that 'he should be reduced from the Office of Principal Warder to that of Tread Wheel Officer of the Penitentiary…at the yearly salary of £50…vice Cambridge who is nominated for Head Officer of the Gaol'.[34]

Ten years later in 1871, Frederick Ursell was the Under Warder at Gloucester. He resigned from his post after twenty-one years' service 'in consequence of illness and inability (from a severe injury in the head received from a fall when on duty in the prison) to continue [his] duties'. He was granted a superannuation allowance of £30 per annum.[35]

In August 1870, the governor of Worcester Prison recorded that he had 'Reported Subwarder Bray to the Visitors on Saturday next for bringing food into the prison for William Webb a convicted prisoner contrary to the 22nd Regulation Schedule 1 of the Prison Act 1865, Bray was dismissed and the arrears of pay due to him forfeited'.[36]

Another sub-warder at Worcester was also in trouble in the same month. On 9 August, Subwarder Bache who had been absent from duty all the day without leave returned to the prison at 9 p.m. The governor suspended him until the next meeting of the Visiting Justices. Four days later, Subwarder Bache was fined one week's pay.[37]

IMPROVEMENTS IN WORKING LIFE

Working conditions for prison warders gradually improved from the 1860s onwards. An increase in staff at the convict prisons meant that by 1864, at Millbank 'every officer was able to have a half-day off during the week if he was on duty on Sunday'.[38] At around this time, 'compulsory dining in messes was abolished'[39] and by 1877, all prison staff were salaried, regardless of whether they worked in a convict or local prison.[40]

There continued to be a disparity between the pay and working conditions of local and convict prison warders. In 1891, convict prison staff were paid 20 per cent more than warders in local prisons and they also had a free issue of boots.[41] The local prison staff argued that '…their duties were as arduous and dangerous as those of the convict staff, and that the local staff had to handle the convicts for the first nine months after sentence when 'they are more careless of their own lives and other people's'.[42] Convicts were confined to local prisons for their nine months' separate confinement from 1886-87.

However, the convict staff argued that '…the work in convict prisons was much more difficult and dangerous, because the men worked in association, and were in possession of tools which could be used…as weapons. Furthermore convict officers frequently had to work in the open air'.[43]

While the local prison officers were rewarded with a slight increase in pay and free boots, by the end of the nineteenth century, there was still a significant difference between the pay of staff in convict and local prisons.

FEMALE STAFF

It has been argued that women recruited as female warders were 'from a social background scarcely distinct from that of the prisoners themselves, and many lacked the education, intelligence or ability to meet the demands made of them'.[1]

Whichever social background she came from, one prison governor noted that, 'Female prisoners often like to be under the care of a good-looking officer, and will obey her and conduct themselves properly with her, though she may be a very indifferent disciplinarian. It has been said, and often confirmed, that a plain-featured officer of unsympathetic address finds it difficult to discipline her charges'.[2]

The staffing of each wing in a female prison required at least three female officers to provide twenty-four-hour coverage. This was 'the bare minimum necessary to maintain constant supervision, and to allow the warders to be relieved in rotation, and to carry out court, identification and escort duty'.[3]

THE MATRON

The matron of a prison had the same onerous responsibilities as the governor. However, she did not share the same status as she was subservient to the governor. She was required to live in the prison and 'have the care and superintendence of the whole female department'. She was to keep the keys for the locks of the wards, cells and yards where the female prisoners were confined, and these were to be secured by different locks from those allotted to the male prisoners. Whenever the female prisoners were at chapel, she was to attend with them 'unless absent by leave, or prevented by some duty'.[4]

Like the governor, the matron was required to inspect the female section of the prison daily and could not be absent without prior agreement from the Visiting Justices. She also had to appoint a deputy matron to act in her absence. Unlike the governor, the matron had just one journal to keep in which she had to record 'all occurrences of importance within her department, and punishments of female prisoners'. This was to be inspected daily by the governor.[5] As the matron was under the direction of the governor, a good working relationship between governor and matron was vital for the smooth running of a prison.

CHARACTERISTICS OF FEMALE WARDERS

In contrast with male prisons, female warders were encouraged to form relationships with the prisoners based on trust and loyalty. They were expected to set themselves up as 'models of feminine decorum, good temper, and compassion, traits that inmates might then seek to emulate'.[6]

Mrs Florence Maybrick, who spent time in Walton, Woking and Aylesbury Prisons, was generally impressed with the warders. She commented on 'the patience, civility and self-control which the officers exhibit under the most trying circumstances' which 'as a rule, mark them as men and women possessing a high sense of duty, not only as civil servants, but as Christians'.[7]

Above left: An unidentified prison warderess, dating from the early twentieth century.

Above right: The principal matron at Brixton Prison. (From Mayhew & Binny)

The directors of the Millbank convict prison insisted that staff should show 'patience, a disposition to discover, and give credit for, the least evidence of improvement, and a sympathy which can understand and feel for the trials and difficulties even of the outcast'.[8]

Mary Ann Beer, whose husband Edward was a warder at Millbank, was also recorded as a warder at the same prison on the 1851 census. She was registered at her home address and Edward was listed at the prison. As it was extremely unusual for a married couple to be employed at a prison, being recorded separately on the census may have been an attempt to disguise the fact that they were husband and wife. Another possible explanation is that Edward was on night duty at the time of the census.

The length of Mary Ann's prison service is not clear as she gave birth to three daughters in 1849, 1852 and 1854. It would appear that she possessed the empathetic nature required of a female prison warder. An unsubstantiated family story tells that Mary Ann felt so sorry for the prisoners at Millbank that she baked cakes and hid them up the chimneys for the prisoners to find.[9]

Like warders in male prisons, female warders were expected to work long hours, sometimes twelve or even fifteen hours a day.[10] A prisoner noted, 'One class of people who have my sympathy in prison are the wardresses. Their work is monotonous, and their lives are spent with the undeveloped and disharmonised souls on life's ocean. They are on their feet all day, and their pay when I was in prison was poor...Some of them were far too good to be wasted there...'[11]

It is perhaps unsurprising that another observer commented: 'Towards the close of the day...some of the officers get irritable and extremely cross with the prisoners, and...other officers get so tired out, they really do not much care whether the prisoners about them conduct themselves ill or well'.[12]

By the beginning of the twentieth century, *Living London* reported that 'The female officers have a life full of anxieties, even dangers, for assaults are not uncommon, yet they are mild mannered, forbearing to their troublesome sisterhood, and have strong claims to the respect and esteem of the public at large'.[13]

PROMOTION

Prior to joining the prison service, some female prison warders gained experience of managing an institution by taking up a post in a workhouse. Like the prison, the workhouse was also peopled with sometimes difficult inmates. Elizabeth Sweetland, a miller's daughter born in West Harpitree, Somerset, joined the prison service in June 1871 as an assistant warder and laundry officer at Gloucester Prison. Elizabeth was unmarried and aged thirty-four at the time. She had previously worked as an assistant matron at Bedminster Union Workhouse in Long Ashton, Somerset.

By August 1873, Elizabeth was classed as a 'Warder, Nurse & Schoolmistress' and at the end of the year, she was promoted to the position of under matron. Elizabeth's sister Emily came to work at Gloucester in December 1873 as the nurse and schoolmistress, staying until May 1877.

Elizabeth herself left Gloucester Prison in July 1874 after three years to take up the position of matron at Worcester Prison. By looking at her career progression, it is obvious she was ambitious and wanted a post of greater responsibility. At the time, the matron at Gloucester was Emily Marshall, who had been promoted from assistant matron in 1873 and she was still the matron in 1891. The only chance Elizabeth had of promotion was to move prisons. She stayed at Worcester for at least seven years.[14]

Above: The female prison officers at Aylesbury Prison. (Supplement to *The Sphere*, 12 December 1908, courtesy of Karl Vaughan)

Right: Warders' terraced houses at the Grove, Portland. (Courtesy of Wendy Corbett Kelley)

SUCCESSFUL FEMALE STAFF

In June 1874, Miss Walker, matron of the Salford Hundred County Prison, was forced to resign from her post after thirty-five years' service on account of ill health. The surgeon certified her illness and found her to be 'suffering from Chronic Bronchitis and Disease of the Arteries of the Brain, rendering her liable to attacks of giddiness and unconsciousness'. On these grounds, he was of the opinion that she was 'no longer capable of efficiently discharging the duties of her office'. In her letter of resignation, Miss Walker urged the Visiting Justices to take into account her thirty-five years at the prison 'and that in deciding upon the scale of retiring allowance you may be enabled to grant me, my services will be deemed of a character to bring me favourably before you'.[15]

COMPLAINTS

Like male warders, female prison officers had strict rules and regulations to adhere to and faced serious consequences if they failed to do so. At Michaelmas 1845, the Visiting Justices of Gloucester Gaol and Penitentiary reported that they had 'carefully investigated the complaints made by Eliza Beames, a penitentiary prisoner that she had been employed during the last nine months by the Matron (Susan Peel) and by the Under Female Officer (Eliza Williams) to perform Fancy and other Sewing Work for the advantage of those officers and not for the County and that the Matron upon questioning her had acknowledged the same'.

Susan Peel and Eliza Williams had broken one of the prison regulations which stipulated that no officer could employ a prisoner. The Visiting Justices decided the offence was so serious that they immediately dismissed Susan Peel and Eliza Williams resigned from her post.[16]

It has been argued that reports of organised trafficking in female prisons were so frequent, and the penalties imposed so minor, that one can only assume that such illegalities were very common.[17] Such trafficking involved prisoners' friends outside prison paying a warder to bring illicit goods into the prison.

At Tothill Fields Prison, a warder named Charlotte Howe 'posed as a potential trafficker and was offered ten shillings and a gold watch by one woman to take in "some Grub, Meat and a little Wine" to a relative inside. At the same prison, an inmate, Emma Steiner, told the authorities that warder Ann Bailey was trafficking goods to a number of her peers, though, significantly, not to Steiner herself'. She said: 'The prisoners say sub warder Bailey receives so much a week to bring parcels into them: it is talked about outside, and when a prisoner gets her sentence they say never mind she has a good screw inside.'[18]

In September 1860, four female prisoners at Tothill Fields 'confessed they had done both plain and embroidery work for these Officers in return for which they received bread, butter, cheese, tea, fruit and cake'. The opportunity to augment the meagre prison diet with such rich luxuries must have been great.[19]

Drunkenness was another offence some female warders committed. In December 1854, a complaint was made against the under matron of the Gloucester County Gaol and Penitentiary, Ann Wigmore, of being 'on the evening of 20th December…so intoxicated as to be wholly incapable of receiving a female Prisoner from the custody of a Sheriff's Officer from Bristol'. She was immediately dismissed on account of her drunkenness.[20]

During their investigations, the Visiting Justices discovered that the lodge keeper had been 'greatly culpable in yielding to the urgent request of the Matron to keep secret his knowledge of this discreditable transaction, and the scene he witnessed in the Female Prison'. For her part, Mrs Mary Bedwell, the matron, from 'the state of her health & increasing infirmities since her paralytic seizure, [has] for some time past, clearly indicated to us the necessity of her early resignation'. Mary Bedwell was quick to resign.[21]

24

CHAPLAINS

The chaplain held a powerful position within the prison. His good opinion of a prisoner or convict could positively influence whether he or she received aid from a charitable society on release. He also directed the schoolmaster in his duties, thereby determining the kind of education the prisoners received

The calibre and personality of the prison chaplain was paramount to the spiritual welfare of the prisoner. A passionate, committed chaplain could inspire his charges to seek redemption and reformation. On the other hand, a chaplain who gave mechanical sermons and rarely visited prisoners in their cells was more likely to inspire indifference.

DUTIES

The duties of a prison chaplain were many and varied. He was required to perform the appointed morning and evening services every Sunday and on Christmas Day and Good Friday. In addition, he was to give religious and moral instruction to 'the prisoners who are willing to receive it' and to administer the Holy Sacrament of the Lord's Supper on suitable occasions to 'such prisoners as shall be desirous'.[1]

Prayers and portions of the scriptures were to be read daily by the chaplain himself or by the governor or other such person appointed by the Visiting Justices. The chaplain also had a special duty to see the sick daily and was required to visit all prisoners under punishment. He was expected to pay particular attention to the juvenile offenders in prison, hence the very detailed reports about them in the journals of most prison chaplains.[2]

Another special responsibility of the chaplain was to attend to the condemned prisoners sentenced to death, to whom he was expected to 'particularly afford his spiritual assistance'. In addition, he was required to keep a journal and, later, a character book of prisoners.[3]

While chaplains had a great deal of responsibility in prisons, some tried to overstep the mark. At Easter 1846, the chaplain of Gloucester Gaol was reprimanded for questioning Daniel Evans, a penitentiary prisoner, 'as to his Commission of a Crime for which he was not suffering, first by himself in the Chapel and next in the presence of his Master'. It was pointed out to the chaplain that 'in the solemn discharge of his Office, [he] may recommend to a distressed Prisoner to relieve his mind by a confession of his Sin but he cannot be permitted to interrogate and ask for the confession of a Prisoner as to his commission of a particular crime not for spiritual but for secular purposes'. It was presumed that the chaplain had 'through ignorance assumed a power with which the law has not invested the Magistracy, namely, the questioning of a Prisoner as to an offence with which he is not charged upon oath'.[4]

VISITS TO PRISONERS IN THEIR CELLS

One of the aims of the separate system was to give the prisoner or convict time alone for reflection on his or her crime and to awaken the conscience. Visits by the chaplain were meant

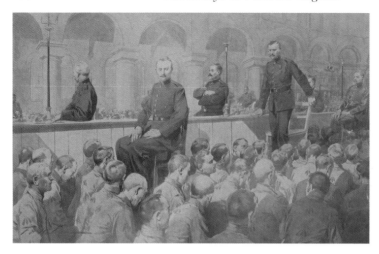

'Watched by Warders
on Raised Seats:
Convicts Offered
the Consolation of
Religion' drawn by
Frederic de Haenen.
(*Illustrated London News,*
15 April 1911)

to be an essential part of this spiritual reawakening. However, regularly visiting hundreds of
prisoners in their cells to have meaningful conversations was a tall order for any chaplain,
especially in prisons where there was no assistant chaplain. Priority was always given to the sick,
the condemned and those prisoners in punishment cells. In local prisons particularly, short-term
prisoners might not receive a cell visit from the chaplain at all.

In July 1850, when the Visiting Justices threatened to take away the post of assistant chaplain at
Gloucester, the prison chaplain the Revd Robert Jermyn Cooper resigned. The Revd Cooper
had been in the post for twenty-eight years and he had had an assistant chaplain for the previous
six years. He explained: 'I feel that my strength will be wholly inadequate to the discharge of the
increased duties which will devolve upon me, and which will be rendered additionally onerous
by the removal of the Assistant Chaplain.' When it came to appointing a new chaplain for the
prison, the Visiting Justices had the luxury of choosing from sixty-four candidates. Their choice,
the Revd John Francis Herschell, was appointed at a salary of £250 per annum.[5]

The zealous chaplain at Pentonville between 1844 and 1859 was the Revd Joseph Kingsmill.
A passionate advocate of the separate system, he was not one to shirk his responsibilities.
During the time he was chaplain, Pentonville 'held a daily average of 500 men all sentenced to
transportation…'[6] In the decade 1845 to 1855, the Revd Kingsmill 'carried out over 100,000
cell visits and spent between ten and twelve hours daily at the prison.'[7]

INFLUENCE ON EDUCATION

The chaplain had an enormous amount of influence over the education of the prisoners and the
school teaching staff as he was required to 'direct the disposal of the time of the Schoolmaster
and Schoolmistress, and the course of instruction to be pursued by them, and frequently
examine the prisoners as to their progress'.

He was also expected to frequently visit every room and cell of the prison occupied by
prisoners and to 'direct such books to be distributed and read and such lessons to be taught in
the prison as he may deem proper for the religious instruction of the prisoners'.[8]

OPINIONS ABOUT CAUSES OF CRIME

Via their regular reports to the Visiting Justices, prison chaplains had an influential voice. In
1849, the Revd John Clay, the chaplain of the Preston House of Correction, put forward his
argument that alcohol was the main cause for crime.

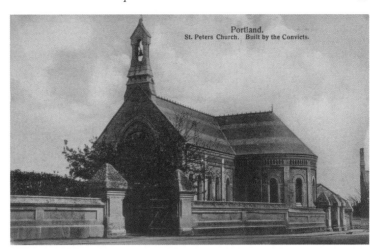

St Peter's Church at
Portland which was
built by the convicts.

Whether taken in beer-shops, public houses, gin-palaces or singing-rooms, DRINK is the great destroyer. We have received into our care 50 Government convicts – men under sentence of transportation, some for 21 years, and some for <u>life</u> – from York, Worcester, Essex and Stafford. In their cases, as in those belonging to our own county, drink has stimulated to crime. Out of the whole 50, only 5 venture to claim credit for sober habits, and 2 drank a little.

The Revd Clay believed strongly that the 'reformatory discipline of a prison must, necessarily, be a religious one, and must greatly depend, humanly speaking, upon the zeal and judgment of the Chaplain…'[9]

For the Revd Richard Appleton, chaplain of the Kirkdale House of Correction, the 'offenders' first fall from grace' could be traced to 'the absence of all religious principles in the mind, owing to the culpable neglect of parents…exposed, as he must be under such circumstances, without any moral guard, to the varied seductive temptations which a large town presents in the form of cheap theatres, tavern, concert-rooms and similar attractive places of concourse'.[10]

SUCCESSFUL CHAPLAINS

After thirty-six years as the chaplain at Preston, the Revd John Clay resigned in January 1858. He had been suffering with depression. In his last report to the Visiting Justices he wrote:

…it has been only during the intervals of freedom from pain and depression that I have felt able to commit my thoughts to writing and use some of the materials I had collected. I have often been on the point of throwing my task altogether aside, and might have given way to the impulse, but for the fixed and deeply felt desire to prove to all…among the multitude of our prisoners and outcasts, there are many…yet capable of being brought, by God's grace, within the Christianfold.[11]

Almost twenty years after his death, the Revd Clay was remembered as an 'able indefatigable and tender-hearted chaplain…who rendered the Prison famous not only in the annals of the County but of the whole kingdom, and who spent his life in endeavouring to ameliorate the lot of the erring creatures who were the objects of his solicitude…'[12]

One Who Has Endured It greatly admired the chaplain at Newgate:

…I received from him the very kindest treatment. Without being obtrusive, he kindly and lovingly urged his great Master's message. …Never have I met a man more fitted for his office than he is. Few men have the gift – and it is a gift which many good men try in vain to attain – of dropping in a few seasonable words, conveying comfort judiciously mingled with reproof, that Mr Jones possesses. Without being obtrusive, with a complete absence of anything approaching to 'cant', he has the happy knack of just saying to an erring man the right thing at the right time, and in the right way.[13]

This chaplain offered One Who Has Endured It some useful advice to get through his sentence of five years' penal servitude:

> You must just consider yourself as a slave till your time is out. Every action of your life will have to be just what your taskmasters may command you to do. Try and bear up meekly and submissively. Avoid giving offence to any of the officials, and remember that, though your body is condemned to slavery, your thoughts, your mind, and heart are free – free to commune with God, free to pray, free to praise, and free to repent. You may in after-life reclaim yourself and actually look back upon this very punishment as a blessing. Blessings you little dream of may, by God's mercy, arise out of what is now so bitter a trial.[14]

COMPLAINTS ABOUT CHAPLAINS

The main complaint about prison chaplains from prisoners and convicts was their indifference and their lack of cell visits. Ticket-of-leave Man recalled:

> I am sorry to say that during my long experience in two convict prisons I never knew a chaplain voluntarily to enter a prisoner's cell and have a little rational talk with him about the good policy of honesty and truth. I am sure not one of them ever came in this way to me. I never heard of one going to any other prisoner.[15]

It was also argued that prisoners were getting a second-class service from their chaplains because 'those who seek office in prisons, asylums and workhouses have failed to obtain a hearing in the outside world, the assumption being that anything will *do* for prisoners, lunatics and paupers'.[16] Oscar Wilde agreed. He thought: 'The prison chaplains are entirely useless. They are, as a class, well-meaning, but foolish, indeed silly, men. They are of no help to any prisoner'.[17]

Although One Who Has Endured It found the chaplain at Dartmoor to be 'most assiduous in his duties, very earnest, and a most obliging gentlemanly fellow', he was also a 'great stickler for rules, and on one occasion I felt he did not quite do his Christian duty in adhering too closely to the strict prison rules'.[18] One of the convicts needed to contact his wife urgently because:

> …she had written to her husband saying she should leave her mother's and go into lodgings by herself unless she heard from him to the contrary. Unfortunately he would not be privileged to write for nearly four months. He was most anxious she should not leave her mother's house and go to live by herself, and he consulted me as to what was best to be done.

One Who Has Endured It urged the chaplain either to back up the young man's request to the governor to be allowed to write to his wife earlier than his privilege, or to write to the man's wife himself. The chaplain replied: 'I cannot see it is my duty to transgress the strict rules of the prison'. As a result of not receiving a letter from her husband, the wife left her mother's and eventually went to live with another man. One Who Has Endured It was convinced that 'had the Chaplain transgressed that one little prison law, he would have saved the wife from transgressing God's law and the husband from becoming a reckless man'.[19]

25

MEDICAL OFFICERS

The health and wellbeing of the prisoners depended to a great extent on the calibre, character and efficiency of the medical officer (sometimes called the surgeon). This varied enormously from prison to prison.

George Bidwell, a prisoner at Woking Hospital Prison, had a very poor opinion of Dr Campbell, the medical officer there. He 'resigned from the service and retired to private life with a pension and the inexpressible hatred and contempt of all prisoners who ever had the misfortune to come under his treatment'.[1] He was much more complimentary about the medical officer at Dartmoor, commenting 'with no exception…never saw among prison authorities a nobler-hearted Christian gentleman than Dr P. Power…'[2]

DUTIES

The prison medical officer had a seemingly endless list of duties to undertake. On admission to prison, he had to examine each prisoner and to record the prisoner's name, age, state of health on admission and 'any disease of importance which he may have been subject'. The prisoner's state of health would have a bearing on whether he or she was capable of undertaking hard labour tasks.[3] The medical officer had to examine all convicted prisoners sentenced to hard labour periodically to ensure they were fit enough to carry it out. He was to enter in his journal the name of any prisoner 'whose health he thinks to be endangered by a continuance at hard labour of either class…' Any such named prisoners were not to be employed at hard labour until the surgeon certified he was fit for such employment.[4]

Among the many duties of the medical officer, he was required to visit the prison at least twice in every week, 'and oftener if necessary, and shall see every prisoner in the course of the week'. He had to visit all prisoners confined in punishment cells and all those deemed to be sick, daily or oftener if necessary. This must have been difficult as the medical officer was not usually resident in the prison, and, in some cases, had a practice outside prison to attend to.[5]

The medical officer had to keep a daily journal in which he wrote 'an account of the state of every sick prisoner, the name of his disease, a description of the medicine & diet, and any other treatment which he may order for such prisoner'. At least every three months, he had to inspect every part of the prison and record in his journal 'any observations he may think fit to make on any want of cleanliness, drainage, warmth or ventilation; any bad quality of the provisions, any insufficiency of clothing or bedding, any deficiency in the quantity or defect in the quality of water, or any other cause which may affect the health of the prisoners'.[6]

In his weekly inspection of the prisoners, the medical officer was required to report to the governor in writing the names of any prisoner he believed was or was likely to be 'injuriously affected by the discipline or treatment…together with such directions as he may think proper'. He was also to notify the chaplain of any prisoner who appeared to require his special notice.[7]

If the medical officer or surgeon considered it beneficial to a prisoner's health to prescribe tobacco or spirituous liquor, he could order it by officially entering it into his journal. He

Left: The interior of a Victorian prison, possibly Wakefield. Notice the wire netting fitted across the galleries which was installed to prevent suicides.

Below: The New City Prison, Holloway (*Illustrated London News*, February 1853)

could also order 'the supply of flannels, and such other things as he may deem requisite, in cases where the health of the prisoner, is suffering, by the want of them'. The medical officer could direct 'that every prisoner take daily as much exercise in the open air as may be necessary for health'.[8]

When convicts were transferred between prisons, the medical officer had to certify their fitness. Sometimes medical officers and governors of prisons had differing opinions. In April 1852, the governor of Preston House of Correction recorded that James Fox and John Wilson were removed to Millbank Prison but 'by the stupidity of the Medical Officer there, were ordered back…'[9]

If any prisoner exhibited any case of danger or difficulty, the medical officer was entitled to call in additional medical assistance if he required it. In any case, he was not allowed to perform any serious operation without consulting another medical practitioner 'except under circumstances not admitting of delay'. This was all to be recorded in his journal.[10]

In the event of the death of any prisoner, it was the medical officer's responsibility to enter into his journal the time the deceased was taken ill, when he first knew of the prisoner's illness, the nature of the disease and when the prisoner died. If a post-mortem examination was made, he also had to provide details of the appearance of the prisoner after death.[11]

Whenever the medical officer required leave of absence or was himself ill or had a necessary engagement which prevented him from visiting the prison, he had to appoint a substitute who had to be approved by the Visiting Justices.[12]

In addition to his duties regarding the prisoners, medical officers had staff obligations. They had to attend to all officers and prison employees, and their families, within the immediate area of the prison (except for midwifery), and also had to examine all candidates for employment. Lest anything should have been overlooked he was reminded that the list did not 'purport to comprise the whole of the duties of the Medical Officer'. He was expected at all times to 'carry out his instructions with good will and to the best of his ability, and (to) spare no effort to promote the wellbeing of the persons under his charge'.[13]

DIFFERENCES BETWEEN LOCAL AND CONVICT PRISONS

One issue which does not appear to have been considered by prison authorities was that medical problems in local prisons were vastly different from those in convict prisons, and therefore demanded different skills. Medical officers of a local prison arguably had a more difficult job because local prisoners came straight from the streets and were the 'destitute, hungry, dirty and diseased'.[14]

The governor of Clerkenwell reported that:

> I have myself known five prisoners received here at the same time who on examination were all found to be covered with lice. I have also seen prisoners brought down in such a filthy state that the lice dropped off their clothes going down the passage. A prisoner once told me that his only reason for breaking a window was to get into prison, so that he might get rid of the vermin with which he was covered.[15]

The local prison medical officer had to cope with a high turnover of prisoners as sentences could be anything from a few days or weeks to two years. This must have made it very difficult for the medical officer to form anything other than a cursory opinion of each prisoner's medical condition.

By contrast, when prisoners reached the convict prison, they had already passed through one of the local prisons. This meant that the convict prison medical officer was better informed about each convict's medical condition. Given the length of convict sentences, the medical officer had time to get to know the convicts under his charge. One problem the medical officer of a convict prison faced was the malingerer, who daily took up his valuable time.

LACK OF TIME FOR DUTIES

The medical officers of both local and convict prisons shared a common difficulty: that of finding enough time to examine each prisoner efficiently to assess his or her medical condition and fitness for hard labour. This was especially problematic with cases of suspected insanity.

In the 1890s, Dr Walker, the medical officer at Holloway, gave evidence to the Gladstone Committee about his working day. Starting at around 9.30 each morning and finishing at the same time in the evening, he examined between twenty and ninety new arrivals at the prison every day. He also had many clerical responsibilities and had to carry out 'a good deal of official writing' at home. Dr Walker did not have time to examine the remanded prisoners unless they complained of feeling ill and he only examined the heart and lungs of the convicted prisoners. He added that: 'There is a certain delicacy with regard to examining women which there is not with regard to men'[16] and implied that 'they did not receive a full examination'.[17]

For Dr Walker, determining the mental state of the prisoners was 'by far the most important duty of the medical officer of the prison' and in some cases 'two or three examinations are occasionally necessary'. By 1894, Holloway received between three and thirteen mental cases every day.[18]

The medical officer's lack of time could explain One Who Has Endured It's view that 'The visit of the Doctor is in many, aye, most cases, nothing but a brutal farce. The Doctor, the apothecary, and a hospital orderly carrying a tray with a few bottles of medicines, and a hospital warder came round, attended by the principal of the prison on duty'. Prisoners were given hartshorn and oil, ointment, pills or castor oil.[19]

Dr Tennyson Patmore, the medical officer of Wormwood Scrubs, had similar difficulties in fulfilling his role. His initial examination was designed to ensure that prisoners 'were in a condition to sleep the night safely in the prison rather than the prison hospital' and to identify any risk of suicide or infectious disease. For those prisoners received in the evening, there was a follow-up examination in the morning. Dr Patmore admitted to the Gladstone Committee that he had a limited amount of time for examinations so he had to 'hurry it'.[20] He was also expected to undertake routine surgery and attend to the females in the prison.[21]

SUCCESSFUL PRISON MEDICAL OFFICERS

Despite the onerous responsibilities, many prison medical officers stayed in their posts for a considerable period of time. Thomas Chalmer had been the surgeon at the Kirkdale House of Correction since it opened in the 1820s. In 1859, he petitioned the Visiting Justices for a superannuation allowance and highlighted the reason he was still working at the advanced age of seventy-one. In 1832 he had placed his son as a resident surgeon at the prison:

> where the labour was so constant and severe that at the expiration of his duties he was rendered unable for twelve months to pursue his studies in the University and laid the foundation of that disease which caused his death in his thirty-ninth year leaving his Widow to the care of your Memorialist and compelling him to pursue his profession at his present advanced age.

It was also stated that Thomas Chalmer was much crippled in his limbs.[22]

Thomas Hickes was a long-serving medical officer at the Gloucester Gaol and Penitentiary. In October 1874, he resigned after thirty-five years at the age of sixty-nine and was rewarded with a superannuation allowance of £120 per annum.[23]

Walter Barton Stott was the surgeon at the New Bailey Prison in Salford for twenty-three years, starting in 1843. His report to the Visiting Justices of April 1866 is typical of those produced by prison medical officers and indicates the number of prisoners he was required to treat in the hospital wing:

The disorder the most prevalent has been as usual at this season Bronchitis – acute and chronic – numerous cases of which have required much care and attention during the recent inclement weather. The number of cases admitted into Hospital during the quarter has been 80 – 50 males & 30 females. The daily average has been 23. Four deaths have occurred. One however was not a Prisoner at the time of his decease. When his imprisonment expired he was not in a fit state for removal and at his own request he was retained in hospital.[24]

Walter Stott was forced to resign as surgeon in 1866 'in consequence of impaired vision and the general state of his health'. The Visiting Justices recorded that he had 'uniformly discharged his duties in a most efficient manner'. He was granted an annuity of £120 per annum (or two-thirds of his salary) by way of a superannuation allowance, under the provisions of the Prison Act, 1865.[25]

COMPLAINTS

The huge burden of work placed upon prison medical officers was undoubtedly the reason for the majority of complaints about their negligence. John Hay, a convict in the 1890s, 'petitioned the governor' complaining he was 'suffering from sciatica', after treading the wheel for a week. He recalled: 'The doctor ordered me to strip, and, having made me get on the scales, said that I was four pounds heavier than when I entered the prison. I don't know how this showed I was not suffering from sciatica'.[26]

Another convict, David Fannan, recalled how he reported sick to the medical officer because of 'a slight spitting of blood that I feared was a symptom of lung sickness…he immediately ordered me off to plank bed and bread and water for imposition…' It was only when his cough and blood spitting did not improve that the doctor was 'compelled to put me on the sick list and send me to hospital'.[27]

One of the more extreme cases of neglect and cruelty on the part of a prison surgeon was found at Birmingham in 1854. Along with the governor, the prison surgeon, Mr Blount, was singled out as being extremely negligent in his duties, particularly regarding the physical examination of prisoners. The Commissioners reported that:

> Until a recent period, he had not kept any records of the health of the prisoners, on their admission into the prison, and on their discharge from it; and his examination of prisoners on their admission, one object of which ought certainly to have been the ascertaining whether they were in a fit state to undergo the ordinary discipline, and to perform the ordinary labour, seems to have been made in a most careless and superficial manner… from the admission of Mr Blount himself…his inspections of prisoners, when performed, were of such a character as to be generally quite useless as means of detecting illness, and that although instances of great suffering and injury to health from excessive labour and want of food, must constantly have come under his notice, he rarely interfered to relieve the prisoners from the operations of a discipline and modes of punishment which few could have been capable of supporting….[28]

Mr Blount's negligence extended to the treatment of prisoners who were genuinely sick or complaining of illness. It was reported that: 'It is very doubtful whether such as daily complained of illness, and desired medical aid, were regularly visited by Mr Blount. It is certain that he frequently refused them means of relief when he did visit them…'[29]

Although there was an infirmary for the sick in part of the prison, the Commissioners were particularly horrified that 'on three occasions prisoners have died in their cells with no fellow creatures present; being found dead by the warder entering some time afterwards'. This was a direct contravention of prison regulations.[30]

Both the governor and the surgeon were forced to resign. However, although they were both criminally proceeded against, and found guilty, Mr Blount 'was never even called up to receive sentence, and was allowed to go unpunished'.[31]

SCHOOLMASTERS AND SCHOOLMISTRESSES

Schoolteachers in prisons were members of the warder grade who worked under the direction of the chaplain. By no means all prisons had a schoolmaster or schoolmistress to educate the prisoners. When the remaining 113 local prisons came under government control on April 1878, 'there were 53 male schoolmasters, 3 clerk/schoolmasters, 8 warder/schoolmasters, 25 female schoolmasters and 8 warder/schoolmistresses'.[1]

DUTIES

For six hours a day, schoolmaster warders devoted themselves to teaching, letter-writing and distributing books. In the 1890s, according to the the Revd W.N. Truss of Knutsford Prison, the duties of his schoolmaster warder were long and arduous:

> He comes on duty at 8 o'clock and from 8 to 8.25 he prepares a list of admissions and discharges…Then he rings the bell for chapel, and he attends, of course, daily service; and at 9.15 he examines all receptions as to their education, and distributes educational and other books, and examines all books from prisoners on discharge; at 10.15 he attends to all applications for letters and petitions, and serves out the different forms to prisoners in their cells; and I should say he often has to write petitions for prisoners who could not write themselves…From 12 to 1.15 he has dinner. Then from 1.30 to 2 writes any letters for prisoners who cannot write, and from 2 to 2.30 withdraws all convicted prisoners' letters, and reads them before they are posted. From 3 to 3.30 gives school instruction where required; 3.30 to 5 distributes library and other books daily to each prisoner having his book renewed every seven days. On Sunday he is on duty from 9 to 12…and from 1.30 to 4.15.[2]

In 1896, the schoolmaster warder 'had time to give them only seven minutes' instruction each per week' for the twenty-five out of 370 who were eligible for instruction.[3]

The schoolmaster had to keep a record of the numbers of prisoners he taught and comment on their standard of literacy. In April 1866, the schoolmaster of the New Bailey Prison in Salford was Thomas Blizard. His regular report to the Visiting Justices indicates the number of male prisoners he was required to educate. At the time of his report, he taught twenty-seven prisoners under seventeen years of age, mostly taught in separate confinement. He also taught seventy-seven adult prisoners who mostly attended the classes for instruction in the schoolroom for one hour per day.[4]

He commented on the state of instruction of five juvenile prisoners awaiting trial:

> Alfred Hannan is able to read the New Testament with difficulty & to repeat the Lord's Prayer & Creed. Parslow, Roughin & Hooley read easy words & repeat the Lord's Prayer – and Ludlow, knows only the alphabet in other respects they all appear quite destitute of useful school instruction – Excepting Hooley all have been previously committed here or elsewhere.[5]

The boys' schoolroom at Tothill Fields. (From Mayhew & Binny)

Schoolmasters and schoolmistresses worked warders' hours and, when not undertaking their instructor role, were available for general duties. They were supposedly not available for night-duty which 'displeased some of their colleagues'.[6] Other duties might include attendance at court with prisoners. In 1854, at the Gloucester County Gaol and Penitentiary, the schoolmistress was expected to attend the Assize courts and Quarter Sessions with female prisoners for trial. During this time, it was reported that 'her duties as Schoolmistress [are]…during such times dispensed with'. To compensate, she was to receive an increase of salary from £30 to £32 per annum.[7]

Some schoolmasters made the prison service their lifelong career. William Davis was a long-serving schoolmaster at the Gloucester Gaol and Penitentiary. He resigned after thirty-two years 'in consequence of illness and inability from Bronchitis and Debility to continue [his] duties'. He was rewarded with a superannuation allowance of £33 per annum.[8]

INFLUENCE OF THE CHAPLAIN

The chaplain had a huge influence over the schoolmaster. It was the chaplain who directed him in his duties and who, in many cases before 1877, appointed him. As a result, the good opinion of the chaplain was an asset to the schoolmaster as he could influence pay increases or promotion.

When the schoolmaster at Worcester resigned in March 1860, the chaplain was asked to find a replacement. He recorded in his journal: 'By the desire of the Magistrates I have been in correspondence with two Candidates for the Situation of Schoolmaster. I have informed them that the salary will be £50 per annum…The Duties to be the same as were performed by the late Schoolmaster, under my direction'.[9]

By the end of the year, the chaplain was satisfied with his new recruit, writing in December 1860 that:

During the Quarter of the year the Schoolmaster has been employed under my direction, in giving instruction to the Male Prisoners, in reading, and writing on Slates; in occasionally reading from the Bible to the Sick – and in exchanging tracts and books in the Cells. He has also acted as Chapel Clerk and has assisted me in keeping the character & other books. The conduct of the Prisoners has been orderly under instruction.[10]

The chaplain at Worcester had to look for another schoolmaster in April 1864 when 'The Schoolmaster Mr Woodward informed me that he had been offered a situation in an office, worth £60 a year'.[11] Evidently, a clerk's position in an office offered better working conditions and a higher salary.

In the 1840s, the Revd Clay, the chaplain at the House of Correction in Preston, was very pleased with his schoolmaster. He reported that his:

attention to his duties, and the interest which he takes in the moral and spiritual welfare of the prisoners are all that I could desire. He devotes himself principally to prisoners under separation; and where there is anything like ordinary capacity; the progress which they make in reading and writing is highly satisfactory. In short no prisoner is permitted to remain in the jail without due pains being taken to cultivate whatever mental power or religious sentiment he may possess.[12]

CHANGES AFTER 1877

After 1877, every prison was to have a school staff 'at an additional expense of £2,230'. Schoolmasters had been recruited from the ranks of convict warders since 1870. This was extended to local prisons from 1879. The governor and chaplain recommended local prison warders as schoolmasters who were 'tested by an Inspector of the Education Department'.[13] At this time, the prison schoolmasters 'were on "the same footing" as elementary teachers'.[14]

There was some hostility between the warders and the schoolmasters, largely because, 'the feeling, expressed by discipline staff and Inspectors [was] that they had an easy job'. This was compounded by the fact the schoolmasters were exempt from night duty. They were, however, required to undertake sleeping-in duty from 1883. At the end of the nineteenth century, there was still a disparity between the local schoolmasters and convict schoolmasters in terms of pay, hours, leave and promotion.[15] In addition, '…the schoolmasters in the local prisons who had been appointed by the local authorities before 1877, and were still employed as schoolmasters' continued to be better paid than those recruited after this date.[1]

NOTES

INTRODUCTION

1. Hawkings, David T., *Criminal Ancestors: A Guide to Historical Criminal Records in England and Wales* (Sutton Publishing, 1992), pp223-224
2. QJC 2 (Lancashire Record Office)
3. Dickens, Charles, 'The Great Penal Experiments', *Household Words*, 8 June 1850
4. Dickens, Charles, 'Pet Prisoners', *Household Words*, 27 April 1850

CHAPTER 1 – THE COURT SYSTEM AND SENTENCING

1. Thomas, J.E., *The English Prison Officer Since 1850 – A Study in Conflict* (Routledge & Kegan Paul, 1972), pp17-18
2. McConville, Sean, 'The Victorian Prison – England, 1865-1965' in Morris, Norval and Rothman, David J. (eds), *The Oxford History of the Prison: The Practice of Punishment in Western Society* (Oxford University Press, 1998), p117
3. *ibid.*, p120
4. Quoted in *ibid.*
5. *ibid.*, p123
6. May, Trevor, *Victorian and Edwardian Prisons* (Shire Publications, 2006), p23
7. McConville, op. cit., p135
8. Thomas, J.E., op. cit., pp127-128

CHAPTER 2 – TYPES OF PRISON

1. May, Trevor, *Victorian and Edwardian Prisons* (Shire Publications, 2006), p18
2. *ibid.*, p11
3. *ibid.*, p7
4. McConville, Sean, 'The Victorian Prison – England, 1865-1965' in Morris, Norval and Rothman, David J. (eds), *The Oxford History of the Prison: The Practice of Punishment in Western Society* (Oxford University Press, 1998), p120
5. Thomas, *The English Prison Officer Since 1850 – A Study in Conflict* (Routledge & Kegan Paul, 1972), p11
6. McConville, op. cit., p122
7. One Who Has Endured It, *Five Years' Penal Servitude* (Richard Bentley & Son, 1877), p150
8. Zedner, Lucia, 'Wayward Sisters – The Prison for Women' in Morris, Norval and Rothman, David J. (eds), *The Oxford History of the Prison: The Practice of Punishment in Western Society* (Oxford University Press, 1998), p306
9. *ibid.*, p307
10. McConville, op. cit., p119
11. Thomas, op. cit., p13
12. *ibid.*, p14
13. *ibid.*
14. *ibid.*, p16
15. McConville, op. cit., p124
16. Report of Visitors in Worcester Prison 1867 - 1873, 496.5, BA 9360 A8 Box 9 (Worcestershire Record Office)
17. McConville, op. cit., p17
18. Thomas, op. cit., p19
19. *ibid.*
20. *ibid.*, p54
21. *ibid.*, pp232-234
22. *ibid.*, p54
23. *ibid.*, pp130-131
24. *ibid.*, pp127-128

CHAPTER 3 – THE SILENT AND SEPARATE SYSTEMS

1. Priestley, Philip, *Victorian Prison Lives – English Prison Biography 1830-1914* (Pimlico, 1999), p35
2. ibid., p36
3. QGR 2/33 Chaplain's Report, Preston (Lancashire Record Office)
4. Thomas, *The English Prison Officer Since 1850 – A Study in Conflict* (Routledge & Kegan Paul, 1972), p17
5. Priestley, op. cit., p36
6. May, Trevor, *Victorian and Edwardian Prisons* (Shire Publications, 2006), p14
7. Thomas, op. cit., p17
8. May, op. cit., p16
9. Mayhew, Henry and Binny, John, *The Criminal Prisons of London and Scenes of Prison Life* (1862), p115
10. ibid., pp142-143
11. ibid., p142
12. QGR 2/33 Chaplain's Report, Preston (Lancashire Record Office)
13. QGR 2/31 Chaplain's Report, Preston (Lancashire Record Office)
14. QGR 3/45, Chaplain's Report, Kirkdale House of Correction (Lancashire Record Office)
15. Thomas, op. cit., p23
16. ibid., p31
17. McConville, Sean, *English Local Prisons 1860-1900: Next Only to Death* (Routledge, 1995), pp237-238
18. QGR 2/42 Chaplain's Report, Preston (Lancashire Record Office)

CHAPTER 4 – ARRIVAL IN PRISON

1. QGV 3/9 Rules and Regulations for Kirkdale House of Correction, 1866 (Lancashire Record Office)
2. One Who Has Endured It, *Five Years' Penal Servitude* (Richard Bentley & Son, 1877), p6
3. QGV 3/9 Rules and Regulations for Kirkdale House of Correction, 1866 (Lancashire Record Office)
4. One Who Has Endured It, op. cit., pp38-39
5. QGV 3/9 Rules and Regulations for Kirkdale House of Correction, 1866 (Lancashire Record Office)
6. One Who Has Endured it, op. cit., pp3-4
7. QGV 3/9 Rules and Regulations for Kirkdale House of Correction, 1866 (Lancashire Record Office)
8. ibid.
9. One Who Has Endured it, op. cit., p48
10. Priestley, Philip, *Victorian Prison Lives – English Prison Biography 1830-1914* (Pimlico, 1999), p22
11. QGV 3/9 Rules and Regulations for Kirkdale House of Correction, 1866 (Lancashire Record Office)
12. One Who Has Endured it, op. cit., pp40-41
13. ibid., p68
14. Priestley, op. cit., p20
15. Brunton, Alan, *Bodmin Gaol Cornwall* (Orchard Publications, 1992), p19
16. ibid.
17. Priestley, op. cit., p21
18. One Who Has Endured it, op. cit., p71
19. Priestley, op. cit., p23
20. QGV 3/9 Rules and Regulations for Kirkdale House of Correction, 1866 (Lancashire Record Office)
21. Information provided by Caroline Haycock
22. QGV 3/9 Rules and Regulations for Kirkdale House of Correction, 1866 (Lancashire Record Office)

CHAPTER 5 – DAILY ROUTINE

1. Priestley, Philip, *Victorian Prison Lives – English Prison Biography 1830-1914* (Pimlico, 1999), p82
2. One Who Has Endured It, *Five Years' Penal Servitude* (Richard Bentley & Son, 1877), pp86-87
3. ibid., p82
4. ibid., p172
5. Priestley, op. cit., p84
6. QGV 3/9 Rules and Regulations for Kirkdale House of Correction, 1866 (Lancashire Record Office)
7 One Who Has Endured It, op. cit., p110
8. Quoted in Jones, Steve, *Capital Punishments: Crime and Prison Conditions in Victorian Times* (Wicked Publications, 1998), p69
9. One Who Has Endured It, op. cit., p81
10. ibid., p72
11. ibid., p109
12. DeLacy, Margaret, *Prison Reform in Lancashire, 1700-1850: A Study in Local Administration* (Manchester University Press, 1986), p197
13. One Who Has Endured It, op. cit., p170
14. ibid., pp218-219
15. ibid., p279
16. ibid., p282

17. QGV 3/9 Rules and Regulations for Kirkdale House of Correction, 1866 (Lancashire Record Office)
18. One Who Has Endured It, op. cit., p36
19. Priestley, op. cit., p198
20. QGV 3/9 Rules and Regulations for Kirkdale House of Correction, 1866 (Lancashire Record Office)
21. Priestley, op. cit., p198
22. One Who Has Endured It, op. cit., p84
23. Priestley, op. cit., p198
24. QGV 3/9 Rules and Regulations for Kirkdale House of Correction, 1866 (Lancashire Record Office)
25. One Who Has Endured It, op. cit., p98

CHAPTER 6 – LIVING CONDITIONS

1. Priestley, Philip, *Victorian Prison Lives – English Prison Biography 1830-1914* (Pimlico, 1999), p27
2. *ibid.*, p29
3. *ibid.*, p27
4. *ibid.*, p29
5. One Who Has Endured It, *Five Years' Penal Servitude* (Richard Bentley & Son, 1877), p78
6. *ibid.*, p80
7. McConville, Sean, 'The Victorian Prison – England, 1865-1965' in Morris, Norval and Rothman, David J. (eds), *The Oxford History of the Prison: The Practice of Punishment in Western Society* (Oxford University Press, 1998), p134
8. Webb, Sidney and Beatrice, *English Local Prisons Under Local Government* (Frank Cass & Co. Ltd, 1963), p212
9. One Who Has Endured It, op. cit., p99
10. Priestley, op. cit., p30
11. QGV 3/9 Rules and Regulations for Kirkdale House of Correction, 1866 (Lancashire Record Office)
12. One Who Has Endured It, op. cit., p79
13. McConville, op. cit., p134
14. *Ibid.*
15. QGV 3/9 Rules and Regulations for Kirkdale House of Correction, 1866 (Lancashire Record Office)
16. Quoted in McConville, Sean, *English Local Prisons 1860-1900: Next Only to Death* (Routledge, 1995), p286
17. *ibid.*
18. One Who Has Endured It, op. cit., p169
19. Extracts from 'Pentonville Prison From Within' quoted in Jones, Steve, *Capital Punishments: Crime and Prison Conditions in Victorian Times* (Wicked Publications, 1998), p68
20. Priestley, op. cit., p45
21. One Who Has Endured It, op. cit., p168
22. *ibid.*, p166
23. Extracts from 'Pentonville Prison From Within' quoted in Jones, Steve, op. cit., p82
24. DeLacy, Margaret, *Prison Reform in Lancashire, 1700-1850: A Study in Local Administration* (Manchester University Press, 1986), p176
25. *ibid.*
26. McConville, op. cit., p283
27. *ibid.*, pp283-284
28. *ibid.*, p284
29. Extracts from 'Pentonville Prison From Within' quoted in Jones, Steve, op. cit., p68
30. *ibid.*
31. McConville, op. cit., p283
32. *ibid.*, p287
33. *ibid.*, p286
34. *ibid.*, pp285-286
35. *ibid.*, p289
36. *ibid.*, p297
37. *ibid.*

CHAPTER 7 – DIETARY AND HEALTH

1. Thomas, J.E., *The English Prison Officer Since 1850 – A Study in Conflict* (Routledge & Kegan Paul, 1972), p59
2. McConville, Sean, *English Local Prisons 1860-1900: Next Only to Death* (Routledge, 1995), p310
3. Priestley, Philip, *Victorian Prison Lives - English Prison Biography 1830-1914* (Pimlico, 1999), p151
4. McConville, op. cit., p310
5. Priestley, op. cit., p151
6. McConville, op. cit., p312
7. *ibid.*, pp313-314
8. One Who Has Endured It, *Five Years' Penal Servitude* (Richard Bentley & Son, 1877), pp82-83
9. Mayhew, Henry and Binny, John, *The Criminal Prisons of London and Scenes of Prison Life* (1862), p130
10. Priestley, op. cit., p152
11. *ibid.*, p153

12. McConville, op. cit., p313
13. One Who Has Endured It, op. cit., p106
14. McConville, Sean, 'The Victorian Prison – England, 1865-1965' in Morris, Norval and Rothman, David J. (eds), *The Oxford History of the Prison: The Practice of Punishment in Western Society* (Oxford University Press, 1998), p133
15. *ibid.*
16. McConville, Sean, *English Local Prisons 1860-1900: Next Only to Death* (Routledge, 1995), p319
17. *ibid.*
18. Extracts from 'Pentonville Prison From Within' quoted in Jones, Steve, *Capital Punishments: Crime and Prison Conditions in Victorian Times* (Wicked Publications, 1998), pp66-67
19. *ibid.*, p67
20. *ibid.*
21. McConville, Sean, 'The Victorian Prison - England, 1865-1965' in Morris, Norval and Rothman, David J. (eds), *The Oxford History of the Prison: The Practice of Punishment in Western Society* (Oxford University Press, 1998), p134
22. *ibid.*
23. *ibid.*
24. *ibid.*, p133
25. Jones, op. cit., p69
26. DeLacy, Margaret, *Prison Reform in Lancashire, 1700-1850: A Study in Local Administration* (Manchester University Press, 1986), p178
27. *ibid.*
28. *ibid.*, p179
29. *ibid.*
30. Report by Dr Edward Smith on the Food of the Poorer Labouring Classes in England quoted in McConville, Sean, *English Local Prisons 1860-1900: Next Only to Death* (Routledge, 1995), p317
31. *Sheffield & Rotherham Independent*, 28 February 1878, with thanks to Lyn Howsam
32. *Justice of the Peace*, 'Casual Paupers', 31 March 1866
33. Dickens, Charles, 'Pet Prisoners', *Household Words*, 27 April 1850
34. *Justice of the Peace*, op. cit.
35. McConville, Sean, 'The Victorian Prison – England, 1865-1965' in Morris, Norval and Rothman, David J. (eds), *The Oxford History of the Prison: The Practice of Punishment in Western Society* (Oxford University Press, 1998), p136
36. Q/GC 20/1 Easter Sessions 1845 (Gloucestershire Archives)
37. Q/GC 20/1 Easter Sessions 1845 (Gloucestershire Archives)
38. Q/GC 20/1 Easter Sessions 1846 (Gloucestershire Archives)
39. Report of Visitors in Worcester Prison, 1867-1873, 496.5, BA 9360, A8 Box 9 (Worcestershire Record Office)

CHAPTER 8 – DISCIPLINE

1. McGowen, Randall, 'The Well-Ordered Prison – England 1780-1865' in Morris, Norval and Rothman, David J. (eds), *The Oxford History of the Prison: The Practice of Punishment in Western Society* (Oxford University Press, 1998), p95
2. McConville, Sean, *English Local Prisons 1860-1900: Next Only to Death* (Routledge, 1995), p238
3. Priestley, Philip, *Victorian Prison Lives – English Prison Biography 1830-1914* (Pimlico, 1999), p194
4. One Who Has Endured It, *Five Years' Penal Servitude* (Richard Bentley & Son, 1877), pp84-85
5. *ibid.*
6. *ibid.*, p86
7. *ibid.*
8. *ibid.*, p64
9. McConville, op. cit., p238
10. *ibid.*, p239
11. *ibid.*, pp239-240
12. *ibid.*
13. *ibid.*
14. *ibid.*
15. *ibid.*, p240
16. *ibid.*, p244
17. *ibid.*, p245
18. Priestley, op. cit., p206
19. QGV 3/9 Rules and Regulations for Kirkdale House of Correction, 1866 (Lancashire Record Office)
20. McConville, op. cit., p248
21. *ibid.*, p248
22. Worcester Governor's Journal (Worcestershire Record Office)
23. *ibid.*
24. *ibid.*
25. Davies, Paul P., *History of Medicine in Great Yarmouth Hospitals and Doctors*, (2003), p472
26. Worcester Governor's Journal (Worcestershire Record Office)

CHAPTER 9 – WORK

1. McConville, Sean, *English Local Prisons 1860-1900: Next Only to Death* (Routledge, 1995), p252
2. QGV 3/9 Rules and Regulations (Lancashire Record Office)
3. McGowen, Randall, 'The Well-Ordered Prison – England 1780-1865' in Morris, Norval and Rothman, David J. (eds), *The Oxford History of the Prison: The Practice of Punishment in Western Society* (Oxford University Press, 1998), p94
4. McConville, op. cit., p249
5. *ibid.*
6. QGV 3/9 Rules and Regulations (Lancashire Record Office)
7. QGV 3/9 Rules and Regulations (Lancashire Record Office)
8. QGV 3/9 Rules & Regulations Kirkdale 1866 (Lancashire Record Office)
9. House of Commons Parliamentary Papers 1852-1853 Vol. L II Northern and Eastern Yorkshire
10. House of Commons Parliamentary Papers 1852-1853 Vol. L II Northern and Eastern Yorkshire
11. House of Commons Parliamentary Papers 1852-1853 Vol. L II Southern and Western District
12. House of Commons Parliamentary Papers 1852-1853 Vol. L II Southern and Western District
13. McConville, Sean, 'The Victorian Prison – England, 1865-1965' in Morris, Norval and Rothman, David J. (eds), *The Oxford History of the Prison: The Practice of Punishment in Western Society* (Oxford University Press, 1998), p132
14. *ibid.*
15. Priestley, Philip, *Victorian Prison Lives - English Prison Biography 1830-1914* (Pimlico, 1999), p127
16. *ibid.*
17. *ibid.*
18. QGC 20/1 (Gloucestershire Archives)
19. Report of Visitors in Worcester Prison 1867 - 1873, 496.5, BA 9360 A8 Box 9 (Worcestershire Record Office)
20. *ibid.*
21. Webb, Sidney and Beatrice, *English Local Prisons Under Local Government* (Frank Cass & Co. Ltd, 1963), p149
22. Priestley, op. cit., p128
23. Report of Visitors in Worcester Prison 1867 - 1873, 496.5, BA 9360 A8 Box 9 (Worcestershire Record Office)
24. *ibid.*
25. McConville, Sean, *English Local Prisons 1860-1900: Next Only to Death* (Routledge, 1995), p250
26. *ibid.*, p251
27. Priestley, op. cit., p129
28. *ibid.*
29. *ibid.*, p130
30. House of Commons Parliamentary Papers 1852-1853 Vol. L II Northern and Eastern Yorkshire
31. QGR 3/45 Chaplain's Report (Lancashire Record Office)
32. Webb, op. cit., p170
33. Priestley, op. cit., pp131-132
34. *ibid.*, p124
35. *ibid.*
36. Webb, op. cit., p197
37. *ibid.*, p207
38. One Who Has Endured It, *Five Years' Penal Servitude* (Richard Bentley & Son, 1877), pp44-45
39. *ibid.*, pp46-47
40. *ibid.*
41. QGC 20/1 (Gloucestershire Archives)
42. McConville, op. cit., p251
43. Webb, op. cit., pp196-197
44. One Who Has Endured It, op. cit., p93
45. *ibid.*, p189
46. *ibid.*, pp176-177
47. Priestley, op. cit., p132
48. One Who Has Endured It, op. cit., p152
49. *ibid.*, p176

CHAPTER 10 – RELIGION

1. Jones, Steve, *Capital Punishments: Crime and Prison Conditions in Victorian Times* (Wicked Publications, 1998), p95
2. QGR 2/42 Chaplain's Report, Preston 1847 (Lancashire Record Office)
3. One Who Has Endured It, *Five Years' Penal Servitude* (Richard Bentley & Son, 1877), p87
4. Priestley, Philip, *Victorian Prison Lives – English Prison Biography 1830-1914* (Pimlico, 1999), p92
5. *ibid.*
6. *ibid.*
7. McConville, Sean, *English Local Prisons 1860-1900: Next Only to Death* (Routledge, 1995), p278
8. Priestley, op. cit., p94
9. Mayhew, Henry and Binny, John, *The Criminal Prisons of London and Scenes of Prison Life* (1862), p163

150   *Prison Life in Victorian England*

10. QGR 2/42 (Lancashire Record Office)
11. *ibid.*
12. McConville, op. cit., p281
13. *ibid.*, p279
14. *ibid.*
15. *ibid.*, p277
16. *ibid.*
17. *ibid.*, p278
18. *ibid.*

CHAPTER 11 – EDUCATION

1. Priestley, Philip, *Victorian Prison Lives – English Prison Biography 1830-1914* (Pimlico, 1999), p109
2. One Who Has Endured It, *Five Years' Penal Servitude* (Richard Bentley & Son, 1877), p97
3. QGR 2/42 (Lancashire Record Office)
4. QSP 3638/6 Preston Chaplain's Report 1861 (Lancashire Record Office)
5. 28 & 29 Vict., c. 126, Sch. 1, clause 53 quoted in McConville, Sean, *English Local Prisons 1860-1900: Next Only to Death* (Routledge, 1995), p265
6. *ibid.*
7. House of Commons Parliamentary Papers 1852-1853 Vol. L II Northern and Eastern Yorkshire
8. McConville, op. cit., p267
9. *ibid.*, p269
10. *ibid.*, p270
11. One Who Has Endured It, op. cit., p205
12. *ibid.*, pp206-207
13. McConville, p271
14. *ibid.*
15. *ibid.*, pp273-274
16. QGV 3/9 Rules & Regulations Kirkdale 1866 (Lancashire Record Office)
17. Chaplain's Journal 122 - BA 249/6a (Worcestershire Record Office)
18. QGR 2/42 Preston Chaplain's Report (Lancashire Record Office)
19. QGR 3/45 Chaplain's Report, Kirkdale House of Correction (Lancashire Record Office)
20. Priestley, op. cit., p113
21. One Who Has Endured It, op. cit., p109

CHAPTER 12 - RELEASE

1. Priestley, Philip, *Victorian Prison Lives – English Prison Biography 1830-1914* (Pimlico, 1999), p284
2. JAPR 5/1 (Lancashire Record Office)
3. McConville, Sean, *English Local Prisons 1860-1900: Next Only to Death* (Routledge, 1995), p320
4. *The Times*, 21 January 1878 quoted in *ibid.*
5. Priestley, *ibid.*, p278
6. QGV 3/9 Rules & Regulations Kirkdale 1866 (Lancashire Record Office)
7. Priestley, *ibid.*, p278
8. One Who Has Endured It, *Five Years' Penal Servitude* (Richard Bentley & Son, 1877), pp352-353
9. *ibid.*, pp356-357
10. *ibid.*, pp358-359
11. QGV 3/9 Rules & Regulations Kirkdale 1866 (Lancashire Record Office)
12. McConville, op. cit., p320
13. *ibid.*, p323
14. *ibid.*, p324
15. Webb, Sidney and Beatrice, *English Local Prisons Under Local Government* (Frank Cass & Co. Ltd, 1963), p185
16. Report of Visitors in Worcester Prison 1867 - 1873, 496.5, BA 9360 A8 Box 9 (Worcestershire Record Office)
17. *ibid.*
18. McConville, op. cit., pp320-321
19. Appendix to QGR 2/42 Preston Chaplain's Report 1847 (Lancashire Record Office)
20. *ibid.*
21. QGR 2/42 Preston Chaplain's Report 1847 (Lancashire Record Office)
22. One Who Has Endured It, op. cit., p362

CHAPTER 13 – THIEVES AND PICKPOCKETS

1. JAPR 1/7 (Lancashire Record Office)
2. QJC 19 (Lancashire Record Office)
3. QJC 21 (Lancashire Record Office)
4. Hawkings, David T., *Criminal Ancestors: A Guide to Historical Criminal Records in England and Wales* (Sutton

Publishing, 1992), pp223-224

5. Mayhew, Henry and Binny, John, *The Criminal Prisons of London and Scenes of Prison Life* (1862), pp89-90

6. *The Bedford Times*, 10 January 1865, information provided by Sharon Floate

7. *Jack's Reference Book for Home and Office*, T.C. & E.C. Jack Ltd, 1923, p494

8. QJC 13 (Lancashire Record Office)

9. *The Times*, 17 November 1852 and Calendar of Prisoners, Clerkenwell December 1852, information provided by Carolyn Alty

10. *The Times*, 17 November 1852, information provided by Carolyn Alty

11. Marlborough Examinations 2 March 1861, information provided by Carolyn Alty

12. *Bradford Observer*, 31 May 1866, information provided by Carolyn Alty

13. QGC 13/1 (Gloucestershire Archives)

14. Cambridge County Gaol Nominal Registers 1885-1887, 1888-1890, information provided by Sharon Floate

15. One Who Has Endured It, *Five Years' Penal Servitude* (Richard Bentley & Son, 1877), pp299-300

16. QJC 25 (Lancashire Record Office)

CHAPTER 14 – MURDERERS AND VIOLENT OFFENDERS

1. The National Archives <http://www.learningcurve.gov.uk/victorianbritain/lawless>

2. JAPR 5/24 (Lancashire Record Office)

3. *The Times*, 9 March 1889

4. Godwin, John, *The Pocket Palmer – The Story of Rugeley's Infamous Character* (The Benhill Press Ltd, 1992), p29

5. *The Times*, 16 June 1856

6. *The Times*, 3 January 1863

7. *ibid.*

8. Chaplain's Journal - 122 BA 249/6a (Worcestershire Record Office)

9. *The Times*, 3 January 1863

10. CRIM 4/774 Indictments Central Criminal Court – 4 April 1870 (The National Archives)

11. *The Times*, 7 April 1870

12. Information provided by Christopher J. Hogger

13. PRO/CRIM/1/12/7, information provided by David Fry

14. *ibid.*

15. *ibid.*

16. *ibid.*

17. PRO/CRIM/4/940, information provided by David Fry

18. Information provided by David Fry

19. *The North London Guardian*, 17 May 1901, information provided by Rita Richardson

20. *ibid.*

21. *ibid.*

22. *The North London Guardian*, 30 April 1901, information provided by Rita Richardson

23. *The North London Guardian*, 17 May 1901, information provided by Rita Richardson

24. *The North London Guardian*, 30 April 1901, information provided by Rita Richardson

25. *The North London Guardian*, 17 May 1901, information provided by Rita Richardson

26. Information provided by Rita Richardson

27. JAPR 5/24 (Lancashire Record Office)

28. QJC 14 Q.S. Castle of Lancaster (Lancashire Record Office)

29. *The Times*, 25 May 1895

30. JAPR 5/1 (Lancashire Record Office)

31. JAPR 1 /2 (Lancashire Record Office)

32. Hawkings, David T., *Criminal Ancestors: A Guide to Historical Criminal Records in England and Wales* (Sutton Publishing, 1992), p263

33. *The Times*, 11 and 18 December 1895

CHAPTER 15 – FRAUDSTERS AND EMBEZZLERS

1. *The Times*, 24 November 1900, information provided by Peter Smith

2. *The Times*, 7 November 1900, information provided by Peter Smith

3. *The Times*, 7 November 1900, information provided by Peter Smith

4. Information provided by Peter Smith

5. Information provided and transcribed by Anthony Baker

6. Longmate, Norman, *The Workhouse*, (2003), p99

7. G/DU 1/3, 11 February 1853 (Dudley Archives)

8. G/DU 3/1/22, 6 July 1863 (Dudley Archives)

9. DP 376/6 (Lancashire Record Office)

10. *ibid.*

11. *ibid.*

12. *ibid.*

13. *ibid.*
14. JAPR 1/7 (Lancashire Record Office)
15. DP 376/6 (Lancashire Record Office)
16. One Who Has Endured It, *Five Years' Penal Servitude* (Richard Bentley & Son, 1877), p3
17. *The Times*, 10 July 1868
18. *The Times*, 9 July 1868
19. One Who Has Endured It, op. cit., pp42-43
20. *ibid.*, p60
21. *ibid.*, p129
22. *ibid.*, pp204-205
23. *The Times*, 5 April 1858
24. Hawkings, David T., *Criminal Ancestors: A Guide to Historical Criminal Records in England and Wales* (Sutton Publishing, 1992), pp239-240
25. *The Times*, 5 April 1858
26. Hawkings, op. cit., pp239-240

CHAPTER 16 – TRANSPORTED CONVICTS AND EXILES

1. Bateson, Charles, *The Convict Ships 1787-1868* (Brown, Son & Ferguson Ltd, 1985), p59
2. *ibid.*, pp61-62
3. *ibid.*, p65
4. *ibid.*, p73
5. *ibid.*, p82
6. 1845 Gaol Calendar, information provided by Jim Halsey
7. Information provided by Jim Halsey
8. Jim Halsey freewebs
9. Information provided by Jim Halsey
10. Hawkings, David T., *Criminal Ancestors: A Guide to Historical Criminal Records in England and Wales* (Sutton Publishing, 1992), p19
11. Information provided by Brian Randle
12. Hawkings, op. cit., p19
13. Information provided by Brian Randle
14. Information provided by John Brake
15. Chandler, Jennifer and Daniels, Barbara, *The Transports are Here – Convicts and the Colony A - Z*
16. Information provided by John Brake
17. McConville, Sean, 'The Victorian Prison – England, 1865-1965' in Morris, Norval and Rothman, David J. (eds), *The Oxford History of the Prison: The Practice of Punishment in Western Society* (Oxford University Press, 1998), p121
18. *The Sheffield & Rotherham Independent*, 6 April 1865, information provided by Lyn Howsam
19. *The Sheffield & Rotherham Independent*, 1 April 1865, information provided by Lyn Howsam
20. *The Sheffield & Rotherham Independent*, 6 April 1865, information provided by Lyn Howsam
21. *ibid.*
22. *The Sheffield & Rotherham Independent*, 1 April 1865, information provided by Lyn Howsam
23. *ibid.*
24. *The Sheffield & Rotherham Independent*, 6 April 1865, information provided by Lyn Howsam
25. Information provided by Lyn Howsam
26. Bateson, op. cit., p305
27. Information provided by Lyn Howsam

CHAPTER 17 – JUVENILE OFFENDERS

1. Priestley, Philip, *Victorian Prison Lives – English Prison Biography 1830-1914* (Pimlico, 1999), p55
2. *ibid.*, p56
3. McConville, Sean, *English Local Prisons 1860-1900: Next Only to Death* (Routledge, 1995), p360
4. Priestley, op. cit., p56
5. QGR 2/32 Chaplain's Journal 1842, 22 July (Lancashire Record Office)
6. QGR 2/31 Chaplain's Report, Preston House (Lancashire Record Office)
7. Report of Visitors in Worcester Prison 1867-1873, 496.5, BA9360 Box 9 (Worcestershire Record Office)
8. *ibid.*
9. *ibid.*
10. Q/AG 31 1849-1854 Answers from local authorities as to salaries of officials (Gloucestershire Archives)
11. McConville, op. cit., p355
12. Priestley, op. cit., p56
13. Report of Visitors in Worcester Prison 1867-1873, 496.5, BA9360 Box 9 (Worcestershire Record Office)
14. Q/GC 10/1 (Gloucestershire Archives)
15. G/DU 1/8, 30 December 1870 (Dudley Archives)
16. One Who Has Endured It, *Five Years' Penal Servitude* (Richard Bentley & Son, 1877), p31

17. Duckworth, Jeannie, *Fagin's Children: Criminal Children in Victorian England* (Hambledon and London, 2002), p73

18. Q/GC 20/1 (Gloucestershire Archives)

19. Webb, Sidney and Beatrice, *English Local Prisons Under Local Government* (Frank Cass & Co. Ltd, 1963), p171

20. The Revd J. Kingsmill quoted in Priestley, op. cit., p57

21. McConville, *op. cit.*, p359

22. *ibid.*

23. Hawkings, David T., *Criminal Ancestors: A Guide to Historical Criminal Records in England and Wales* (Sutton Publishing, 1992), pp216-218

24. Duckworth, op. cit., p109

25. Hawkings, op. cit., p23

26. Duckworth, op. cit., p176

27. *ibid.*, pp177-178

28. *ibid.*, p174

29. Q/GC 20/1 (Gloucestershire Archives)

30. Prochaska, Frank, 'Carpenter, Mary (1807-1877)' in *Oxford Dictionary of National Biography*

31. QSP 3747/18 Governor's Report 9 April 1866, New Bailey Prison (Lancashire Record Office)

32. Report of Visitors in Worcester Prison 1867-1873, 496.5, BA9360 Box 9 (Worcestershire Record Office)

33. JAPR 1/7 (Lancashire Record Office)

34. Report of Visitors in Worcester Prison 1867-1873, 496.5, BA9360 Box 9 (Worcestershire Record Office)

35. McConville, op. cit., p357

36. *ibid.*, p355

37. *ibid.*, pp357-358

CHAPTER 18 – WOMEN

1. May, Trevor, *Victorian and Edwardian Prisons* (Shire Publications, 2006), p34

2. *Cornhill Magazine* 1866 quoted in *ibid.*

3. Zedner, Lucia, 'Wayward Sisters – The Prison for Women' in Morris, Norval and Rothman, David J. (eds), *The Oxford History of the Prison: The Practice of Punishment in Western Society* (Oxford University Press, 1998), p312

4. *ibid.*, p319

5. *ibid.*, p315

6. McConville, Sean, *English Local Prisons 1860-1900: Next Only to Death* (Routledge, 1995), pp342-343

7. *ibid.*

8. Zedner, op. cit., p305

9. *ibid.*, p297

10. *ibid.*

11. Jones, Steve, *Capital Punishments: Crime and Prison Conditions in Victorian Times* (Wicked Publications, 1998), p91

12. Priestley, Philip, *Victorian Prison Lives – English Prison Biography 1830-1914* (Pimlico, 1999), p72

13. *Huddersfield Examiner*, information provided by Roger Harpin

14. Information provided by Roger Harpin

15. Zedner, op. cit., p319

16. *ibid.*

17. *ibid.*

18. QJC 23 Preston Quarter Sessions (Lancashire Record Office)

19. *ibid.*

20. QJC 12 (Lancashire Record Office)

21. *ibid.*

22. *The Times*, 22 July 1869

23. Report of Visitors in Worcester Prison 1867-1873, 496.5, BA9360 Box 9 (Worcestershire Record Office)

24. Zedner, op. cit., p312

25. *ibid.*

26. *ibid.*, p313

27. *ibid.*, p314

28. McConville, p350

29. *ibid.*

30. *ibid.*

31. *ibid.*, p340

32. *ibid.*

33. *ibid.*, p341

34. QGV 3/9 Rules and Regulations Kirkdale 1866 (Lancashire Record Office)

35. DeLacy, Margaret, *Prison Reform in Lancashire, 1700-1850: A Study in Local Administration* (Manchester University Press, 1986), p194

36. Zedner, op. cit., p307

37. *ibid.*

38. McConville, op. cit., p342

39. Mayhew, Henry and Binny, John, *The Criminal Prisons of London and Scenes of Prison Life* (1862), p191
40. *ibid.*, p471
41. Jones, op. cit., pp92-93
42. HO27/118, information provided by Heather Leonard
43. Information provided by Heather Leonard
44. Hurley, Beryl (ed.), *Fisherton Anger Gaol – Matron's Journal* (Wiltshire Family History Society, 1997), p5 and p18
45. McConville, op. cit., pp338-339
46. *ibid.*, p344
47. *ibid.*, p348
48. Zedner, op. cit., pp314-315

CHAPTER 19 – LUNATICS

1. McConville, Sean, *English Local Prisons 1860-1900: Next Only to Death* (Routledge, 1995), p290
2. *ibid.*
3. QSP 3944/26 (Lancashire Record Office)
4. McConville, op. cit., p300
5. DeLacy, Margaret, *Prison Reform in Lancashire, 1700-1850: A Study in Local Administration* (Manchester University Press, 1986), p198
6. *ibid.*
7. McConville, op. cit., p300
8. *ibid.*, p301
9. Chaplain's Journal - 122 BA 249/6a (Worcestershire Record Office)
10. Extracts from 'Pentonville Prison From Within' quoted in Jones, Steve, *Capital Punishments: Crime and Prison Conditions in Victorian Times* (Wicked Publications, 1998), p84
11. McConville, op. cit., p290
12. *ibid.*
13. *ibid.*, p292
14. *ibid.*, p294
15. Report of Visitors in Worcester Prison 1867-1873, BA9360 A8 Box 9 (Worcestershire Record Office)
16. Roberts, Andrew 1981-/timeline - Mental Health History Timeline <http://www.mdx.ac.uk/www/study/mhhtim.htm> Middlesex University)
17. DP 376/6/P47and DP 376/5/P47 W. Bowdler Cuttings (Lancashire Record Office)
18. Hawkings, David T., *Criminal Ancestors: A Guide to Historical Criminal Records in England and Wales* (Sutton Publishing, 1992), pp192-194
19. Webb, Sidney and Beatrice, *English Local Prisons Under Local Government* (Frank Cass & Co. Ltd, 1963), pp225-226

CHAPTER 20 – DEBTORS

1. QGV 3/9 Rules & Regulations Kirkdale 1866 (Lancashire Record Office)
2. *ibid.*
3. *ibid.*
4. Sketches in London, James Grant, 1838 quoted by Jackson, Lee – The Victorian Dictionary <http://www.victorianlondon.org/prisons/queensbench>
5. *Illustrated London News*, 17 January 1880
6. *ibid.*
7. Sketches in London, James Grant, 1838 quoted by Jackson, Lee – The Victorian Dictionary <http://www.victorianlondon.org/prisons/queensbench>
8. *ibid.*
9. Information provided by Noelene Cummins
10. DeLacy, Margaret, *Prison Reform in Lancashire, 1700-1850: A Study in Local Administration* (Manchester University Press, 1986), p192
11. *ibid.*, p190
12. *ibid.*
13. *ibid.*, pp192-193
14. *ibid.*, pp191-192
15. *ibid.*, p193
16. McConville, Sean, *English Local Prisons 1860-1900: Next Only to Death* (Routledge, 1995), pp362-363
17. *ibid.*, p367
18. *ibid.*, p369
19. *ibid.*

CHAPTER 21 – GOVERNORS

1. Thomas, J.E., *The English Prison Officer Since 1850 – A Study in Conflict* (Routledge & Kegan Paul, 1972), p42
2. Report of Visitors in Worcester Prison 1867-1873, BA9360 A8 Box 9 (Worcestershire Record Office)
3. McConville, Sean, *English Local Prisons 1860-1900: Next Only to Death* (Routledge, 1995), p111

4. *ibid.*
5. Report of Visitors in Worcester Prison 1867-1873, BA9360 A8 Box 9 (Worcestershire Record Office)
6. Thomas, op. cit., p115
7. QGV 3/9 Rules & Regulations Kirkdale 1866 (Lancashire Record Office)
8. *ibid.*
9. *ibid.*
10. QSP 3747/18 Governor's Report 9 April 1866 (Lancashire Record Office)
11. QGV 3/9 Rules & Regulations Kirkdale 1866 (Lancashire Record Office)
12. One Who Has Endured It, *Five Years' Penal Servitude* (Richard Bentley & Son, 1877), p196
13. QGV 3/9 Rules & Regulations Kirkdale 1866 (Lancashire Record Office)
14. Priestley, Philip, *Victorian Prison Lives – English Prison Biography 1830-1914* (Pimlico, 1999), p271
15. *ibid.*
16. One Who Has Endured It, op. cit., pp252-253
17. *ibid.*, pp252-253
18. Q/AG 31 1849-1854 Answers from local authorities as to salaries of officials (Gloucestershire Archives)
19. Q/GC 20/1 (Gloucestershire Archives)
20. McConville, op. cit., pp112-113
21. *ibid.*, p113
22. *ibid.*
23. *ibid.*
24. Q/GC 20/1 (Gloucestershire Archives)
25. *ibid.*
26. Webb, Sidney and Beatrice, *English Local Prisons Under Local Government* (Frank Cass & Co. Ltd, 1963), p171
27. *ibid.*, pp173-174
28. *ibid.*, p175
29. Q/GC 20/1 (Gloucestershire Archives)
30. *ibid.*
31. *ibid.*
32. *ibid.*
33. Priestley, Philip, *Victorian Prison Lives – English Prison Biography 1830-1914* (Pimlico, 1999), p270

CHAPTER 22 – WARDERS

1. Thomas, J.E., *The English Prison Officer Since 1850 – A Study in Conflict* (Routledge & Kegan Paul, 1972), p41
2. Information provided by Wendy Corbett Kelley
3. Q/AG 31 - 1845-1854 Gloucester – Answers from local authorities as to salaries of officials (Gloucestershire Archives)
4. Joy, Ron, *Dartmoor Prison A Complete Illustrated History Volume Two – The Convict Prison 1850-The Present Day* (Halsgrove, 2002), p15
5. *ibid.*
6. One Who Has Endured It, *Five Years' Penal Servitude* (Richard Bentley & Son, 1877), pp314-315
7. Information provided by Patrick Thomas
8. Information provided by Lyn Owers
9. Information provided by great-great-great grandson Dominic Pinto
10. Information provided by Kenneth Scott
11. Q/AG 31 - 1845-1854 Gloucester - Answers from local authorities as to salaries of officials (Gloucestershire Archives)
12. Thomas, op. cit., p46
13. McConville, Sean, *English Local Prisons 1860-1900: Next Only to Death* (Routledge, 1995), p211
14. Thomas, op. cit., p98
15. McConville, op. cit., p211
16. Information provided by Garry Morton
17. One Who Has Endured It, op. cit., pp77-78
18. Mayhew, Henry and Binny, John, *The Criminal Prisons of London and Scenes of Prison Life* (1862), p118
19. Information provided by Garry Morton
20. May, Trevor, *Victorian and Edwardian Prisons* (Shire Publications, 2006), p32
21. McGowen, Randall, 'The Well-Ordered Prison – England 1780-1865' in Morris, Norval and Rothman, David J. (eds), *The Oxford History of the Prison: The Practice of Punishment in Western Society* (Oxford University Press, 1998), p95
22. QGV 3/9 Rules & Regulations Kirkdale 1866 (Lancashire Record Office)
23. One Who Has Endured It, op. cit., p172
24. QGV 3/9 Rules & Regulations Kirkdale 1866 (Lancashire Record Office)
25. One Who Has Endured It, op. cit., pp122-123
26. May, op. cit., p33
27. *ibid.*

28. *The Times*, 11 September 1866
29. Information provided by Brian Wollaston
30. QJC/21/2 (Gloucestershire Archives)
31. Thomas, op. cit., p62
32. Information provided and transcribed by Graham Wells
33. Q/GC 20/1 (Worcestershire Record Office)
34. *ibid.*
35. *ibid.*
36. Worcester Governor's Journal (Worcestershire Record Office)
37. *ibid.*
38. Thomas, op. cit., p61
39. *ibid.*
40. *ibid.*, p35
41. *ibid.*, p95
42. *ibid.*
43. *ibid.*

CHAPTER 23 – FEMALE STAFF

1. Zedner, Lucia, 'Wayward Sisters – The Prison for Women' in Morris, Norval and Rothman, David J. (eds), *The Oxford History of the Prison: The Practice of Punishment in Western Society* (Oxford University Press, 1998), p309
2. Priestley, Philip, *Victorian Prison Lives – English Prison Biography 1830-1914* (Pimlico, 1999), p266
3. McConville, Sean, *English Local Prisons 1860-1900: Next Only to Death* (Routledge, 1995), p338
4. QGV 3/9 Rules & Regulations Kirkdale 1866 (Lancashire Record Office)
5. *ibid.*
6. Zedner, op. cit., p308
7. Priestley, op. cit., p266
8. Zedner, op. cit., p308
9. Information provided by Patrick Thomas
10. Zedner, op. cit., p309
11. Priestley, op. cit., p267
12. Zedner, op. cit., p309
13. May, Trevor, *Victorian and Edwardian Prisons* (Shire Publications, 2006), p33
14. Q/GC 21/2 (Gloucestershire Archives)
15. QSP 3944/28 (Lancashire Record Office)
16. Q/GC 20/1 (Gloucestershire Archives)
17. Zedner, op. cit., p310
18. *ibid.*
19. *ibid.*
20. Q/GC 20/1 (Gloucestershire Archives)
21. *ibid.*

CHAPTER 24 – CHAPLAINS

1. QGV 3/9 Rules & Regulations Kirkdale 1866 (Lancashire Record Office)
2. *ibid.*
3. *ibid.*
4. Q/GC 20/1 (Gloucestershire Archives)
5. *ibid.*
6. Forsythe, Bill, 'Kingsmill, Joseph (1805/6-1865)' in *Oxford Dictionary of National Biography* (Oxford University Press, 2004)
7. *ibid.*
8. QGV 3/9 Rules & Regulations Kirkdale 1866 (Lancashire Record Office)
9. QGR 2/42 Chaplain's Report, Preston (Lancashire Record Office)
10. QGR 3/45, 1843 Report of Chaplain, Kirkdale House of Correction (Lancashire Record Office)
11. QGR 2/42 Chaplain's Report, Preston (Lancashire Record Office)
12. QSZ4/46 Report of Visiting Justices 1877-78 Preston (Lancashire Record Office)
13. One Who Has Endured It, *Five Years' Penal Servitude* (Garland Publishing, 1984), pp20-21
14. *ibid.*, p47
15. Priestley, Philip, *Victorian Prison Lives – English Prison Biography 1830-1914* (Pimlico, 1999), p113
16. *ibid.*
17. *ibid.*, p114
18. One Who Has Endured It, op. cit., p209
19. *ibid.*, pp209-213

CHAPTER 25 – MEDICAL OFFICERS

1. Priestley, Philip, *Victorian Prison Lives - English Prison Biography 1830-1914* (Pimlico, 1999), p186
2. *ibid.*, p187
3. QGV 3/9 Rules & Regulations Kirkdale 1866 (Lancashire Record Office)
4. *ibid.*
5. *ibid.*
6. *ibid.*
7. *ibid.*
8. *ibid.*
9. QSP/3410/85 Preston 13th April 1852 (Lancashire Record Office)
10. QGV 3/9 Rules & Regulations Kirkdale 1866 (Lancashire Record Office)
11. *ibid.*
12. *ibid.*
13. McConville, Sean, *English Local Prisons 1860-1900: Next Only to Death* (Routledge, 1995), pp298-299
14. *ibid.*, p294
15. *ibid.*
16. *ibid.*, p299
17. *ibid.*
18. *ibid.*
19. One Who Has Endured It, *Five Years' Penal Servitude* (Richard Bentley & Son, 1877), pp196-197
20. McConville, op. cit., pp299-300
21. *ibid.*, p300
22. QSP 3572/7 Memorial of Thomas Chalmer, Surgeon of Kirkdale Prison (Lancashire Record Office)
23. Q/GC 20/1 (Gloucestershire Archives)
24. QSP/3747/25 Surgeon's Report 1866 (Lancashire Record Office)
25. QSP 3753/25 Visiting Justices Report
26. Priestley, op. cit., p186
27. *ibid.*
28. Webb, Sidney and Beatrice, *English Local Prisons Under Local Government* (Frank Cass & Co. Ltd, 1963), p173
29. *ibid.*
30. *ibid.*
31. *ibid.*, p175

CHAPTER 26 – SCHOOLMASTERS AND SCHOOLMISTRESSES

1. Thomas, J.E., *The English Prison Officer Since 1850 A Study in Conflict* (Routledge & Kegan Paul, 1972), p73
2. McConville, Sean, *English Local Prisons 1860-1900: Next Only to Death* (Routledge, 1995), pp270-271
3. *ibid.*
4. QSP/3747/26 Schoolmaster's Report Salford County Prison (Lancashire Record Office)
5. *ibid.*
6. McConville, op. cit., p270
7. Q/GC 20/1 (Gloucestershire Archives)
8. *ibid.*
9. Chaplain's Journal - 122 BA 249/6a Worcester (Worcestershire Record Office)
10. *ibid.*
11. *ibid.*
12. QGR 2/33 Chaplain's Report Preston (Lancashire Record Office)
13. Thomas, op. cit., p73
14. *ibid.*
15. *ibid.*, p99
16. *ibid.*, p100

BIBLIOGRAPHY

BOOKS

Bateson, Charles, *The Convict Ships 1787-1868* (Brown, Son & Ferguson Ltd, 1985)

Brunton, Alan, *Bodmin Gaol Cornwall* (Orchard Publications, 1992)

Chandler, Jennifer and Daniels, Barbara, *The Transports are Here – Convicts and the Colony A – Z* (Jennifer Chandler, 1996)

Davies, Paul P., *History of Medicine in Great Yarmouth Hospitals and Doctors* (2003)

DeLacy, Margaret, *Prison Reform in Lancashire, 1700-1850: A Study in Local Administration* (Manchester University Press, 1986)

Duckworth, Jeannie, *Fagin's Children: Criminal Children in Victorian England* (Hambledon and London, 2002)

Emsley, Clive, 'The History of Crime and Crime Control Institutions' in Maguire, Mike, Morgan, Rod and Reiner, Robert (eds), *The Oxford Handbook of Criminology* (Oxford University Press, 2002)

Fitzgerald, Mike, McLennan, Gregor and Pawson, Jennie (eds), *Crime and Society: Readings in History and Theory* (Routledge, 1981)

Forsythe, Bill, 'Kingsmill, Joseph (1805/6-1865)' in *Oxford Dictionary of National Biography* (Oxford University Press, 2004)

Freeman, John (ed.), *Prisons, Past and Future* (Heinemann, 1978)

Godwin, John, *The Pocket Palmer – The Story of Rugeley's Infamous Character* (The Benhill Press Ltd, 1992)

Graham, Anne E. and Emmas, Carol, *The Last Victim: The Extraordinary Life of Florence Maybrick* (Headline, 1999)

Harrison, J.F.C., *Early Victorian Britain, 1832-1851* (Fontana Press, 1989)

Hawkings, David T., *Criminal Ancestors: A Guide to Historical Criminal Records in England and Wales* (Sutton Publishing, 1992)

Hayes, David, *Inveraray Jail: County Prison of Argyll 1820-1889* (Landmark Press)

Hurley, Beryl (ed.), *Fisherton Anger Gaol – Matron's Journal* (Wiltshire Family History Society, 1997)

Jack's Reference Book for Home and Office, (T.C. & E.C. Jack Ltd, 1923)

Jones, Steve, *Birmingham – The Sinister Side* (Wicked Publications, 1998)

Jones, Steve, *Capital Punishments: Crime and Prison Conditions in Victorian Times* (Wicked Publications, 1998)

Jones, Steve, *London – The Sinister Side* (Wicked Publications, 1993)

Joy, Ron, *Dartmoor Prison A Complete Illustrated History Volume Two – The Convict Prison 1850-The Present Day* (Halsgrove, 2002)

Lewis, Geoffrey, *Behind The Walls – A Chelmsford Turnkey of the Nineteenth Century* (Ian Henry Publications, 1996)

Longmate, Norman, *The Workhouse* (Pimlico, 2003)

Maguire, Mike, Morgan, Rod and Reiner, Robert (eds), *The Oxford Handbook of Criminology* (Oxford University Press, 2002)

May, Trevor, *Victorian and Edwardian Prisons* (Shire Publications, 2006)

Mayhew, Henry and Binny, John, *The Criminal Prisons of London and Scenes of Prison Life* (1862)

McConville, Sean, *English Local Prisons 1860-1900: Next Only to Death* (Routledge, 1995)

McConville, Sean, 'The Victorian Prison – England, 1865-1965' in Morris, Norval and Rothman, David J. (eds), *The Oxford History of the Prison: The Practice of Punishment in Western Society* (Oxford University Press, 1998)

McGowen, Randall, 'The Well-Ordered Prison – England 1780-1865' in Morris, Norval and Rothman, David J. (eds), *The Oxford History of the Prison: The Practice of Punishment in Western Society* (Oxford University Press, 1998)

Morris, Norval and Rothman, David J. (eds), *The Oxford History of the Prison: The Practice of Punishment in Western Society* (Oxford University Press, 1998)

One Who Has Endured It, *Five Years' Penal Servitude* (Richard Bentley & Son, 1877)

Priestley, Philip, *Victorian Prison Lives – English Prison Biography 1830-1914* (Pimlico, 1999)

Prochaska, Frank, 'Carpenter, Mary (1807-1877)' in *Oxford Dictionary of National Biography*

Royston Pike, E., *Human Documents of the Age of the Forsytes* (Unwin Brothers Ltd, 1969)

Royston Pike, E., *Human Documents of the Victorian Golden Age* (George Allen & Unwin Ltd, 1967)

Southerton, Peter, *Reading Gaol by Reading Town* (Berkshire Books, 1993)
Thomas, J.E., *The English Prison Officer Since 1850 – A Study in Conflict* (Routledge & Kegan Paul, 1972)
Webb, Sidney and Beatrice, *English Local Prisons Under Local Government* (Frank Cass & Co. Ltd, 1963)
Webster, Paul, *The Bridewell Prison* (Aberdeen and North-East Scotland Family History Society, 2000)
Zedner, Lucia, 'Wayward Sisters – The Prison for Women' in Morris, Norval and Rothman, David J. (eds), *The Oxford History of the Prison: The Practice of Punishment in Western Society* (Oxford University Press, 1998)

ARTICLES IN PERIODICALS

Dickens, Charles, 'The Great Penal Experiments', *Household Words*, 8 June 1850
Dickens, Charles, 'Pet Prisoners', *Household Words*, 27 April 1850
Hawkings, David T., 'The Story of Millbank Penitentiary', *Family Tree Magazine*, April/May 2005
MacDougall, Philip, 'The Origins of Convict Abel Magwitch', *Bygone Kent*, Volume Twenty One, Number Ten, 2000
Storey, Neil, 'The Prison Warder', *Family Tree Magazine*, October 2005

CONTEMPORARY PERIODICALS AND NEWSPAPERS

Bradford Observer
Household Words
Huddersfield Examiner
Justice of the Peace
The Bedford Times
The Cambridgeshire Weekly News
The Graphic
The Illustrated London News
The North London Guardian
The Sheffield & Rotherham Independent
The Sphere
The Times

WEBSITES

Jackson, Lee - The Victorian Dictionary <http://www.victorianlondon.org/prisons/queensbench>
Roberts, Andrew 1981-/timeline - Mental Health History Timeline <http://www.mdx.ac.uk/www/study/mhhtim.htm> Middlesex University)
The National Archives <http://www.learningcurve.gov.uk/victorianbritain/lawless>

INDEX